ONE MISSION

ONE MISSION

HOW LEADERS BUILD A TEAM OF TEAMS

CHRIS FUSSELL

With C. W. GOODYEAR

WITHDRAWN

PORTFOLIO / PENGUIN

Portfolio / Penguin
An imprint of Penguin Random House LLC
375 Hudson Street
New York, New York 10014
penguin.com

Most Portfolio books are available at a discount when purchased in quantity for sales promotions or corporate use. Special editions, which include personalized covers, excerpts, and corporate imprints, can be created when purchased in large quantities. For more information, please call (212) 572-2232 or e-mail specialmarkets@penguinrandomhouse.com. Your local bookstore can also assist with discounted bulk purchases using the Penguin Random House corporate Business-to-Business program. For assistance in locating a participating retailer, e-mail B2B@penguinrandomhouse.com.

Images on pages 69, 70, 71: Intuit Inc.
Chart on page 122: 2016 State of Oklahoma

Library of Congress Cataloging-in-Publication Data

Names: Fussell, Chris, author. | Goodyear, C. W., author.
Title: One mission : how leaders build a team of teams / Chris Fussell, with C.W. Goodyear.
Description: New York, NY : Portfolio/Penguin, [2017]
Identifiers: LCCN 2017013769 (print) | LCCN 2017021010 (ebook) | ISBN 9780735211360 (EPub) | ISBN 9780735211353 (hardcover : alk. paper)
Subjects: LCSH: Teams in the workplace. | Military administration—United States—Case studies. | Organizational effectiveness. | Organizational behavior. | Leadership.
Classification: LCC HD66 (ebook) | LCC HD66 .F87 2017 (print) | DDC 658.4/022,dc23
LC record available at https://lccn.loc.gov/2017013769

Printed in the United States of America
1   3   5   7   9   10   8   6   4   2

Illustrations by Daniel Lagin

*To the men and women, on the battlefield and throughout industry,
who are fighting every day to define the future of leadership.*

CONTENTS

FOREWORD

We first met in a time of great uncertainty. It was 2004, and our initial expectations of rapid victory in Iraq and Afghanistan had faded into reluctant recognitions that the fight ahead would be long, brutal, and unlike anything we'd seen before.

In many ways we were very different. I was a fifty-year-old soldier just completing my first of what would ultimately be almost five years commanding an elite counterterrorist Task Force. Chris Fussell was a Navy SEAL in this organization and was twenty years younger than me. We crossed paths for only an hour at his small team's outpost along the Afghanistan-Pakistan border, but even in this brief initial encounter I recognized a reflective nature that struck me.

We would meet again, less than a year later, in Iraq. Chris had moved up in the organization and was serving as an operations officer at one of the three regional headquarters our Task Force had in the country. In this context he was responsible for reallocating resources, staying attuned to operations, and sharing intelligence. In such a managerial role it was natural, and almost expected, to become ruled by the tyranny of the here and now. Chris was certainly masterful in his conduct of the current fight, but it was his uncommon curiosity about the larger *how* behind it all that stood out to me.

Chris's constant questioning revealed a unique interest in the design and experimentation taking place at the Task Force's strategic level. For example, he wanted to know how we managed the decentralized decision making that he and his peers had become accustomed to; how we maintained awareness of, but did not impede, the resourcing decisions taking place at the small unit level; and where I saw the broadest gulfs in information sharing between our organization and outside partners. His queries were informed, but in the context of the overwhelming tasks of the daily fight he was orchestrating, to find the time and willpower even to ask them was notable.

Chris was therefore a natural selection to be the aide-de-camp for my final year in command. If he truly wanted to see behind the organization's strategic curtain, a year at my side in Iraq would be a grand opportunity to round out his learning. His primary assigned duty was to manage the logistics of the Task Force's senior leadership team, and ensure that we were spending our time in accordance with the organization's priorities around the world. In addition, I advised him at the outset to exploit this opportunity—to actively learn how it all *actually* worked.

And that is what he did. For a year Chris took it all in, observing the nuances of our organization's process and structure with keen interest. He then went on to graduate school and, still not satisfied, wrote a master's thesis on how our Task Force had organized our intelligence fusion centers around the globe to identify and capture best practices throughout our teams.

So perhaps it was inevitable that over time Chris and I found ourselves connected after the war by a shared fascination—almost a fixation—on the disorienting new phenomenon of *complexity* that we'd faced on the battlefield, and could see across almost every facet of life now that we'd left the service.

In the autumn of 2010, six years after we'd first met, Chris and I sat at my kitchen table and talked about how the special operations community had made such a significant organizational leap in the post-9/11 years.

"If this doesn't get captured in a book, history will get it wrong," he said. By "it" Chris meant how our Task Force had adapted to an insurgency in Iraq that was a technologically enabled, interconnected network of highly autonomous individual actors. More akin to mobs or violent gangs than a traditional understanding of insurgency would have led us to believe, its membership was motivated by an extremist ideology to foster unconstrained violence wherever possible. To combat the speed and effectiveness of this type of adversary, we'd shifted, reluctantly, from a masterfully constructed, purpose-built, centralized structure to a decentralized but deeply interconnected entity whose distributed teams could move with the fluidity of a network while retaining the focus and stability of a bureaucracy.

At the time of that conversation, I was just beginning to write my memoirs, which would consume my efforts for the next two years. But underlying that biographical work was an alternate story, the one that I most wanted to tell, and in the spring of 2013, we told it via the writing project that Chris had first suggested: *Team of Teams: New Rules of Engagement for a Complex World,* which would be released in the spring of 2015, reflecting years of thought and extensive research on the topic we'd first considered at my bland kitchen table.

Team of Teams met our intent to lay out a case about environmental change in modern competitive realms, and deeply resonated with leaders across a wide spectrum of organizations. The consistent "You described my organization's problem" type of feedback we received reinforced our conclusions that the challenge the Task Force had encountered was not unique to combat but rather reflected the common conditions of our era.

The hierarchical organizational models and leadership norms that we all grew up in were designed for a different type of environment from what we're now all facing. Organizations must adapt to the realities of the information age or face existential risk. Our "team of teams" approach, with its emphasis on shared consciousness and empowered execution, was an important framing and gave language to this universal threat.

Though we didn't call it such at the time of the Iraq war, a team of teams is an operating framework for an organization that we've seen work on the battlefield and in industry. It is grounded in the creation of true strategic alignment across an organization; executing disciplined, broad, and transparent communications; and decentralizing decision making to the edge of the enterprise. It allows traditional organizations to retain the strength of their bureaucracy while moving with the speed of a network.

But *Team of Teams* was not written to address a possibly more important follow-up question: *How, exactly, do you create an adaptable organization?*

When we realized that there was a clear need for a book to address the specific practices and behaviors that made our transition possible, I immediately thought that the right person to take on this project was Chris.

Chris has been more acutely focused on the *how* of our organizational transformation than anyone else I knew. Sure, other officers might have led at higher levels, had more intense battlefield stories, or saw parts of the war that Chris did not; but in my many years within the special operations community, I didn't know a single leader who was more intellectually curious as to what was practically taking place at an *organization-wide* level, across all tiers and different perspectives that our hierarchy offered.

Of equal importance, Chris will offer a view on what behaviors a team of teams model requires from its leaders if it is to truly thrive. In the Task Force, we had not only to *create* a new series of practices but also to leverage that model through the communalization of new cultural norms and behaviors.

Among the Task Force's senior leadership, it was obvious that the various parts of the organization were, in the early days of the fight, both unable and *unwilling* to connect and collaborate. We had to redesign ourselves and create not only the *capability* to connect, but the *willingness* to create a new culture, one populated by exceptionally powerful tribes. Without both aspects in place, the effort to establish either one is redundant.

The pages ahead offer, in my opinion, a critical response to one of the most difficult questions that the world is currently wrestling with—how must our models for leading and managing large systems evolve? Chris and his coauthor, Charlie Goodyear, a brilliant young Yale graduate, map the course toward a hybrid structure that is, more through disciplined trial and error than through academic forethought, what we eventually created within the Task Force.

I believe that organizations hoping to survive in today's increasingly complex world will need to (as we did on the battlefield) retain the strength and stability of a hierarchy while simultaneously adopting the speed and decentralization of a network—as well as the behaviors necessary for them to function.

If you're a leader looking to build your own team of teams, Chris and Charlie offer you a road map.

—General Stanley McChrystal (Ret.), March 2017

ONE MISSION

INTRODUCTION

In 2014 I was invited to join my former commanding officer, Stan Mc-Chrystal, as a coauthor in writing *Team of Teams*. Our goal in writing it was to offer our view on why the military models of the twentieth century were fundamentally misaligned with the realities of an information-age battlefield. The speed and interconnectivity of this new type of conflict forced the senior leadership within our branch of the special operations community to make a choice: lead us through a culture change or potentially lose the fight against Al Qaeda. They chose the former.

Team of Teams explored a simple idea that sat at the epicenter of the challenge in making this culture change: *How can large organizations move with the speed and agility of a small team?*

In that vein, our writing team laid out the reactive small-team dynamics that are so powerfully highlighted within special operations units, as well as in any number of other high-performing teams. We explained that a small team's ability to quickly adapt comes from the combination of four key drivers.

First, their members trust one another. Second, they are bound by a sense of common purpose—a shared ideology or purposeful trait. Third, given the small size and rich interconnectivity of a small team, they can create a sense of shared consciousness among the group: a state in which all members have a common understanding of their mutually-held problem set, a shared access to key information, and are aligned in the direction they need to move next. You've felt this, most likely, in small teams you've been on, but re-creating this state at scale, and with necessary regularity, is a far greater challenge.

With these three initial factors in place, the fourth and final quality can exist: empowered execution. The ultimate goal in today's quickly changing environment for an organization is the ability to decentralize decision-making rights down to those actors closest to the issues: empowered execution was, for the special operations community, the key to moving as fast as or faster than the rate of change of our external environment. Empowered execution creates the space for teams to act with autonomy, but as it is coupled with the influence of shared consciousness, it is *high-accountability* (and therefore risk-reduced) autonomy.

The book we wrote found an audience with senior leaders across many industries. From the reading list of commandant of the Marine Corps to Walmart CEO Doug McMillon's 2016 list of "must reads," the book's ideas found receptive audiences in some of the world's most seasoned and credentialed leaders.

Even with *Team of Teams* as a frame, however, readers have continued to ask us a common series of questions: *I accept the premise, but how exactly do we implement this model?* Or *What are the most important steps to focus on when attempting a team of teams?* And even *How does a forum with thousands of people not devolve into total chaos?*

To this day, I'll also often get another line of questioning meant to be respectful of our teams' efforts in conflict, but which expresses a healthy skepticism about whether lessons from a modern battlefield can truly apply to other realms: *What your organization did was impressive, but it's different here. In the military you can just give orders, and subordinates have to follow. It's not like that in the civilian world.*

If there are any former military folks in the room, they'll invariably chuckle at this.

I was on active duty for just over fifteen years, and I can't think of a single time that I ever truly gave or received an "order" like the one you might imagine from watching a war movie, in which a higher-ranking officer's harsh words are universally adhered to and respected by those under their command. That approach doesn't work well in the conventional military, and it falls even further short in the special operations community—where triple-selected, highly qualified, and deeply experienced personalities don't take kindly to being *ordered* by an officer with less practical experience than they possess.

Regardless of context, a leader cannot simply *command* people what to do and expect them to wholeheartedly follow. Rather, their task should be to guide teams, influence their decision making, and give them appropriate but not overly restrictive guardrails. But guardrails like this are impossible to establish without one critical factor—an organizational model that retains stability where necessary while also allowing for the distributed decision making that is mandated by our information age.

Many of the questions I've received, of course, can be compounded into the following line: *What are the practical and tangible steps that business leaders must take if they are to build their own team of teams?* *Team of Teams* told our story and made an argument about the final state that modern organizations need to arrive at to succeed, but it was not a practicum on how to reach that goal. Our intent in the pages ahead is to offer just that; to provide leaders with a sense of the necessary steps to creating a team of teams.

Having spent several years both experiencing and observing as this change took hold in its original context, I had the good fortune to be exposed to the inner workings of this model. As a tactical-level, junior leader in our organization, I was positioned to *feel* the impact that these practices were having on the organization. As an operational-level leader, I was responsible for helping implement these changes. But most interestingly, as McChrystal's aide-de-camp during his final year commanding our Task Force, I had a front-row seat to how these practices were working from a strategic perspective.*

After spending a year perched at this tier of our organization, as an observer of the systems that made the enterprise work, I had finally completed a kaleidoscopic view of our reformation. Having ricocheted from leading SEAL elements on the ground to helping synchronize these efforts from different operational-level positions to finally facilitating our senior leadership's interaction with our thousands-strong, globally distributed enterprise, I now had a multi-lensed view on how our organization had once operated, how it changed, and what "right" looked like.

If you're interested in a firsthand narrative about counterterrorism raids or tracking down Al Qaeda cells, writings by other service members offer much better perspectives on the ground-level realities of our fight than I could ever hope to produce. Their invaluable stories have shaped our generation's understanding of recent conflict, and their voices are increasingly critical to ongoing discussions about national roles in an in-

---

* Such a chief-of-staff-type role is becoming more in-demand in private-sector organizations. For readers interested in better understanding the nuances of this position in an organization, I've included an appendix detailing the process for serving most effectively in that function.

creasingly complex world. Instead, the pages ahead discuss the transformation of an organization, and are intended as a practicum for how that evolution might be replicated by others.

The book ahead will communicate those lessons and offer you a tangible guide to building your own team of teams, walking you through the process of transforming from traditional silos into what we will refer to as a "hybrid" organizational model.

In chapters 1 and 2, we'll explore the critical concept of "one mission," which must sit at the heart of a team of teams. We will also explore the history of traditional bureaucratic models, then show why today's environment is simply misaligned with such systems, which so many of us have been conditioned to accept.

After these first two chapters will come the heart of this work—an introduction to the concrete practices that, when used, will help an organization form networks among its teams, and embody a hybrid model.

Each of these practice-focused sections, dedicated to exploring one specific process or concept, will also be accompanied by a case study from a civilian organization that has successfully implemented the subject matter.

These case studies will follow a consistent pattern, providing background on the organization ("The Setup"), the issue it was working to solve ("The Problem"), the solutions that were implemented ("The Solution"), and the results that ultimately followed ("The Outcome").

The first of the core chapters of the book will detail the creation of an **aligning narrative**—determining the unifying, empowering *narrative* that can deliver an organization to a state of "one mission" and how it can be leveraged to create buy-in among influential members of the organization who might otherwise default to their own tribal norms. We will show the role that *social contagion* plays in the spread of this narrative, the importance of network influencers within your enterprise, and the limits of colocation in changing behaviors and attitudes in organizations.

In the subsequent chapter on **interconnection** we will explore actual social network formation. Where narrative alignment provides a common foundation from which teams are empowered to network with one another outside their conventional lines of authority, this chapter explores the *means* by which this interconnection can take place, free from bureaucratic oversight, once that story is set.

In the Task Force, our interconnection was enabled by physical and virtual forums, as well as supplementary online chat rooms, intranet portals, and information databases. Nevertheless, it was in our forums that the Task Force's aligning narrative could be periodically recontextualized by our senior leadership, and scattered teams could be given a platform to exchange information and become familiar with one another's needs. This results in the creation of a state of shared consciousness.

In this chapter we will discuss how to lay the groundwork for the proper application of these technologies—including how to select and use a "controller," how to build participation in forums, how to ensure that supplementary technologies are available for all members of an organization, and how a leader overseeing all of these technologies should modify his or her behavior to encourage teams to form networks appropriately.

That will all raise the question, naturally, of how often an organization must strategically realign itself. Therefore, in the subsequent chapter we will discuss the **operating rhythm** needed in an effective team of teams model. Finding the cadence-based balance between the creation of shared consciousness and windows of empowered execution is critical to the success of a hybrid model of leadership, as is knowing when to adjust this balance.

Here we will explore how leaders must resist the strong urge to use interconnecting technologies to exert greater control of their teams' operation, the ways in which a well-set operating rhythm can ensure more efficient vertical communication in an organization, and how it can reduce the amount of time teams take to identify ("X_1") and exploit ("X_2") new developments in their environment.

After that, we'll dive into the creation of **decision space** within your teams—exploring how organizations can expand and control the decision-making authority that networks of teams are expected to act on during periods of empowered execution. Although the networks that exist in a hybrid model are expected to work free from bureaucratic oversight in order to problem-solve in a complex environment, there must be nuance about when they'd need to report back to their bureaucratic command chain.

Finally we'll look at how to expand a hybrid model beyond a single enterprise, diving specifically into the creation and distribution of **liaison networks** across different bureaucratic command chains and functional silos. The variously specialized individuals who fill these formalized roles are expowered to act as "point people" for lateral collaboration during periods of *empowered execution*—helping coordinate joint action, accelerate information sharing, and generally increase interpersonal familiarity across silos. We will discuss the nuance to how these individuals are selected and leveraged and how their role was transformed over time in the Task Force from a symbolic position to one having a genuine practical function.

Our conclusion will show what the simultaneous use of all of the key practices looks like, demonstrating how each part of the model can work in conjunction with the others to unite teams under one mission.

Keep in mind that each practice we detail is insufficient in and of itself to drive true and lasting culture shifts. For example, narratively aligned teams will never reach their full potential for organic collaboration if they forgo the practices for establishing and leveraging internal networks (such as a virtual forum). As all of these practices come into place together, they create a feedback loop with one another, alignment on the narrative deepens, and the symbiotic operation of a team of teams model will intensify.

Whereas these practices are presented in a linear manner, it does not necessarily mean that every organization looking to adopt this model should implement them in this exact order. Their order of use is *relative,* despite the sequence that this writing endorses.

Per my experience in the civilian world studying and re-creating this model, some enterprises may find it easier to adopt certain practices first, based on the nuances of their current structure or environment. My best advice on this front is to consider the same approach that the Task Force's leadership initiated: just start with the practices that you believe are most needed in your organization, and self-critically iterate as you go along.

My military recollections are told in broad terms and written to maintain appropriate distance from actual personalities, times, and locations. Everything herein is representative of countless real-life events during the time period discussed, but specific details are blurred by design.

Implicit in all of this, though, is the true question we wrestled with and we see so many other organizations also addressing: how can a strong, stable, well-built global enterprise unify around a single mission?

Distribution, tribalism, complexity, and change in the external environment are all forces that sit in opposition to creating this type of narrative unity. Our early conversations on the battlefield circled around the very difficult question of how we could be so highly competent at the small-team level yet incapable of moving with the same agility as an enterprise. Ultimately it was our senior leadership, leveraging the inclusion and transparency of the team of teams model, who began to insert a constant reminder that if we did not align behind *one mission*, the individual capabilities of our elite teams would prove insufficient. We could all be great and still lose.

Our leaders did not direct us but rather *invited* us to be part of this cultural and operational excursion. The invitation was simple but its demands were not easy; we would change ourselves in the middle of the fight of our generation, we would break down tribal barriers and align upon one mission, and we would win.

Ahead you'll find our story. We wish you luck in your own.

CHAPTER 1

ONE MISSION

I'd learned, over the years, that nighttime in the open deserts of Iraq could be surprisingly beautiful and still.

Perched on the edge of an empty airfield, with one knee on the ground and my weapon slanted at the half ready, I gazed through my lime green night-vision goggles at the dark sky. It was the spring of 2008, and such a respite from the speed and noise of our war was a rare pleasure. I took a deep breath, and appreciated the momentary calm.

My boss, U.S. Army general Stanley McChrystal, knelt in the dirt beside me as we waited. For nearly five years, he had commanded a Special Operations Task Force dedicated to eliminating extremist insurgent cells in the country.

On this cool night, I was entering the final two weeks of my yearlong tour as McChrystal's aide-de-camp. A traditionally unglamorous position, this role had added a final lens to my appreciation of the Task Force's operation, and had been the most formative experience of my military career.

Having begun, years earlier, as a tactical-level platoon leader before gradually working up our bureaucratic ranks, I'd watched as McChrystal had transformed the organization from a coalition of tightly siloed units into a united team of teams. Now with a year of access to our commander's inner circle, I'd been able to observe our transformed organization in its full scope, and had helped with the large-scale implementation of the practices that had made it all possible.

That night McChrystal and I had gone on a foot patrol with an infantry unit out of their farmhouse headquarters and into a nearby village that had been decimated by insurgent groups over the past several years. Now we were awaiting the arrival of our predawn flight back to the Task Force's headquarters in Balad—a small town located north of Baghdad. The logistics for an excursion like this were my responsibility as his aide, and tonight's dictated that we fly aboard a compact MH-6 "Little Bird" helicopter, a spartan form of travel for a three-star general.

A Little Bird resembles a horizontal, jet-black dewdrop. Its cramped interior has room only for two pilots, while park bench–like seating runs along its exterior sides. These force passengers to dangle their legs into empty air once in flight, making for a dramatic ride that forces even the proudest operators to instinctively tighten their grip. These machines are built for agile attack rather than comfortable transport and are not a normal mode of transportation for VIPs.

The night remained still as we awaited their arrival. Then, exactly on schedule, we heard the distinct, angry *whirrrrrrr* of two Little Birds' high pitch rotors fill the air. The pair touched down lightly nose to tail, their rotors cutting green halos through my night vision. My commander and I split up to run to either side of the first aircraft, crouching to avoid the buzzing blades overhead before sitting down on our respective benches.

From where I sat on the Little Bird's exterior, I turned to look toward the aircraft's cockpit. Just eighteen inches in front of me, our copilot's arm was stuck outside the aircraft, parallel to the ground, fist clenched and thumb pointing skyward. He was awaiting my grasp, a signal from me that his two passengers were secure and ready for takeoff. I watched the copilot's arm remain stark still, his camouflaged sleeve flapping under the rotor wash.

Nothing, not an approaching enemy fighter, not a bullet hitting the Little Bird's globular windshield, would cause that pilot to withdraw his fist or pull the aircraft into flight—he wouldn't move, not until he felt the anticipated signal from his passenger. My life was in his hands, and he in turn trusted me.

Once secure, I leaned forward, grabbed the copilot's outstretched fist, and squeezed once. This seemingly small interpersonal gesture implied a deeper meaning—*I'm ready when you are.* McChrystal did the same on the other side of the aircraft, with slightly larger significance—a multistar general was clasping the hand of a young pilot many organizational tiers below him, but the faith demonstrated between these two people on the battlefield defied conventional understandings of rank.

Our pilots reacted swiftly. The aircraft quickly lifted and began on a heading back to Balad, followed closely by the second Little Bird. The air whipped my face beneath my goggles, and my legs became pinned back by the wind of the Iraqi night sky.

Small moments like this capture why soldiers can sometimes miss being in war. Just as the pressure of that moment locked the pilot and I into a mutually dependent relationship, so too had our leadership found a way to scale such intimate trust through our global enterprise. I would miss more than just the passing moments of intensity like this one; I would miss the intimacy of our *organization* once I was home.

Each of us, to our core, is drawn to being part of something larger than ourselves, something with purpose, something we can believe in. The Task Force had become exactly that for its membership. We shared one mission, and this culture shift had augmented the way we operated as an organization—to tangible results. The rate at which our teams would go out on raid-type Direct Action (DA) missions in the early days of the war were roughly ten per month—but with minimal increases in personnel and funding, that same figure had reached *three hundred* per month by 2006.

The pilot's clenched fist, awaiting my signal, represented a standard operating procedure that predated the Task Force's reformation, but back in 2003 relationships within our organization as a whole did not embody the trust and unity of that gesture.

Five years before the night of that Little Bird rendezvous, on March 20, 2003, I listened to a radio call echo through a darkened, crowded Joint Operations Center (JOC) close to the border of Iraq. Its tone was fuzzed with static, but the words were still intelligible to those assembled: "Shots fired."

With that, all of us in the large hangar knew we might be hearing the first combat of a new war, as our forces entered the western Anbar Province of Saddam Hussein's Iraq.

Yet, as you likely know today, the enemies who were the subject of that night's radio call were not the ones the invading Coalition would be most troubled by in the years to come. Though beating Hussein's military was no small challenge, the greatest long-term obstacles to peace in Iraq would be the various Sunni and Shi'ite insurgencies that sprouted organically across the long-mismanaged nation in the aftermath of the Ba'athist regime's collapse. These networks' amorphousness, opacity, and then-

novel ability to exploit modern technology made them especially dangerous and complex foes.

Prime among these weirdly webbed organizations was Al Qaeda in
Iraq (AQI), a regional franchise of the greater international Al Qaeda
terror conglomerate. Known before the invasion as Tawhid w'al Jihad
and initially headed by a charismatic young Jordanian, AQI's brutal actions contributed significantly to spiraling levels of sectarian violence in
Iraq, which peaked between 2007 and 2008. Sadly, the influence of this
organization in Iraq grew exponentially *after* the invasion, benefiting
from the complex conditions that the Coalition's presence unintentionally
helped foster.

Entering the military in 1997 after my graduation from college, I
served as an officer in the Navy SEAL Teams until 2012. A year after the
invasion of Iraq, I joined the Task Force, whose mission was to disassem-
ble Al Qaeda's expansive networks in Iraq, Afghanistan, and other parts
of the world. The bread and butter of our work, historically, was deploying small groups of operators in DA counterterrorism operations against
enemy leaders and influencers within these confusingly clustered networks.

However, in a way that sometimes mirrored the Sunni/Shi'ite divide
that helped define the civil chaos that engulfed Iraq, the Task Force's
constituent teams naturally clung strongly to their respective tribal
norms. In each of these factions there existed deeply enshrined unit his-
tories, myths of legendary heroes who once walked among members, as
well as jealously guarded traditions and rituals. Young members of these
units were advised and influenced by close mentors to think of these tales
and practices as inspiration for how to conduct themselves over the
course of their careers.

We even had mascots and totems of honor, handed out to members
of our microcommunities as a reward for loyalty to their home units—
hanging on the wall of my home office in D.C., to my wife's dismay, is
(among other memorabilia) a four-foot-long battle-ax from my time with
one such tribe, a subunit of one of the SEAL Teams I spent time with. Not
unlike the prized ornaments some white-collar professionals receive for
working on different deals, experience within a certain military clan was
often rewarded with physical reminders of the bonds you shared with
your teammates.

Much like Khan's Mongols, Boudicca's Iceni, and Shaka's Zulus, our
Ranger units, CIA analyst teams, State Department liaisons, and SEAL

platoons were distinct examples of proud clans that trusted only their own and lived within well-established norms of their group's functions. In our complex battlefield, though, these tactical distances would soon lead to broader and more dangerous strategic divides.

Today the term "echo chamber" is commonly used in association with politics or social media or both, especially in the aftermath of the 2016 U.S. presidential election. An article in *Wired* magazine on November 25, 2016, accurately summarized the scale of this problem on these fronts, noting that many Americans today "seem to feel trapped in a filter bubble created by the personalization algorithms owned by Facebook, Twitter and Google. Echo chambers are obviously problematic; social discourse suffers when people have a narrow information base with little in common with one another." More recent discussions regarding "fake news" seems to confirm that this trend will continue to remain relevant in different forms in the foreseeable future.

In the Task Force, though, our insulated cultures on the small-team level unintentionally contributed to the formation of **strategic** echo chambers, with the "filter bubbles" in our case being actively maintained by influential members of our teams and passively allowed to exist by our organization's bureaucracy.

Our various isolated teams, not surprisingly, could quickly become spaces where only one view of our organization's complex problem sets and overall strategy was discussed and socially accepted among close peers. These spaces then became stand-alone strategic echo chambers, further constraining their relations with teams in the larger Task Force.

A common, generalized refrain you might hear across these spaces would be *Everybody else is at fault, and only we have the best understanding of what's going right and wrong in this war. If everyone listened to and thought like us, then this war would be going smoothly.* As with like-minded political echo chambers, wherein those inside bounce and magnify prefiltered viewpoints off each other, strategic echo chambers can serve to reinforce and exaggerate divergent thoughts on what an organization's strategy or culture should be like and exacerbate operational distance between teams.

These differences had led to the formation of multiple *narratives* within our Task Force: distinct, unit-specific stories broadcast to and accepted by a critical population, in which listeners would inevitably cast themselves as actors playing a tribally accepted part. From army platoons to CIA human-intelligence analysts to NSA signals intelligence partners, each internal and partner unit associated with the Task Force held its own *distinct* history and sense of culture. This informed each unit's narrative, which in turn increased members' sense of tribal identity, which contributed to an echo chamber effect across different parts of our organization's bureaucracy.

For my first few years of the post-9/11 wars, I'd summarize my own narrative—the guiding story that motivated me and many of the SEALs I worked with, influenced my interactions with outside entities, and defined my sense of culture—as follows: *I am part of an elite tribe made up of great individuals who are the best at what they do. Each of us needs to earn their place in this tribe every day. Each of us needs to exceed the expectations of our SEAL teammates, and we expect them to do the same for us.*

This powerful, unit-based ethos had subconsciously been burned into our psyches and was reinforced constantly—to the extent that even the physical "territory" of our units would drive our tribal independence home to us. Above the front entrance of the first SEAL Team to which I was assigned in Little Creek, Virginia, there was an etched reminder on the doorframe that asked a daily question of those who passed under it:

DID YOU EARN YOUR TRIDENT TODAY?

The trident, a gold-plated special warfare insignia worn on the chest of every Navy SEAL, has a long and proud history and is earned only after nearly two years of training, which has an attrition rate that can reach the 80 percent mark. The trident is earned, not granted. Constantly being reminded to live up to the significance of this insignia, none of us ever felt the chance to rest on our laurels or forget to do well by those who also wore it. Totems like this served to strengthen and inform the narrative of our isolated community, as was the case for others we were expected to work seamlessly with.

But mine was an ill-informed narrative, though I did not recognize it as such early in my career. I, and others like me, were living to a "best in class" standard without ever spending substantive time with other special operations units or other teams whose work informed and enabled our own. My narrative was inwardly focused, myopic, and selfish; while certainly motivating, it did not align with building collaborative teams and offered no room for, or even acknowledgment of, other important tribes in our organization. Similarly, their narratives had no room for me or my kind.

Yet the Task Force still *functioned* with our many narratives, with its teams working through the limited bureaucratic highways that organizationally connected us.

For generations our model worked. We could function with our many narratives in a twentieth-century world that was complicated but not complex.

But then we encountered a change in the pace and complexity of our environment and found in the midst of that change an enemy with a truly unified membership. In contrast to our own individual stories, the narrative that aligned AQI's dispersed, unprofessional, and poorly resourced network was exponentially better than any one of ours. It may have been best summarized by Ayman Al-Zawahiri—the Egyptian physician-turned-terrorist regarded at the time as Osama Bin Laden's second-in-command of Al Qaeda's international umbrella organization. Following the 2011 death of Bin Laden, Al-Zawahiri, long a leading strategic voice for the organization, has gone on to inherit the executive command of Al Qaeda.

Al-Zawahiri's inclusive, empowering words, delivered by Internet broadcast in the early days of the conflict in Iraq, reveal a powerful organizational juxtaposition when compared to the personal, myopic stories of our teams:

> Those fighters in Iraq, we greet them and salute them and support them, and ask God to bless their efforts and their bravery in fighting the crusaders. And we tell them God is with you and the nation is supporting you. Depend and rely on God. And attack and devour the Americans . . . and bury them in the graveyard of Iraq.

AQI's members—though geographically dispersed—were all synchronized around an inclusive shared narrative, paired with a well-communicated strategic vision. Their organization's extremely fluid, freely designed operational structure helped ensure that the narrative of their leadership consistently permeated their distributed membership, enabling their rank and file to move with speed and individual initiative, collaborating with one another and aligning their otherwise-isolated actions with one another's efforts, free from formalized approval chains.

Contrasting my unit-centric narrative as a young SEAL officer with what was being broadcast by Al Qaeda's strategic leadership, it is not surprising that the first few years of the Coalition's occupation in Iraq were an exercise in futility. Levels of violence in the country continually hit new heights, despite the best efforts (and on-paper successes) of still-bureaucratic entities like the Task Force to remove key nodes from AQI's network and ideologically similar groups. In early January of 2004, roughly 200 attacks per week were being launched by insurgents against Iraqi government targets. By mid-June of 2007, this figure had increased by about eightfold, reaching more than 1,700 attacks per week. Large sections of the country were home to ethnic cleansing, pocketed with torture chambers, left without power during soaring summer heat, and lacking basic services for years on end.

The pooled stenches of death, heat, and decay seemed to fill the air. It was hell on earth.

Simply put, the Task Force was exponentially more capable on paper yet more culturally disparate than the enemies we were encountering, whereas AQI's far less prepared members were nevertheless all aligned under one narrative. We had excellence, talent, and capability; they had a uniting calling. Our many unit-centric narratives excluded one another and outsiders; their singular one invited anyone who identified with their purpose to play a role in their success. We were a strictly ordered machine equal only to the sum of our parts; they were an organic movement.

The condition of the country around us indicated how these two systems matched up against one another.

But in time the Task Force learned from this new enemy. As I was fortunate to witness firsthand, our leadership established what we'd later call a team of teams organizational model, in which our units and their leaders were not only given unprecedented access to one another's intelligence and senior decision makers but were also encouraged to form organic interpersonal relationships with one another outside the enterprise's bureaucratic lattice. This allowed our organization to dramatically increase each element's productivity and, in time, contributed to the quelling of Al Qaeda's influence on the insurgency.

Whereas an entire series of innovative organizational practices (each of which will be detailed in this book) was responsible for this shift, one process was critical to laying the foundation for the rest. This was the attempt by our senior leadership to introduce and consistently reinforce an *aligning narrative* that would override those held by our individual component units.

The aligning narrative they would build into our lexicon, and would ensure was circulated in our echo chambers, forced each of us in the enterprise to make a choice; we could either hold on to our myopic cultures and risk losing the war, or we could begin to interact with one another and commit to being a part of the team of teams we saw being created.

Our organization's new aligning narrative, which posed us this choice, began with the following simple equation, presented to all of us repeatedly by our senior leadership through a wide variety of mediums:

Credibility = Proven Competence + Integrity + Relationships

On its face this is a simple equation rather than a deeper qualitative narrative. But in practice this became the backdrop for a conversation we would have every day. As we'll discuss in later chapters, thousands of us would connect and resynchronize in inclusive forums every twenty-four hours, but at the heart of this communication wasn't transactional information but informed interaction derived from the above principles. Each day these were expanded into coaching conversations, contextualizing what was and wasn't working.

We talked about results not only for the operation's sake but to tell the story of how a given action had enhanced or harmed relationships across the organization, or deepened credibility with key stakeholders. We were asked hard questions by our leadership not so they could demonstrate power but so they could give us room to be honest and vulnerable about what we did or did not know. Teams didn't brag about successes but willingly exposed lessons so that the competence of the force could rise based on one group's challenges. If the equation had been put on the wall for reference, it would have been meaningless; but leveraged as the backdrop for how we prioritized our efforts and communicated across tribes, it became a more powerful tool than I comprehended even in the moment.

Our leadership knew that credibility was something our teams, and our broader organization, had long looked for in those we worked with—other leaders in the case of our teams and external stakeholders in the case of our organization. After all, credibility would allow us to move with more speed and decentralized autonomy—something we all had long desired.

But what had been preventing this from occurring?

Credibility was now framed as having three component factors:

proven competence, integrity, and *relationships.* Competence and integrity were not the limiting factors—our teams, while poorly interconnected, were each extremely selective and possessed strong moral fiber. What was missing were the *relationships* through which these other qualities could be proven to other tribes; these were needed to earn credibility with decision makers and with each other.

These relationships would need to extend far beyond those already established among members of the same unit and reach those on other teams and in critical partner organizations. Therefore many of us were encouraged to interconnect, expose ourselves to other closely-held viewpoints across our organization, and transform these connections into tangible operational benefits for each team.

In a way, this approach relates to the naturally social aspect of human identity. In 2014 Israeli historian Yuval Noah Harari ascribed our species' success to what he refers to as a "revolution in Sapiens' cognitive abilities," a possible product of the theorized "Tree of Knowledge mutation"—an anomaly in early *Homo sapiens* DNA that enabled our ancestors "to think in unprecedented ways, and to communicate using an altogether new type of language."

Per Harari, our forebears used their unparalleled intelligence to create not just physical tools but also social bonds of culture and identity, which eventually wrought huge benefits for their long-term ability to thrive. Essentially, they created stories that allowed small pockets of tribes to interconnect. In short order our ancestors, while physically slower and weaker than the threats around them, thrived by creating order and enforcing behaviors. They became bigger than their tribe.

In the Task Force our eventual strength came from this same biologically ingrained driver. We were not being solely given a transactional end state or directive-like strategy, as we had been before—instead, our leaders were giving us a well-contextualized vision of a new, more inclusive behavioral culture to create, which they cast as critical to ensuring our goals were attainable.

After several years of focus by McChrystal and our senior leaders, this new narrative created cultural, then operational unity, breaking down the bureaucratic walls that had once blocked our ability to communicate, collaborate, and trust. This newfound connectivity enabled us, among other things, to increase the rate of our DA operations so that our teams on the ground could move and adapt faster than the *leaderless* insurgent cells they faced on the battlefield.

But increases in quantitative measures of operational speed and efficiency were simply one type of outcome. An additional result of our experience was culture change, though we did not directly address it in the moment. Under the pressure of war and seemingly insurmountable challenges, we'd transitioned from a disparate series of high-performing elements to a purpose-bound, interdisciplinary team with singular focus on mission. We transitioned from a coalition whose capability was simply the sum of its parts to a cohesive enterprise driven by trust-based relationships. Most important, each of us evolved in our views from a tribal, small-team optic to a newfound feeling of higher purpose and calling.

The fruits of our teams' labors in this new model held, right up until the Coalition withdrew from Iraq in December of 2011. Since then, with the pressures that the Task Force and other entities helped exert removed from their immediate environment, AQI's membership has metastasized into a yet-more-notorious, networked, narrative-driven form, that of the Islamic State of Iraq and the Levant (ISIL). But ISIL is simply another chapter, whose days are clearly numbered in the long story of a new world we all now share.

A CHANGING LANDSCAPE

The types of problems presented to the Task Force in Iraq reach far beyond the world of military conflict, puzzling and challenging leaders in every industry.

The realities of competing in the twenty-first century are unavoidable, for the outside world has changed drastically: it is flatter, faster, more interconnected than ever before. As a result, some organizations that once functioned well are finding themselves where the Task Force found itself in 2003—possessing all of the talent and resources they need but unable to break out of silos and respond quickly to a shifting environment.

Many thinkers have recognized the drastic changes happening in our world and have helpfully ascribed terms to them.

Financial trader–turned–writer Nassim Taleb coined the term "black swan" to describe high-impact, unpredictable events that have nonlinear (i.e., exponentially disproportionate) consequences. He defines them by a "triplet" of qualifications: "rarity, extreme impact, and retrospective (though not prospective) predictability." The idea has caught on and many since have built upon it—with some adding the nuance of foreseeable "grey swans."

Further back on the timeline (1962 to be exact), American physicist and scientific historian Thomas Kuhn introduced a nuanced take on the word "paradigm" in his book *The Structure of Scientific Revolutions,* which he believed formed from two essential characteristics. A new scientific achievement must be "so unprecedented to attract an enduring group of adherents away from competing modes of scientific activity . . . (and) sufficiently open-ended to leave all sorts of problems for the redefined group of practitioners to resolve" in order to form a paradigm. You may recognize the significance of Kuhn's work when you consider how his writing gave rise to the term "paradigm shift."

This theory can get redundant after a while though—the practical takeaway is that the actions or words of one can now easily set off a cascading chain of consequences for others in ways not previously possible. For example, the self-immolation of a lowly fruit seller in a small Tunisian town can fuel a regionwide series of civil upheavals, whereas the negative experience of a single individual in one part of the globe can exert downward pressure on the responsible company's stock.

Clearly, part of the issue we all face comes down to the speed and scale of information flow. This was certainly a harsh revelation on our information-age battlefield in Iraq and Afghanistan. For hundreds of years, orders between even the best-organized military units (like Rome's legionnaires or Napoleon's *levée en masse* armies) could move only at the pace of the fastest couriers, be they on foot or on horseback. Even thinkers who are extremely hesitant to agree with arguments about how our environment newly challenges organizations (like the *Economist*'s current Schumpeter op-ed writer) have proven grudgingly willing to admit "there is some truth to this"—i.e., it is clear how changes in the speed of information flow have changed how organizations must operate.

Kissinger Associates vice chairman Joshua Cooper Ramo summarized the rate of this change deftly in his 2009 work *The Age of the Unthinkable:*

A letter carried on horseback 150 years ago would have moved information at a rate of about .003 bits per second (the average note carrying, say, 10 kilobytes of data, though of course that measure didn't yet exist). As late as the 1960s those same 10 kilobytes might have moved at 300 bits per second. Today global telecom cables transmit at a rate of billions of bits per second.

At closer ranges it was always semaphore, bugle cries, and drumbeats that allowed large groups of individuals in war to assemble, move, and fight with sufficient speed to react to other actors. Only the most organized, equipped, and professionally drilled armies, maintained by nation-states capable of levying taxes on a willing population, could master these centrally controlled processes—and only the best of these could maintain their armies' readiness during peaceful periods.

Thus these types of militaries, and the formalized nation-states they served, dominated war for millennia. This status quo was further set by technological innovations in the twentieth century, which allowed wealthy nations to replace horse-mounted couriers with increasingly far-reaching communication systems—a capability that no actor beneath a state level could possibly attain or hope to outmaneuver.

But suddenly, in the blink of an eye relative to many generations of human history, communication became democratized. As we entered the twenty-first century, the ability to share information with millions in real time began to emerge at every person's fingertips. A stand-alone idea or experience of one person could suddenly reach tens, thousands, or millions with the touch of a button or the click of a camera.

In the unconventional wars of Iraq and Afghanistan, the Task Force's long-standing organizational structure—purpose-built to prioritize ordered command and control interactions among teams—was quickly overwhelmed by the speed of this new reality, where disorganized collections of individuals could disrupt our operations in a nonlinear manner. The frequent filming on cell phones of improvised explosive device (IED) attacks on our teams and the posting of the video in Internet chat rooms for propaganda purposes were apparently a precursor to the state of civil affairs over a decade later in the United States, where political protest movements regularly use viral videos to fuel their base and attract new membership.

Moreover, it became exceedingly difficult for the Task Force's senior leaders to fully grasp what was happening on our front lines at any time, as conditions around us changed too quickly for our bureaucracy to distribute valid insights to the necessary corners of our organization, adding to the confusion and sluggishness of our decision making.

Our fight against Al Qaeda and its sympathizers was an early example of such a shift. The Arab Spring, beginning in 2011, was a sociopolitical movement spanning continents, prominently enabled by social media, that brought a deliverance from tyranny to some (as in Tunisia) and a devolution to chaos for others (as in Syria). The insurgent ride-sharing industry populated by Uber and Lyft, and sparked by the proliferation of smartphones, has quickly besieged the once-sound industry of taxi services. Traditional transportation may well be next to go, as self-driving technology makes an assumed constant like a driver's license a small relic we'll one day show to our grandchildren as proof of our antiquity, along with stories of speeding tickets, traffic jams, and road rage.

What is common among these cases is that all involve the dethronement of a dominant, incumbent state of reality through the dedicated efforts of a smaller, more fluid few, in ways not possible a mere few years ago. In his 1859 speech to the Wisconsin State Agricultural Society, not-yet-President Abraham Lincoln recalled a story he had heard, in which "an Eastern monarch . . . charged his wise men to invent him a sentence . . . which should be true and appropriate in all times and situations. They presented him the words: 'And this, too, shall pass away.'" Change, in short, is ever-present; but today, the disruption is ceaseless.

Anyone still convinced that the organizational structures and leadership models of the twentieth century will magically work in today's exponentially more complex world will quickly encounter inconvenient truths: as Albert Einstein noted toward the end of his decently fruitful career, "a new type of thinking is essential if mankind is to survive and move toward higher levels." In the early years of the Iraq and Afghanistan conflicts, we were undoubtedly trying to defeat a twenty-first-century threat with a twentieth-century playbook.

We all know the world has changed, and continues to change; a natural next question remains for us to wrestle with, addressing an even more fundamental issue: **how can organizations respond to the changed environment?** Today's organizations clearly face new types of interconnected and complex environments; therefore, they require an organizational model designed to handle such complexity. That is the challenge of our time.

As I prepared to leave Iraq after my year with McChrystal, I believed deeply that our enterprise had arrived at an answer to this question. Our organization had learned to defy our chaotic external environment, which some external observers might have labeled black swan heavy, or subject to paradigm shifts. Human-to-human connectivity and true strategic alignment had been established across our enterprise's teams and around the globe, binding thousands of people from unique and different tribes to a purpose that changed in scope and complexity almost every day. This new culture allowed our enterprise's teams the space to react with speed and autonomy to the unpredictable challenges thrown our way every day. We were thousands of professionals around the globe, but shared the intimacy of a small team sitting around a table.

The dramatic improvement in our monthly rate of direct-action missions, with other variables of cash, equipment, and personnel controlled for, demonstrated that our one-mission approach worked. But a far better testament to our success, in my mind, comes from the qualitative testimony you'd hear from members of the Task Force. Though the integration of their cultural microcosms wasn't always initially welcome, and though the changes needed to align us on one mission weren't always easy, one thing that no former members deny is that our organization had become whole: we were many teams, freely operating and engaging with one another in the pursuit of one mission. We often put other, once-rival tribes ahead of ourselves and knew they would do the same for us.

Normally, strong trust and respect among military members is limited to those who share a unit—those who have been able to fight alongside one another, work in close proximity, and engage in either supportive or argumentative dialogue as necessary. Yet in giving that final squeeze to the hand of the Little Bird pilot, I knew that our organization's new *identity* would be what I would miss more than anything else once I departed for home—a many-leagues-deep interpersonal trust, scaled across an entire enterprise through carefully facilitated, informal, intertribe relationships, that complemented our preexisting bureaucratic norms.

This was what allowed us to stand strong in the midst of a rapidly changing environment and adapt to act on our organization's strategy in a way that exploited the changes that were constantly occurring around us.

In so many ways we'd become a global organization that felt more similar to four people sharing space on a helicopter, entrusting one another with their lives, flying low over the desert sands of a war zone, than a large, hierarchical organization from the complicated world of the twentieth century.

But in reality, we were a bit of both.

QUESTIONS TO CONSIDER:

♦ Do you believe that your organization's external environment is changing in a way markedly different from how it has in the past, or at a greater rate?

♦ If so, do you believe that your organization's teams are currently able to collaborate and adapt as quickly and effectively as they need to in response?

♦ If they can't, what is preventing that adaptation? Lack of familiarity or exposure to one another? Fear of repercussions? Uncertainty about the response of senior leadership? Lack of strategic clarity?

CHAPTER 2

THE HYBRID MODEL

L ike many other military members, I've been in seemingly countless
helicopters over the years, and it is difficult to not appreciate the skill
level of the pilots with whom we entrusted our lives. On any given
helicopter flight, passengers like me could look on as these talented individuals worked hard at the helm of a machine we were all dependent on.

From the ground, an approaching helicopter might look like a gently
descending aircraft; but piloting what is in reality an inherently unstable
platform is anything but a "soft" process. There is no autopilot in helicopters. Their pilots are in constant motion, using all of their limbs to
work the pedals and levers to respond to crosswinds, updrafts off the
desert floor, "brown-outs" upon landing in the dry desert, and countless
other challenges.

Similarly, there is nothing static about being a business leader in today's complex world. Even if conditions seem stable, you'd be wise to
think of yourself as a helicopter pilot on a low-level flight over dangerous
terrain, remembering that any moment of calm is likely to be disrupted
by an unforeseen updraft or sandstorm. It's not that you don't trust your
machine; established business models and helicopters are tested, reliable
structures. Both pilots and business leaders appreciate the strengths of
purpose-built structures, but are also comfortable living in a constant
state of adaptation.

To "pilot" the unsteady Task Force through the complex conditions
we faced in Iraq, our leaders needed to create an entirely new organizational model. The leaders at its helm had to be able to concentrate efforts
along more than one axis: they needed to not only appreciate and lever-

age the strength of the bureaucracy, but to also maintain constant awareness of changes in the environment and empower the organization to adapt.

And that's what they did. Through trial and error, the Task Force transitioned to a hybrid model that combined the best elements of rigid bureaucracy and adaptable networks, becoming a fighting force such as the battlefield had never seen before.

BUREAUCRACY'S BEAUTY

In late 2016 one of my research assistants bought a used car and soon afterward moved to trade his old driver's license for a D.C. one.

He wisely did his research in advance, and after filling out the necessary application and gathering his original Social Security card, his out-of-state license, and copies of two utility bills that had been mailed to his D.C. address, he proceeded to the Georgetown DMV.

Yet after waiting in line for his appointment, he was turned away.

"Your utility bills, sir," he was told, "they both need to be from within the last sixty days." The attendant pointed at one of the two bills and then at a calendar displayed on her desktop. "This one is from *sixty-four* days ago."

It was a minor oversight, and he tried to plead, but to no avail—regulations were regulations, and the system didn't care that he had but one minor irregularity in an otherwise pristine collection of documents.

It was the equivalent of showing up with nothing at all. He was dismissed with a curt "Next." He had experienced bureaucracy at its finest.

For generations, organizational structures have been heavily influenced, if not defined by, the idea of *bureaucracy:* a centrally controlled method of managing sprawling lattices of teams. This method of organization was best framed by German sociologist Max Weber in the late nineteenth and early twentieth centuries.

Weber was born into the German upper middle class in 1864 and lived through the aftermath of the Western industrial revolution. Initially interested in law, he eventually became fascinated with the way private business and civil service could be transformed from disorganized systems into organizations run efficiently at scale.

Weber's theories effectively captured the societal revolution his era had witnessed. In an age where one's future was largely predetermined by familial connections, he suggested that an "impersonal order" was superior to a personal one. In Weber's bureaucracy, authority flowed from "offices" and not from people. He argued that rule and order should ideally come before the individual, and that the holder of an office should be obedient, first and foremost, to the rules of the hierarchy (and the office above his). Weber perceived that this would eliminate cronyism and create meritocratic opportunity for the masses.

In Weber's mind, the ideal relationships between employees, teams, and leaders were rigid, unadaptable, and defined by a distant figure in order to guard against inefficiencies and informalities. His resulting model is a top-down structure in which each member is subservient not only to the higher-ranked leadership above them but also to the formalized responsibilities of their role within the system. A diagram of Weber's resulting *impersonal order* could be presented as follows:

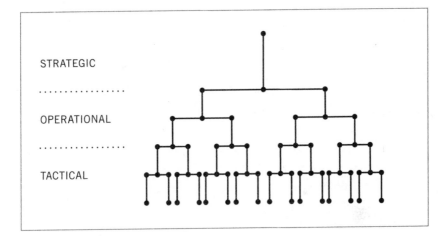

As any business leader will realize, the above diagram doesn't just represent an archaic idea; it is also a simplified rendition of the standard org chart for almost every large company on the planet today. Human subjectivity is (theoretically) minimized and replaced by structured corporate code, and silos are formed. Authority rests with the strategic leadership at the top and flows down to a senior group of middle-management officers (*operational-level* leaders), who in turn lead *tactical* teams. These formalized hierarchical relationships are fixed and unbending, fittingly drawn as solid lines.

Weber recognized that this organizational structure had dangers and could lead to "specialists without mind, [and] pleasure-seekers without heart." Yet he believed that the benefits of bureaucracy outweighed the risks. "The development of bureaucracy," Weber wrote, "greatly favours the levelling of social classes." By viewing employees and leaders and consumers with an objective, unchanging attitude, a bureaucracy ensured fairness and predictable operation.

When my research assistant was refused his D.C. driver's license, he found out what bureaucracies were designed to be: soulless institutions designed to operate without acknowledging personality or identity. His irritation was understandable but might have been tinted with a bit of relief as to *why* he was refused, and its positive implications.

He was treated without annoyance, without warmth, but rather as an objectively faceless customer among the others who would attempt what he had that day. The representative didn't care that he had only a minor abnormality in his application—all that mattered was he wasn't within guidelines.

He (and others looking on) should have taken heart, knowing that there was *no way* the organization they were interacting with could be "gamed" or would treat any one of them inconsistently. In that waiting area they were all equals. Such an operational principle prevented fraudulent vehicle registrations in the city and created a standard by which the organization could scale its function.

The multidivisional firm structure Alfred P. Sloan pioneered while he led General Motors in the 1920s was very much consistent with Weber's concept of the impersonal order.

Sloan transformed GM's structure into what he deemed, "an objective organization, distinguished from the type that get lost in the subjectivity of personalities." His vision was a multidivisional structure staffed mainly by coat-and-tied middle managers—whom John Micklethwait and Adrian Wooldridge deem "Company Men"—and such a change delivered great results. GM seized more than 15 percent of market share from competitors by 1929, merely six years after Sloan's ascendance to its presidency, largely because of increased efficiency as the bureaucratic model enabled centralized scalability.

Sloan's General Motors was not alone in benefiting from this approach to organizational management—elements of what has been deemed "Sloanism" were integrated into the management of peer organizations. The titans of that time—General Electric, U.S. Steel, Standard Oil, and others—all adopted similar practices; and they did so because bureaucracy was the optimal solution—for that time.

In *Team of Teams* we explored the enduring impact of industrialist Frederick Winslow Taylor's reductionist, efficiency-focused management practices. Taylor's method of scientific management standardized previously individualized industrial processes and attempted to do away with individuality—and with great success.

But despite the successes of bureaucracy, it has its dangers. Weber's, Sloan's, and Taylor's management theories, when taken to their extremes, dehumanize teams and individuals in order to ensure centralized control at scale—and limit their interactions to only authority-defined formalistic relationships.

The problem with bureaucratic approaches is that they assume that relationships among an organization's teams should always be formalized and utilitarian. Solid-line operational relationships between teams and leaders were thought to form sufficient structure and community within an organization, which is equivalent to assuming that a skeleton without interconnecting tissue or nervous and circulatory systems is sufficient to make up a whole human body.

Nothing could be further from the truth. Organizations, at the end of the day, are not composed of cogs and gears that remain completely isolated from all those not directly relevant to their operation. Rather, they are staffed by subjective *humans*—sometimes isolated communities of them. A formalized org chart that doesn't account for human and environmental subjectivity can quickly destroy teams' sense of mission.

When left isolated from the rest of the organization, teams become strategic echo chambers, and soon adopt divergent cultures.

This effect is magnified as organizations get larger and bureaucratic lattices grow more complicated, leaving teams in increasingly isolated corners. As Simon Sinek writes, "by its very nature, scale creates distance, and at distance, human concepts start losing their meaning." Once cloistered teams are isolated enough from personal interaction and exchange with one another, senses of "otherness" and impersonality grow.

Not only does pure bureaucracy destroy narrative unity, but it also puts people in positions where they cannot keep up with a rapidly changing environment.

You and your organization likely feel the daily strain of trying to keep pace with rates of external change. Our formalized systems simply aren't built to enable the level of cross-functional response necessary for contemporary problem sets. Impersonal orders are meeting their match—with the Company Men being particular weak points.

LEADERS IN BUREAUCRACY

A mentor of mine once asked me a question regarding Emanuel Leutze's painting *Washington Crossing the Delaware*.

You'd recognize the image. It shows General Washington standing at the prow of a wooden boat crossing the Delaware River, at the head of American revolutionary forces, before the Battle of Trenton in 1776. Including a dramatically iced-over river, the painting depicts Washington gazing into the distance while soldiers alongside him use spiked barge poles to guide their craft.

Now the question I was asked by my friend: how can you tell Washington is the leader in this scene?

The answer? He's the only one who doesn't look like he's doing anything.

The joke reveals much about our shared biases about leaders—we expect them to manage and not "do." Current-day network theorist, sociologist, and physicist Duncan Watts writes about the first time he realized this in his book *Six Degrees: The Science of the Connected Age.*

Boarding a plane one day, Watts noticed the furiously typing, suit-clad Company Men he always found seated beside him on such flights, and he couldn't help but wonder what they did.

> "What," I wondered, squeezed in between parallel displays of urgency, "do these guys actually produce?" If all a person does is rush from one meeting to another, what does he or she actually contribute to the productivity of an organization?

Watts's conclusion is one with which Weber, Taylor, and Sloan themselves would agree:

> The answer, from an information processing point of view, is that a manager's principal task is not production at all but *coordination*, to serve as an information pump between the individuals whose task is production [emphasis mine].

In a bureaucracy, senior leaders are granted authority over tactical units and are expected to play the role of "information pumps" between the units. As a result, managers spend the majority of their efforts facilitating the cooperation of their teams through the limited bureaucratic means available to them.

Cross-functional cooperation among teams is becoming increasingly critical, making the function of information pumps more important. At the same time, the overwhelming amount of information moving in today's environment makes being an effective information pump increasingly time-consuming. The managers who are expected to create and manage cross-functional collaborations or resolve conflicts are increasingly overwhelmed by the noise of the day-to-day. As the level of noise increases, so does the likelihood that leaders will either fail to effectively move information between teams or leave their superiors out of the loop as they scramble to put out fires. This not only takes an obvious short-term operational toll on the organization but also furthers the narrative divide between teams. *Whose fault was that*–type conversations, caused by limited means of connection among different parts of an organization, increase cultural animosity.

This was certainly the state of the Task Force I first joined. It was an impersonally ordered conglomerate staffed by elite operators, analysts, and seasoned leaders. But on the information-age battlefield, its ability to connect across functions was overwhelmed by the speed, complexity, and unpredictability of the competition. Not surprisingly, fingers began to be pointed among tribes.

Though Weber would have looked at our org chart with deep satisfaction, the spiraling sectarian violence we encountered in Iraq and Afghanistan proved that a centrally planned, hierarchy-dependent organizational structure was *insufficient*. The gap was quickly recognized at the tactical level, where the personal losses of close friends that resulted from organizational failure inflicted a type of pain unlike any other. But the solution was not immediately apparent. Our system was working as it was designed, but information pumps in the system were repeatedly confounded in their ability to turn overwhelming amounts of raw intelligence into fast enough action. The threats were changing too quickly, expanding one step faster than we could contain them.

As a leader myself, I experienced the strain of being an information pump unable to keep up with a changing environment. When I applied to become an officer in the SEAL Teams in 1997, my youthful assumption was that if I made it into the SEALs and was given the appropriate rank, I would be put in charge of a small team of operators and thus *become* a *leader*. If, as an officer going through basic training, I'd been asked by an instructor to name the most important leaders who ran our community, I would have requested to see a solid-line org chart of the force and would have proceeded to read out the names of the highest-ranking individuals I could find on it. I would have been mistaken.

Several years into my career, after I passed selection, deployed, and started moving up the solid-line hierarchy of the Task Force toward strategic roles and away from the tactical operations, I felt a different kind of stress and anxiety developing. I was moving away from playing an active, practical role in our organization, away from the tightly clustered, narratively bound work of a small team, and toward becoming a bureaucratic information pump.

This wasn't a welcome change, and whether on the battlefield or in the boardroom, this feeling is common among authority figures in bureaucracies.

When I left the military in 2012, I was surprised to see how prevalent this tension is in other industries—a result of our similar structures. Bureaucratic advancement means fewer peers, more span of control, generally an increasing information-pump function, and increased distance from the actual implementation of whatever it is the organization *actually* does.

When you are in a small team at the tactical level—whatever your industry—you are closest to your organization's pressing problem set, and can see or feel solutions either take hold or fail. The work is firsthand, the feedback direct, and you know quickly whether you are good at the job: you either close deals, build a good product, make your numbers—or you don't. Moreover, you are fully integrated into your team's narrative and act in accordance with it.

If all goes well, strong performance in this specific function gets you promoted, and before long, you're filling an operational-level position on the bureaucratic org chart. Now, like it or not, you're an information-pump *leader* of an increasing number of frontline teams—responsible for enabling the practical work of the units you used to be an integral part of. You increasingly receive only secondhand information about your organization's external environment.

With no real conversations from those above you on the org chart about what it takes to fill this new role, you base your approach to this new job on your observations of new peers in your current tier of the bureaucracy. You reflect the work ethic they demonstrate, being the first at your desk in the morning and the last to leave at night. You communicate, continuing and perhaps tweaking the regular meetings that you were on the receiving end of for the past few years.

But despite your efforts, the frontline issues that you were once immersed in become more blurred every day; anxiety starts to build. Learning secondhand about the state of the teams and environment that you were once a part of, your sense of value and worth is challenged. This sense of separation and isolation can increase in quick leaps as you move up the hierarchy, with personal fear and doubt growing in kind. Impostor syndrome, a sense that everyone but you belongs there, can set in and grow—feeding the urge to micromanage and demand more from your subordinate teams. The impersonally ordered bounds of a bureaucracy assume leaders will be able to identify where and when cross-functional collaboration is necessary, then enable that cooperation and interaction. In a complex environment, this expectation compounds anxiety for leaders. The speed with which humans within the system can connect and solve emerging issues becomes the limiting factor in the bureaucracy.

"I'm the bottleneck" is a common refrain from so many of today's self-aware leaders, all too often said in a way that reflects the leader's belief that her ineffectiveness is her fault. The reality, as the battlefield taught us, is that a twentieth-century organizational system is simply insufficient for the speed of the information age.

COMPLICATED, COMPLEX, AND CYNEFIN

Most of us grew up inside twentieth-century bureaucratic models designed for a world based on predictability. But that environment has changed in front of our eyes, and so too must our organizations. Understanding the precise nature of the shift from complicated to complex systems will help us understand the problems with bureaucracy and its information-pump leaders.

A system is *complicated* when its many different parts interact with one another in a predetermined fashion. This set series of interactions among parts ensures that whatever results are delivered by the system are predictable. Think of a machine you own—be it a printer, a calculator, your car, anything mechanical: it is *complicated,* as its parts interact in a preset, unerring way to produce a predictable outcome (e.g., the printing of a sheet of paper, or a precise digit, or combustion in an internal engine).

Complicated systems are not easy to understand, unless you're an expert in their specific subject matter; but all of us are confident in the cause-effect relationship of complicated systems. We know what will happen when we press our foot down on our vehicle's accelerator—predictable forward motion, provided that the system's complicated parts are put together correctly, as we've learned to expect.

In contrast, in a complex system, parts interact in new and unique ways, which defy preset definitions. Think of an ecosystem, which is inherently *complex*—the different organisms and abiotic conditions that make up a rain forest can interact in an apparently unlimited number of ways, with a nonlinear variety of results. Minute variations in local temperature can create cascading consequences; a few degrees can make the difference between life or death for the many different animals that depend on vegetation growth and their delicate food chains.

Our world, with increasingly widespread access to high-speed information flow and pervasive interconnecting technologies like smartphones and social media platforms, is increasing daily in its complexity. More actors and variables are entering our environment, interacting in unpredictable ways, challenging our old ways of leading. And, as we found in the military, complicated systems don't do well in complex environments.

Some areas of business are also feeling this challenge. Recent data shows that it is becoming increasingly difficult for established businesses to compete in global markets. Whereas the very top tier of modern corporations (especially in the United States) are displaying record profitability, and certain industries are seeing meta-oligopolies emerge through gigantic mergers, a deeper look at the data suggests that life for large companies as a whole is getting harder. The expected life spans of companies have dropped dramatically over the last few decades, a decline that seems to be deepening. According to 2012 estimates by Clark Gilbert, Matthew Eyring, and Richard N. Foster, members of the S&P 500 in 2012 were, on average, expected to remain in the index for only eighteen years, compared with the sixty-one years they could have expected in 1958.

Today, publicly listed corporations in the United States have a one-in-three chance of being delisted from the stock exchanges within the next five years, a rate that has increased sixfold in the past forty years. This nonlinear increase is an indicator that far too many companies have had difficulty becoming truly adaptable. This change can be ignored, but the cliff is very real, and we're moving toward it at ever-increasing speed.

We also see the expansion of complexity in recent high-profile failures of once-sound scientific political polling.

Hours before the results of the June 2016 Brexit referendum were evident, betting markets predicted that the chance of Britain remaining in the EU was about 88 percent. Though the models of news outlets and pollsters significantly discounted the probability of the eventual outcome (voters electing to have the UK leave the European Union), reality diverged from what nearly all experts had anticipated. Speaking for many at the time, France's then–prime minister, Manuel Valls, reflected the disposition of many the morning after the referendum when he described it as "an explosive shock."

Similarly, in October 2016 Colombian voters rejected a referendum for a peace agreement that would have ended their decades-long conflict with the Revolutionary Armed Forces of Colombia (FARC). Polling had predicted that it would pass by a two-to-one margin. On a topic that has undermined Colombia's internal stability and development for decades, the results were a shock to the country's political elite.

And, of course, the vast majority of scientifically sound exit polls, public-opinion pollsters, and election forecasters overwhelmingly failed to predict Donald J. Trump's victory in the 2016 U.S. presidential election. For essentially the entirety of the race, predictive models favored his opponent. On the morning of the general vote, the *New York Times* predicted Hillary Clinton had an 85 percent chance of winning, and pollster Nate Silver (whose models had earned acclaim by correctly calling the 2012 presidential election result for all fifty states) was guardedly but justifiably confident in a Clinton victory. Yet the eventual results, like Brexit and other recent global shifts, highlighted that traditional means for predicting new developments in the world are failing at an alarming rate.

All realms—political, commercial, and social—are thus feeling the impact of our contemporary complexity, but how is a leader supposed to respond?

In 2007 David Snowden and Mary Boone penned a widely read *Harvard Business Review* article titled "A Leader's Framework for Decision Making," in which they offered readers a practical matrix for applying complexity theory to their businesses. The model Snowden and Boone proposed—called "the Cynefin framework" (pronounced *ke-ne-fin* after the Welsh word for "habitat")—suggests that there are several distinct types of environments (which they refer to as "domains") that leaders of organizations may find themselves competing in—not only complicated and complex but also *obvious* and *chaotic*.

A simplified version of Snowden and Boone's Cynefin model is shown below:

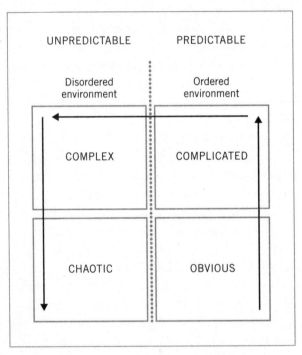

Snowden and Boone argue that the apparent relationships between cause and effect in each of the four quadrants differ. In the obvious quadrant, it is immediately apparent (and predictable beforehand) how and when the causes produced a particular problem set. Yet in the chaotic quadrant, this relationship is virtually unknowable and unpredictable. Per Snowden and Boone, leaders need to determine in which quadrant they're operating and adjust their approach accordingly.

It is relatively easy for leaders to adapt their organizations when they move from working in an obvious environment to working in a complicated one. But the next transition, from complicated to complex, a shift that the information age is forcing upon all of us, is the most difficult. Crossing this divide, the relationship between cause and effect shifts from being somewhat predictable (in a complicated system) to knowable only in hindsight (in a complex environment). Once an organization enters the *complex* space, all challenges are nuanced, and require bespoke solutions.

In a complicated world, where emerging problems often require only solutions similar to those used to solve previous problems, pattern recognition can develop and the bureaucracy can move quickly: *in this type of situation, our teams must react in this way step-by-step.* But in a complex system, each event is its own unique occurrence, and a bureaucracy is quickly overwhelmed; or worse, leaders roll out solutions based on pattern-recognition biases, then wonder *why it didn't work this time.* In a complex world, a dependence on quick pattern recognition can prove fatal.

If your organization is high performing, it is able to react to complex or chaotic events. When these situations arise, all the right folks jump on a conference call or come in on Saturday.

But a few things are happening while you do this. First, depending on the breadth of the issue, other work around the organization slows; key leaders are immersed in the crisis, so they're not focused on their day jobs; members of the broader organization are waiting for their leaders to return, hesitant to go about the day-to-day, uncertain of how the crisis might impact any pending decisions. Authority, in other words, is *further monopolized* when the system goes into crisis mode. The situation is solved because you have smart and talented people in the same room, but at what cost to the broader organization's ability to function?

Moreover, once the situation passes, a bureaucracy is hardwired to return to its *complicated,* business-as-usual structures and await the next crisis; it is not designed to quickly adapt based on the situation it just encountered. But this "crisis mode," you've likely noticed, is becoming the new norm. The day-to-day functions of your enterprise are being interrupted at a feverish pace. Your challenge is to create an enterprise that is comfortable constantly adapting to the complexity around it, while avoiding constant disruption to the parts of the organization that should remain stable.

Early in the post-9/11 conflicts, an army peer and friend told me that he saw the SEAL Teams as "exceptional at reacting to crisis," which I initially thought was a compliment. "The problem is," he continued, "you're so much better at crisis than long-term planning that you turn *everything* into a crisis." It was a biased view of our community, but his point was well taken, and I've seen similar patterns in high-performing companies throughout various industries over the past several years.

Austrian economist Friedrich Hayek forecasted the impacts of misunderstanding complexity in his acceptance speech for the 1974 Nobel

Prize for economics. "To act on the belief," he said, "that we possess the knowledge and the power which enable us to shape the processes of society entirely to our liking, knowledge which we in fact do **not** possess, is likely to make us do much harm." He warned that not all factors that determine events within an economic system are predictable or measurable and thus allow for behavior by actors that is inconsistent with previous norms: "If man is not to do more harm than good in his efforts to improve the social order, he will have to learn that in this, as in all other fields where essential complexity of an organized kind prevails, he cannot acquire the full knowledge which would make mastery of the events possible." A failure to accept that pending impact of unpredictable factors, he argued, could lead to disaster—a frighteningly accurate prediction from one of the key designers of twentieth-century economic theory.

Bureaucratic structures, through no one's fault, are built to incentivize the very type of behavior that Hayek eloquently warned against. Leaders who want to transform their solid-line organizations to better deal with life in the complex quadrant will need a new model.

NETWORKS

In contrast to the steady revelation of the failure of bureaucracies, *networks* are thriving in today's interconnected world. These collections of loosely connected points—people, in the case of social networks—are the antithesis of bureaucracy and are fast becoming a dominant informal organizational model as the technology era affords them the ability to scale at unimaginable speeds. Networks like these can present a great danger if ignored but offer great promise if we're willing to learn from their strengths.

As Watts defines them, networks, unlike bureaucracies, are not "objects of pure structure whose properties are fixed in time." Instead, networks change rapidly, their connections in constant motion based on the surrounding conditions. Bureaucracies, on the other hand, are stable and hard to change.

Moreover, connections among members of a true social network are unmoderated. In bureaucracies, not only are the numbers of interconnections among different teams and leaders carefully controlled, but the nature of these relationships is also carefully managed—solid-line relationships are strictly hierarchical.

In contrast, the connections between a network's various members can be informal and established organically by individual members. A network's shape is self-defined, not centrally controlled. As a result, a common practice among writers and academics is to represent connections within networks as *dotted lines* to reflect their resistance to categorization and their variance in strength.

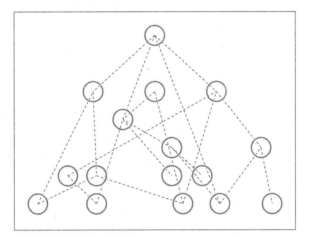

Through their dotted-line relationships, members of a network are free to collaborate with ease. There is no set of rules to govern how information flows among members—no Taylorist standardization, no *need-to-know* governing rules, no Weberian approval chains.

The freedom of movement found among members of networks has a huge impact on this property—because there is no bureaucracy-dependent approval process for which new members (or "nodes") can be added to a given network by existing members, and no internal regulations that govern the interaction of these nodes, the structure of networks can vary greatly, as guided organically by the free choice of their membership.

This can manifest as *clustering*, which network theorist Albert-László Barabási referenced as a state "in which everybody knows everybody else." Clustering exists among small networks of individuals (like families)—and as a result can be often seen on the team level in bureaucracies.

As Anne-Marie Slaughter details in *The Chessboard and the Web*, clusters enable "repeated human interaction," which fosters trust within the cluster but can hamper the flow of information to outsiders. It is here that narrative disconnects between different parts of bureaucratic organizations emerge and bureaucracies degenerate into motley tribal fiefdoms on a team-by-team and silo-by-silo basis. This is because these clusters are insufficiently connected to each other.

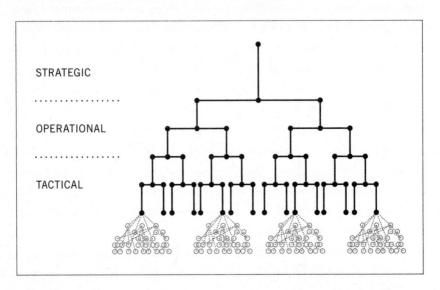

At the small-team level, *impersonal orders* are anything but impersonal; instead, small, closely bound networks spring up within well-ordered systems. It is in our nature to create them, and no amount of rules will break humanity's need to connect with others.

THE PROBLEM WITH NETWORKS

It might seem, then, that the answer for our complex world would be to transition to purely social network–driven systems. Fast and adaptable, they seem to be the perfect solution for today's environment. But recall their weaknesses. They lack central planning and are driven purely by narrative.

A lack of control means any given action might unintentionally prove dangerously out of line with the long-term interests of the network. Narratives are powerful, but when contradictory, they destroy an organization, either by multiplying within small, clustered networks found in silos or by causing critical elements of the organization to become isolated echo chambers.

Networks are best designed for immediate adaptation, not long-term planning. If your organization is considering a multiyear, phased implementation of a new human resources platform, do you think this should be developed and managed with a freewheeling network? If you were considering merging with a competitor, would you want to simply adapt in the moment, or would you want to weigh the long-term effects of the deal? Networks are indeed an exciting model, but for mature leaders in enterprise, they are not an all-encompassing solution.

In order to understand how a network driven by only narrative and ungoverned by any stable structure can go wrong, it's important to understand how network narrative works. Nicholas Christakis and James Fowler describe clustering as a partial product of *"homophily . . . birds of a feather flock together."* Strong social networks are formed when individuals identify with one another and share common traits or focus. They share a basis for their interactions, and their ties strengthen over time.

However, for small teams in the Task Force, clustering was not just a product of like-minded "birds of a feather" organically banding together but was also informed by the influence of preexisting cultural norms. Because members usually do not choose which team would be the best culture fit for *them,* instead being assigned to a team, the individual adapts to the culture of the tribe.

Relationships in clustered social networks where homophily exists— like families, lunch groups, and work teams—are underlain by common narratives. In the SEAL platoons that I was a part of, this narrative clustering drove the cohesion of our tactical units. Whether articulated or not, there was a clear sense of community that bound our memberships together and naturally isolated outsiders from our thinking. In hindsight, as stated earlier in this book, I would describe the narrative that bound me to my immediate peer SEALs as follows:

> *We are an elite tribe, made up by great individuals who have to be the best at what they do. Each of us need to earn their place in this tribe every day. Each of us needs to exceed the expectations of our SEAL teammates, and we expect them to do the same for us.*

If you changed just a few words in that sentence, you could likely apply a similar narrative to each of the highest-performing teams in your own organization. Perhaps it's on their wall, or perhaps it's just the way they would self-describe. This results in an intimate drive toward excellence within a team but implicitly leads to operational *and* cultural isolation from any other team.

In military history these clustered units were the Vikings, Zulus, and Mongols of our world—exposed to the narrative only of their small tribe, bound within their own proud echo chambers. Similarly, these clans were amazingly competent in their age but fell quickly when the world around them changed. MIT researcher Alex Pentland notes in his work *Social Physics,* that "when there are feedback loops in the social network, then the same ideas circle around and come back again and again."

Similarly, the delusion seen in certain clustered circles of investment bankers in the years preceding the financial crisis of 2008 highlights the risk in allowing teams to operate solely within their narrative-centered social networks. But today, whereas bureaucracies have long harbored clustered networks at the team level, external narrative-driven networks are demonstrating a previously unknown degree of scalability.

This is a new phenomenon for humanity, adding an addendum to the oft-cited research of English anthropologist Robin Dunbar, whose 1992 paper "Neocortex Size as a Constraint on Group Size in Primates" has been interpreted as naming an upper limit to the size of humans' social networks. Dunbar concluded that a given human can form close relationships with approximately 150 people at any given time (a figure often referred to as "Dunbar's number") and "can put names to the faces of around 1500" more.

The implication of this is that our ability to independently form large social networks has historically been limited; yet the hundreds of connections you might have on Facebook, the thousands of connections many have on LinkedIn, and the millions of followers that some have on Twitter show us that the ability to influence ever-increasing numbers in real time exists without question. Digital-age technology has enabled the greater interconnection and empowerment of individual actors and eased the means by which they can interact with one another, broadcast narratives, and create and expand social networks on a previously unseen scale. Networks can now draw their membership from a boundary-less geographic and social range.

But with that sudden scalability come nonlinear increases in levels of unpredictability and complexity in these networks. In Snowden and Boone's complex and chaotic domains, as more people are added to these systems, the more likely they are to interact in unique ways, producing a series of unpredictable, nonlinear outcomes. The actions of these large and unpredictable social networks have been proven by reality to pose existential threats to incumbent bureaucracies.

The fascist Egyptian government in 2011 was not exactly an organizational structure that would thrill Weber, Taylor, or Sloan—whereas an impersonal order did exist among officeholders within it, corruption and poor management were endemic in its many branches. Nevertheless, a bureaucracy it was, and, starting in January of 2011, a narrative-driven, young, and technologically interconnected network of protesters successfully overthrew it through smartphone-captured videos and blog posts.

"It came to be known throughout the Middle East as *The Vlog that Helped Spark the Revolution*," Spanish sociologist Manuel Castells recalls. The viral nature of social network platforms spread this powerful narrative at light speed, and in the blink of an eye, masses were gathered in Cairo's Tahrir (Liberation) Square, "calling for the resignation of Mubarak and the end of the regime." The network won, the hierarchy fell, and the world watched with shock, disbelief, and excitement about how quickly the status quo can now change.

Whereas there were countless traditional reasons for these protesters to distrust one another, their once-inward-facing narratives had been superseded by the broader opportunity to align, in massive scale, against a norm they all wanted to change.

The role networks play in different realms is variable—whereas some organizations may find themselves counteracting small, narratively aligned, and agile start-ups, others may be forced to respond to the unpredictable whims of increasingly interconnected, empowered networks of customers, investors, or employees, who can discover common narratives to act upon and quickly find others to add to their social network.

And yet a pure network structure remains a poor, or at least yet-unproven, way of organizing large enterprises for the *long* term. Networks defy centralized control, lack the efficient operation of functional silos, and remove the positive aspects of authority offered by bureaucratic hierarchies. They are complex and ever changing in their structure and produce nonlinear outcomes as a result.

As an example of this, think to the fatally decentralized Occupy Wall Street movement, which originated in 2011 in Manhattan's financial district and spread rapidly to other cities around the country and world. Though the newly networked, tech-assisted movement had great initial momentum, assembling hundreds of thousands of protesters in cities from

New York to Madrid, Barcelona, and Rome, it was defined as "a leaderless movement without an official set of demands." By November 15 of that year, when New York police forcibly removed the original protesters from their central camp in the city's Zuccotti Park, the movement's public face had diminished. It petered out altogether not long after.

A classic pure network organizational structure, the Occupy movement has been evaluated in retrospect through various lenses. By some measures, it ceased having relevance the moment its protesters went home. Others might argue that its principles lived on, as exemplified by current debates (led on one front by politicians such as U.S. Senators Bernie Sanders and Elizabeth Warren) on raising the minimum wage in the United States or easing student loan debt. But either way, the weakness of a pure network structure as an organizational model is clear: though its core narrative cause may be scalable and sustainable, its amorphousness and lack of any central control makes it a poor way of directing an enterprise.

THE HYBRID

So what alternate choices does a leader have?

Bureaucracies made of solid-line connections provide order and enable the objective, efficient delivery of a good or service, but are plagued by interteam disconnect, with informal, isolated networks forming tribal narratives that may undermine the broader strategy of the enterprise and slow their ability to adapt.

Purely social networks of individuals grow rapidly in the information age, easily transmit information, and facilitate decentralized action among their membership, but they are highly disorganized and difficult to focus or control.

These divergent organizational structures are each, in their own ways, both extremely attractive and deeply flawed for leaders looking to adapt their organizational structure to the increasingly complex conditions of the twenty-first century. But a third option holds promise.

The Task Force learned from the networks it fought and adopted many of the best practices associated with their fluid organizational structure, but becoming a pure network was not the end state. The risk of losing control would have exceeded the gains of speed. Rather, the

Task Force adapted certain aspects of networks into its own functionally siloed structure, thereby creating an entirely new *hybrid* model.

Our hybrid model incorporated elements of networks by using an aligning narrative to unite teams, and introducing other practices to foster dotted-line connections between our elite teams. We maintained the predictable structure of our solid-line hierarchy—we could scarcely get rid of that in the military—but the intentional creation of personal relationships among members of the bureaucratically unrelated but functionally interdependent teams allowed us to break down the walls of silos.

The organization became a *hybrid* of bureaucracy and networks, moving away from a traditional method of operation and toward a model that combined the strengths of both opposing systems:

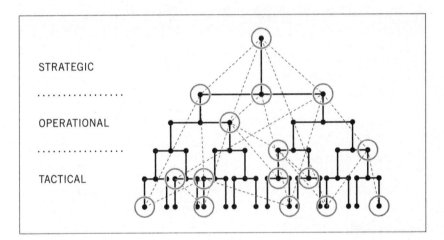

This hybrid structure harnessed the speed and information-sharing capabilities offered by the informal relationships found in networks while retaining the efficiency, reliability, and predictability of a bureaucracy. The impact of this structure was a revolution in the enterprise's agility and operating speed, which was easily perceivable to those of us on the ground, and quantifiable in hindsight.

The hybrid model allowed us to operate the Task Force like a helicopter pilot in low-level flight over hostile terrain. We could both appreciate the deliberately designed aspects of the platform under our control, while also being comfortable in a state of constant adaptation to ever-changing conditions and unpredictable threats. It was this readiness that allowed our organization to maintain its one-mission focus. This is the new model and state to which modern, centrally controlled organizations should aspire to if they wish to compete in the twenty-first century.

In all likelihood you have some characteristics of the hybrid model on the small-team level in various parts of your organization, as did we. But harnessing these clustered small-team networks into an inclusive, aligned whole that can be managed and directed is a unique challenge. At the core of this new organizational model is the idea of maintaining constant one-mission focus.

An *aligning narrative*—a story that forces members to choose between small-tribe norms and the mission of the enterprise—was the linchpin in our evolution—and will be in yours too.

QUESTIONS TO CONSIDER:

♦ What strains are being placed on your information pumps? How often do you personally feel like a bottleneck to cross-functional dialogue and collaboration in your organization?

♦ Where are you seeing complexity enter your environment? How are your teams reacting, and how are the expectations your organization holds for its leadership changing?

♦ Do you have any practices in place that interconnect and force dialogue among different teams and small-team networks in your organization? How might you scale that impact?

CHAPTER 3

AN ALIGNING NARRATIVE

"Cephalopod" is a fancy name for a mollusk with tentacles, like a cuttlefish or octopus. Uniquely, much of their nervous systems are not concentrated within their brains (like ours) but are instead distributed throughout their bodies. In an octopus, for example, the majority of its neurons are in its tentacles—nearly twice as many as can be found in its central brain.

As a result of this distributed nervous system, an octopus's body parts think and act somewhat free from the central brain's direction—to sometimes disconcerting extents. Researchers can surgically remove a tentacle yet still watch the now-severed arm not only move off by itself but also grasp any food it comes across and attempt to pass it back to where the octopus's mouth would be were the tentacle still connected to the body. Each appendage seems to be able to "think" for itself and make decisions on how best to react to what it comes across, and yet when attached to the octopus's body, they coordinate their efforts in such a way as to never tangle with one another.

When I joined the Task Force, I joined a masterfully designed bureaucratic military, a top-down vertebrate with the thinking at the top and the actions at the limbs. We encountered in Al Qaeda a distributed cephalopod, whose limbs could continue to act when severed and whose position on the main body quickly regenerated. Facing such a threat, our top-down alignment structure was insufficient.* We all knew on some level

---

* See Ori Brafman's 2006 *The Starfish and the Spider* for one of the earliest twenty-first-century explorations of this concept.

that our singular mission was to defeat Al Qaeda, but our teams, when empowered to act autonomously, too often accidentally worked against one another.

If we were to become a hybrid model that maintained top-down alignment while also empowering our individual teams to make *coordinating* autonomous decisions, each team would need a deep enough understanding of strategy to operationalize it without top-down direction. To do this, we needed to create a powerful narrative that not only would unite our teams on our organization's single mission but would also tell them *how* to achieve that mission.

PROBLEMS WITH TRADITIONAL APPROACHES TO STRATEGIC ALIGNMENT

The idea of strategic alignment is not new; for years, bureaucratic organizations running on a traditional model have worked to make sure their teams are strategically aligned. However, in most cases this alignment comes from the top, and our experiences in the Task Force showed that a traditional top-down approach to vertical strategic alignment can actually *mask* horizontal misalignment and further fuel narrative divide among teams.

In a traditional business model, the company runs like a crew rowing a racing shell, to borrow an analogy used by Robert Kaplan and David Norton, developers of the "Balanced Scorecard" system. Not only are the parallel crew members horizontally aligned in that they do not disrupt one another's strokes as they row, but they are also vertically aligned in that their combined actions jointly contribute to the overall direction and velocity of their boat.

Kaplan and Norton compare the coxswain's role in a crew to that of corporate headquarters. The leader of the racing shell steers the boat and monitors the cadence of the strokes, providing a uniting force to the team on both vertical and horizontal planes. Similarly, the strategic leadership of an organization monitors every silo's actions, motivating them accordingly and ensuring they do not conflict with one another.

This top-down approach has been the standard for strategic alignment since iconic management figure Peter Drucker popularized "management by objectives" through his 1954 tome *The Practice of Management*.

In it Drucker argued that each of an enterprise's teams needed to be able to work toward clearly defined, often self-guided goals that stack upon one another to better achieve the organization's overarching long-term strategy. His description channels Weber:

> Business performance therefore requires that each job be directed toward the objectives of the whole business. And in particular each manager's job must be focused on the success of the whole. The performance that is expected of the manager must be derived from the performance goals of the business, his results must be measured by the contribution they make to the success of the enterprise. The manager must know and understand what the business goals demand of him in terms of performance, and his superior must know what contribution to demand and expect of him—and must judge him accordingly. If these requirements are not met, managers are misdirected. Their efforts are wasted. Instead of team work, there is friction, frustration and conflict.

Vertically cascading alignment like this is a relatively straightforward process, allowing strategic leaders either to individually frame their organization's different objectives or to delegate ideas on how different silos should interact, down a solid-line org chart. But there are drawbacks to placing ultimate decision-making power in the hands of those at the top of the bureaucratic org chart.

Remove the coxswain's guidance from a crew, and inexperienced rowers may descend into misalignment and poor pacing. Similarly, without senior leadership calling the shots, a company's silos may end up misaligning their efforts if the company is operating in a complicated environment. And if the organization is dealing with complexity, traditionally structured teams will certainly lose their alignment if the top-down communication ceases.

In their *Harvard Business Review* article "Why Strategy Execution Unravels—and What to Do About It," Donald Sull, Rebecca Homkes, and Charles Sull note that the traditional approaches to alignment— "translating strategy into objectives, cascading those objectives down the hierarchy, measuring progress, and rewarding performance"—are insufficient to unite a team on one mission. In fact, though they seem to maintain some measure of vertical alignment, they may actually damage horizontal alignment.

In the hundreds of interviews Sull, Homkes, and Sull conducted over the course of nine years, 84 percent of managers expressed confidence in their ability to rely on and trust their solid line–connected bureaucratic superiors or subordinates—but responses reflected serious problems with horizontal alignment; only 9 percent of managers surveyed felt they could "rely on colleagues in other functions and units all the time." Additionally, managers reported that cross-functional collaboration was "handled badly two times out of three."

Our experiences in Iraq mirrored these problems. As complexity increased, so too did horizontal gaps and resultant mistrust among silos. In the early days, it seemed that the Task Force's strategic leadership set a relatively clear guiding objective for our organization. From my perspective, the ultimate, obvious goal that our organization's teams were expected to "self-guide" upon was to "defeat Al Qaeda in Iraq." We believed that strategic leadership could announce this goal and that it would cascade down to the intelligence officers who worked at an operational level and further down to the operators who moved us forward on the tactical level. We can better picture this cascade through the use of an alignment triangle.

But this direction to "defeat Al Qaeda in Iraq" was the equivalent of a multinational firm's dream of "winning market share" or "earning higher levels of customer satisfaction than our competitors"—a lofty, certainly worthwhile goal, but one that is unfortunately bland and narrowly communicated. As a result, this open-ended, vaguely unifying objective actually served to reinforce disconnects among teams in our enterprise, for "defeat Al Qaeda in Iraq" actually meant *different* things to *different* subordinate silos, which worsened horizontal alignment.

In the Task Force's case, my interpretation of a singular mission to "defeat Al Qaeda in Iraq" could feasibly be twisted to serve my unit's own narrative of what was needed, in our view, to win the broader war. Each of us would inevitably retrofit this mandate from senior leadership to augment our preexisting tribal narratives, as I did in my SEAL unit, where "Did you earn your trident today?" was the filter through which we viewed our strategic direction.

With little transparency and few direct lines of communication between our teams and leaders, each of us could use our organization's overarching objective to feed our myopic view of the fight. This strengthened the already-powerful bonds among our clustered teams but weakened connections with the broader Task Force. This was repeated across our enterprise's lattice of teams, narratives, and cultures—leading to conflicting strategic eforts.

Our state of vertical alignment appeared to be fine on the surface level. Our organization's silos could, in a manner that Drucker might have approved of, independently ascribe metrics and quantitative goalposts to the overall objective, but would do so in a way that reinforced the individual tribal narratives of the respective teams. Of course, our strategic leadership would retain approval authority over these proposed goalposts, keeping everything ordered and controlled.

On paper these added up to a cohesive plan, but in practice the lower goals that our many siloed teams would pursue in the effort to "defeat Al Qaeda in Iraq" would inevitably create intertribal conflict. Gradually, despite the fact that teams were consistently meeting their managed objectives, it became obvious that we could have high batting averages but lose the game. As we met our metrics, the violence around us spiraled out of control. Our networked enemy was not fighting us at our strongest points but instead navigating to the gaps.

Without a new type of nuanced management by objectives, one that placed just as much emphasis on lateral, informal information highways as it did on vertically approved, solid-line pathways of approval and authority, we were in trouble—and I remember the first time I realized just how severe this was in the Task Force.

KHOWST

"Chris, are you around?" The handheld radio on my desk crackled.

"Roger," I replied. "What's up?" I recognized the voice. It belonged to a friend of mine from a civilian intelligence team whose headquarters were located just a few hundred meters away.

"Your team's monkey . . ." the voice on the radio came back. "She just stole our laundry."

"On it," I replied with mock intensity. I got up and walked out of my office into the bleaching midday sun of Afghanistan.

It was 2004, and I was based on a small compound on the edge of Khowst—an arid city located on the country's eastern border. It was my first deployment as a part of the Task Force, and the organization was still in the extremely nascent stages of changing its operational approach. Conversations about changing our internal culture were just starting to happen among our senior leadership, but these had not percolated down into tangible changes at our tactical levels.

Our compound sat on the edge of a long-abandoned Soviet airfield with rusted, decaying skeletons of aircraft from past wars scattered around its perimeter—some of which I could recognize, like the bulbous Mi-17 transport helicopter. My morning run, which consisted of laps around the mile-and-a-half outer loop of the base, wove between these wrecks, closely hugging the twelve-foot-high meshed HESCO barriers that lined our compound.

The monkey I pursued had been living in the compound for at least a year, passed down among the Task Force's operators as we rotated deployments, and she'd become a mascot of sorts. Recently, perhaps bored with our area of the base, she'd gotten in the habit of running along the compound's Tetris-block walls and stealing clothes off of the laundry lines of other units. It wasn't uncommon for our intrabase radios to come alive with a complaint about some simian shenanigans.

Responding to the radio call, I started walking across the compound with a half-eaten banana in hand, intent on winning back the monkey's attention. As I walked, I stared to the east, at the permafrost-tipped mountain range ever visible on the horizon. Beyond those peaks lay the Federally Administered Tribal Areas (FATA) of Pakistan.

The FATA was, and remains to this day, an ungovernable space on the Pakistani side of the border. It was there where pockets of anti-Coalition fighters sat, enjoying sanctuary in that rugged no-man's-land separating these two ancient nations. Over there, opaque enemy networks found the freedom to execute attacks against us, dropping mortar shells in our general direction whenever they pleased. Their accuracy, thankfully, wasn't great; but it seemed that they weren't trying to strike us directly, but instead to remind us that they were safe, secure, and waiting.

The outstation in Khowst hosted an eclectic mix of personnel, who, in accordance with the teachings of thinkers like Weber, Sloan, and Taylor, were compartmentalized across different teams, each beholden to a different narrative about our collective mission. As I walked through the compound and passed the various cordoned-off sections of the base that were each unit's territory, I could see firsthand where one unit's narrative ceased to apply and another's began.

A few hundred yards away from my team's annex, intelligence analysts from civilian agencies were working to develop a network of locally sourced informants, trying to get a better understanding of the membership of those FATA-based insurgent cells. At the far end of the airfield, a conventional unit—standard infantry soldiers—had been tasked with managing infrastructure reconstruction projects in nearby towns, and so were regularly patrolling outside our compound, interacting with the local populace. On another side of the base, a small team of Army Special Forces soldiers held another center of operations, while integrated across that entire mix was a yet-more-motley assortment of Afghan soldiers, early manifestations of the larger Afghan National Army (ANA) that the Coalition would try to build up in the near future.

The people who made up these teams were outstanding professionals, easy to relate to, and exceptionally dedicated to their jobs. We were all in the same conflict, sharing common facilities, and facing similar pressures to advance our efforts. To distant strategic leaders, these overlaps gave the impression that we were synergized. But despite appearances to the contrary, the units that shared the Khowst compound were poorly interconnected and uncommunicative on matters of true substance.

Unfortunately, it was difficult for us to see this, because the Task Force's examinations of alignment tended to be of the "congressional hearing" style, where our organization's leaders would ask high-level questions of their subordinates. If the answers matched what the examiners want to see, they often wouldn't notice that empirical evidence pointed to an inconvenient truth. These kinds of examinations don't succeed, because they are calibrated to measure vertical alignment only, and miss the evidence of horizontal misalignment altogether.

Consider the discussion that occurred in the Capitol in Washington, D.C., on January 13, 2010, among Goldman Sachs CEO Lloyd Blankfein, JP Morgan CEO Jamie Dimon, Morgan Stanley chairman John Mack, Bank of America CEO Brian Moynihan, and the Financial Crisis Inquiry Commission (FCIC) of the U.S. Congress.

The Commission, a ten-person council of congressional leaders, had organized this initial three-hour gathering to supplement its investigation into the factors contributing to the 2007–2008 global financial crisis. But the Republican vice president of the Commission, California representative Bill Thomas, wisely pointed out the limited utility of the hearing. As he argued, the hearing would not be able to see the "7/8ths of the iceberg underwater," and he was right. Opening comments from those testifying scratched only the surface of factors that contributed to the financial crisis. This was no one's fault but simply a by-product of how difficult it is, in a normal process review, to truly tease out the realities of a complex and interconnected system.

A congressional hearing–style test for connectivity among our teams in Afghanistan would have had similar results. Had the Task Force's leaders administered such a hearing to the teams at Khowst, it would have appeared that our efforts were perfectly aligned. Senior solid-line officers would have asked broad questions of their assembled subordinates, who would have presented a unified front and given prepared answers supporting what senior leaders expected to hear: teams are aligned, sharing information effectively, and working together. But this would have been only half true: whereas our Druckerian metrics did in fact vertically align with the strategy of our parent organization, our horizontal alignment was ineffective. What would have prevented us from disclosing this in a congressional hearing–style test for alignment— similar to that of the FCIC—would be a mix of social pressure, frustration with the narrow questioning, and nervousness about disappointing solid-line leaders.

But had our leadership isolated personnel from one another and initiated a non-blaming, unassuming series of deeper questions, the truth would have quickly emerged. Less guarded, more spontaneous answers regarding the state of alignment among our teams would have been offered. These could have taken the form of open admissions on poor horizontal alignment (*You know what? To be totally honest, sir, we* don't *really have the communication or exposure we need with those guys*) or honest revelations about the narratives that existed at the small-team levels in our organization (*This is how we actually think through problem sets we encounter and who we try to go to in our organization for help in solving them*) or frank finger-pointing (*What baffles and frustrates us is that* those *guys don't talk to us, seem to misunderstand our work, and won't show up when we need them to*). This approach would have found contradictory views, each of which was correct in the eyes of the person offering comment.

Much like the parable of the blind men and the elephant, our various elements were each seeing individual parts of a complex and constantly changing puzzle, which was always placing new and fresh demands on them to work closely with one another. Our intelligence teams were gleaning snapshots of the insurgency's growing influence on criminal networks in both Afghanistan and Pakistan, while our conventional and Task Force units were getting a growing sense of these networks' increasing ability to move across the border, and the experiences with Afghan soldiers on base were indicating a steady rise in the insurgency's ability to disrupt our recruitment of local fighters.

The significance of any one of these activities might have been painfully obvious to the team monitoring it, but tying these smaller events into a fully contextualized picture, which could better inform the operations of all of our teams, required a level of personal relationship–based interconnection among us that didn't exist and that our senior leadership couldn't perceive the need for.

It wasn't necessarily personal animosity that kept us apart. Many members of these distinct teams were friendly with one another. Rather, it was the impersonal bureaucratic stove-piping that prevented us from pooling our knowledge or interacting on a deeper level upon it.

In pursuit of our mascot, I finally arrived at the intelligence team's wing of the base and spotted the primate perpetrator. With a half banana in hand, I moved to coax her off her perch and away from the precious clotheslines. She was sitting atop a tall wall that ringed an intelligence team's workplace, and—hearing them moving about in the courtyard on the other side—I yelled across to the analysts, "Sorry, fellas."

A cipher-locked door sat between us, a security feature that represented the broader cultural and operational divide that was metastasizing across the Task Force's ordered body. Whereas the exterior of the Khowst base might have made it aesthetically *appear* to be a sprawling, open space behind high HESCO barriers, guard towers, and a well-fortified main entrance, a knowing eye walking the interior would instead recognize it as a series of bases *within* bases, defined by cipher locks, guarded doors, and thick walls. Protected and maintained behind these features were the tribal narratives of our different teams.

Eventually my efforts to lure the monkey away from the intelligence analysts' annex worked. She hopped down from the wall and, taking the banana from my hand, perched nimbly on my shoulder. Now reunited, and safe from the intelligence team's retribution, we headed back to the Task Force's side of the compound. I had a conference call to dial in to.

"Chris on the line," I said, after returning to my team's courtyard, dropping the monkey off in our annex, and joining the call from our team room. My solid-line superior—an operations officer in Bagram, Afghanistan—was leading the discussion, and the topic at hand was a recent raid that we'd been forced to cancel the night prior.

The reason for this cancellation was that a conventional unit had, unbeknownst to us, established a temporary outpost in the same area where our operation's target was located. We had identified this issue only just before our team had launched, when I'd put in a call to a contact in the conventional unit's command chain to notify them of our pending mission—an oversight that would have been negated had our teams been better operationally integrated.

Once identified, it was immediately clear that the risk of our forces encountering each other, and the resulting potential for friendly fire, was too high. The conventional team was already established in the area, so we'd decided to stand down. In my mind it had been a successful deconfliction, a sign that the system was working.

"From now on, no more stovepipes," announced an unexpected voice. It had the unmistakably southern drawl of a senior officer in our bureaucracy who was in command of all the Task Force's units in Afghanistan. A colonel, he reported directly to McChrystal, who himself was less than a year into his time as the Task Force's commanding general. It was the first time I'd heard that word—"stovepipe"— used in our organization, but this exchange would be a simple foreshadowing of what was to come.

This tactical slipup was not the type of issue that would normally gain the attention of the colonel overseeing operations around the entire country. But he was, I would understand in hindsight, already involved in deep discussions with McChrystal about the complexity of the fight. He was leveraging this after-action discussion as an opportunity to educate all of us on the direction things would be heading in soon.

Similar discussions were in their early stages across the Task Force. As the colonel spoke about collaboration with other organizations, about early synchronization of efforts versus last-minute deconfliction of actions, and about building truly effective relationships with other organizations, my thoughts drifted to the walls, cipher locks, and security procedures that still separated the various units within the Khowst compound. These were products of, and contributors to, the narrative gulfs that helped keep our organizations compartmentalized.

I realized just how far we had to go. There was no single person who bureaucratically owned this issue, no standalone order that would force us to collaborate. This would be a culture change, something that would take years—but this was a start.

CREATING AN ALIGNING NARRATIVE

The colonel's words over the phone that day were a product of the Task Force's still-emerging aligning narrative, which was being developed within the strategic hallways of our organization and would eventually be used to break down the tribal ones of our teams.

I encountered the new narrative just a few weeks after returning from my first deployment with the Task Force. On a morning like any other, I'd gotten to work and logged on to my desktop to check the morning's e-mail traffic before heading to the gym.

At the top of my inbox was an e-mail marked "high priority," and the sender was none other than McChrystal. Its contents, sent directly to every member of the organization, were straightforward. In one paragraph a few simple facts were laid out, but more important, they were contextualized in a well considered narrative. Having just returned from deployment, I found that these words had an especially deep significance.

> We are at war, and in war, there are winners and losers. We are a force comprised of the most capable, well equipped, and highly trained warriors the battlefield has ever known. Your actions in the fight have shown that this is true.
> But make no mistake—we can win every individual battle, and still lose. To win, we will need to change. If you are not willing to become part of that change, then you will not enjoy being part of this organization moving forward.
> What we are doing now is not working, and I take responsibility for that. I also take responsibility for the change that lies ahead.

McChrystal's tone was not threatening, and he did not cast blame. Rather, he offered a simple statement of fact about where we were in the fight and what would start to be expected from our teams if they truly intended to win. More important, it was an invitation to be part of the process, or to leave, with no middle ground offered.

He laid out our overall goal in no uncertain terms, but then, instead of doubling down on our main goal of defeating Al Qaeda or mandating exactly how teams would interact with one another, he went on to remind us generally of the importance of interpersonal interconnection among our teams. Our overarching goal now was not to simply "defeat Al Qaeda in Iraq" but to become the type of culture that could beat a complex enemy. Our process was as important as our end goal, and defining our process was the equation introduced in chapter 1:

Credibility = Proven Competence + Integrity + Relationships

By emphasizing our new priorities to create relationships, to reach across boundaries, and to form the network half of our hybrid model, the equation changed our narrative in one important way. Instead of talking only about winning, we would talk about changing how we operated *in order to win*. Our alignment triangle would now reflect this change.

Over the next few years, our leadership would leave little room for misinterpretation of what these principles meant or of the necessity of our changing our success-measuring metrics to match them. They would talk

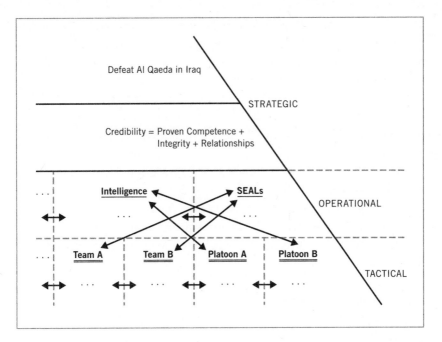

to us, day after day, week after week, about becoming something different, something bigger, and something far more capable than we thought possible.

COMMUNICATING AN ALIGNING NARRATIVE

In openly addressing the need for the Task Force's teams to demonstrate more informal interconnectivity, defy tribal barriers, and eschew reserve in favor of transparency, our leadership began to model a new type of behavior consistent with its still-developing aligning narrative. The implicit hope was that our teams would take this cue and steadily embrace the same behavior among themselves—a trend that would cascade as more and more members of narratively similar peer groups adopted similar behavior, strengthening social pressure on other members to do the same.

For the Task Force, full change would not take hold overnight, but a starting gun had been fired. From that point on, our aligning narrative would be repeatedly, incessantly broadcast into the rank and file of our teams—through e-mail, in-person visits, and daily forums broadcast around the world. Moreover, whenever one of us had a successful operation or result derived from this new type of behavior, our leadership would flag it to the rest of the organization, maximizing the utility of our social learning.

Remember, we started to hear from them, day in and day out, *this is always going to be hard. What makes our organization unique is the way we're trying to communicate, share information, and act as a unified and networked team.*

We have the best fighting force in the world. That is not in question. But we need to become networked. We need to connect our teams and partners around the world in order to win. We're many different teams embarking on a single mission. The way we communicate and share information, the way we protect our relationships with one another, and the way we demonstrate trust—that's what's going to release capacity from within our teams.

This narrative, told to us every day, cast each of us as an actor in an entirely new story. We started to feel what was possible, and the best among us were showing a willingness to forgo concepts of "tribe" in order to become part of this new culture.

Every day, our aligning narrative and its associated behaviors became increasingly ingrained in our thinking, a product of the repetition of messages coming from our leadership and of observing the impact that this new approach began to have on the battlefield. Relationships over missions, trust over individual accomplishment; slowly, we all started to believe that this was the approach that would bring us the tangible progress we were all there to achieve.

Attitudes were changing. There was an evolving willingness to make the changes necessary for true alignment. Our horizontal exposure began to inform our new approach to management-by-objectives.

Now we needed to make the practical changes that would allow us to build trust further and extend dotted-line relationships across our solid-line structure. It was time to act upon our aligning narrative.

QUESTIONS TO CONSIDER:

♦ How does your organization currently measure horizontal alignment among its teams and functional silos? Would your teams be able to demonstrate horizontal alignment in a non-congressional-hearing-style test setting?

♦ Your teams might claim to trust and have open lines of dialogue with one another—but can they demonstrate examples of how this trust is helping accomplish your organization's strategy?

♦ In your organization's current state, how would an aligning narrative be best emphasized and contextualized for your teams?

CASE STUDY:
INTUIT

PREFACE

As you read of Intuit's approach to strategic alignment, keep in mind the concepts we framed in the previous chapter.

In particular, note that whereas this company's environment and strategy had long emphasized to its teams the need for cultural and operational unification, this hadn't taken hold effectively among employees. This organization's misalignment manifested itself in employees being unable to provide clear guidance on strategy or, on the flip side, being confused by the strategy put out by its leadership.

In addition, consider how Intuit's new approach to strategic alignment revolved around clearly communicating its strategy for subordinate silos to follow, and how a traditional cascading approach to strategic alignment was adapted to better effect (through both aligning narrative-style clarification and the use of the alignment triangle tool).

Finally, observe how Intuit used technology to bypass traditional bureaucratic means of communicating strategy, a topic we will discuss in the following chapter.

THE SETUP

I first met Brad Smith, CEO of Intuit, just a few months after I left the military. A focused, people-oriented leader with a subtle, disarming twang in his voice suggestive of his West Virginia roots, he immediately impressed me. It's a well-known fact in the military that when a southern-accented general says with real kindness, "Well, I might not be the smartest one in the room . . . ," you're about to learn something. Smith embodies the same disarming approach, coupled with an incredible leadership acumen. Our early meeting was formative for me, as it introduced me to the passion that existed in the technology space for the study and practice of leadership.

Intuit Inc.'s birth in 1983 was a humble affair. That year the hardware and software giants of today were still in their infancy, staffed by relatively small teams that were barely getting by—Microsoft was only five years old and was still dependent on programming work for IBM, while Apple's most recent venture into the home computer market (the clunky, defect-ridden Apple III) in 1980 had ended with commercial failure.

Founded by Scott Cook (a veteran of the management consulting and household product worlds), who was inspired by his wife's complaint about the burdens of pen-and-paper checkbook balancing, Intuit's motivating purpose was to enable average consumers to manage their own finances at a fraction of the typical cost, hassle, and time. The way to translate this vision into a reality? Cook's answer was to craft radically consumer-friendly personal finance software and offer it to the growing pool of American PC owners.

Cook, an economics and mathematics major, lacked the expertise to start on this path. But through a chance encounter at Stanford University, he connected with programmer Thomas Proulx, and together they founded the company in 1983.

As Intuit first strove for success, it faced existential threats, flirting frequently with disaster. Its close skeleton crew had to work without pay at times, as the company's bank account balance ran as low as fifty dollars. Marriages were jeopardized by the intensity of the work, and employees even suffered physically—Proulx, while trying to adapt Intuit's flagship financial software product (Quicken) to a different PC operating environment, worked his way into developing a bleeding ulcer. He requested access to a computer from his hospital bed so that he could keep coding, and was denied.

In those early days, what bound its small, clustered team together was a widely held focus on serving consumers better than any other competitor could hope to. The low head count of the company prevented echo chambers from forming and diverging from the company's central devotion to optimizing user experience.

There are many examples of how every corner of Intuit's small staff was aligned on what mattered: both on their purpose and on the personal way they approached customers. The company's first marketing officer would regularly call up and interview individual home users who had mailed feedback forms to the company, and employees distributed hundred-dollar software packages for free to attendees of different trade shows. By 1989 Intuit had begun dispatching employees to accompany first-time Quicken buyers home from software stores to assist in the installation process. Ease of use, consumer-friendly packaging, rapid elimination of software bugs, and building brand loyalty—these were the pillars of Intuit's business, all informed by its Cook-and-Proulx-centered devotion to pleasing customers, which was easily propagated through its small size.

Yet once these first battles had been won, a behemoth threat loomed in the early 1990s: Microsoft, by then a vast software giant that had already conquered the word processor and spreadsheet worlds (through its now-ubiquitous Word and Excel programs), was looking to financial management software next via its new Microsoft Money program.

On paper, it should have been no competition. In 1991 Microsoft's revenues were more than forty times those of Intuit, and it had 8,200 employees to Cook's by-then two-hundred-strong team. It had won new markets through similar means—Word and Excel had swept smaller competitors out of the way, and Money was expected to do the same to Intuit's Quicken. Worse yet, Intuit's product for Microsoft-operated PCs (Quicken for Windows) was set to arrive on the market two months *after* Microsoft Money.

Not only was David far smaller than Goliath, but he had arrived on the battlefield later.

And yet, David won.

On closer inspection, the factors behind this upset were clear: not only was Quicken for Windows far better packaged and more user-friendly than Money, but Intuit had also anticipated Microsoft's entry into the market, issuing price rebates in advance for customers to use on Intuit's product. Consumers proved willing to wait out Money for the cheaper, objectively better Quicken for Windows. When Microsoft realized what had happened, it issued its own price rebates, but these backfired. Microsoft's huge, reactive discounting drastically reduced potential profit margins for retailers, prompting them to further prioritize the sale of Quicken for Windows to customers.

The takeaway was that Microsoft's bureaucracy and large size contributed to a lack of reactivity among silos, whereas Intuit's narratively aligned team proved more able to serve customers quicker and better.

Goliath had lost handily, outmaneuvered by a smaller, more reactive foe.

In the meantime, Intuit was still expanding—in 1990, prompted by the large number of small businesses that were using Quicken as an off-brand, programmable corporate accountant, the company created a new Small Business Group (SBG) division. Its central product would be the now-ubiquitous QuickBooks, a reengineered version of Quicken designed for use by businesses rather than families for managing internal finances.

And so Intuit kept growing, adding bureaucratic lattices to its ever-expanding, ever-more-impersonal structure and increasing degrees of separation between teams and leadership across its broadening areas of responsibility.

In 1993 Intuit had its IPO, and by 1994 it was entertaining a nearly $2 billion attempted buyout from Microsoft (that was later blocked by the U.S. government). Goliath, a firm once dedicated to muscling tiny Intuit out of business, was now interested in forging a permanent alliance at no small cost. Cook, Proulx, and Co.'s efforts had paid off, and Intuit had become the undisputed king of its new field within a decade of its founding.

THE PROBLEM

1993 proved to be a watershed year for Intuit. Beginning with its IPO, a new stage of growth began for the company, both organic and inorganic. That year Intuit bought Chipsoft—a company that had invented the tax software TurboTax—reflecting a long-held ambition of Proulx to break into the tax-preparation software business. Moreover, feeling increasingly out of touch with his rapidly changing company as it ballooned to new proportions, Cook came to believe he was no longer the right person to lead it. In mid-1994 he formally ceded his role as Intuit's CEO, retaining a seat on its board of directors as chairman.

For a long time, on paper, things seemed to be going swimmingly, and by conventional metrics they were. In 1999 Intuit bought Rock Financial, quickly rechristening it "Quicken Loans," which gave Intuit exposure to the consumer loans industry. From an outside perspective, and that of Wall Street, things were going phenomenally throughout the first few years of the new millennium—not only was the company valued well into the billions, but it was continuously sustaining aggressive growth, expanding into various business sectors that seemed to offer exciting new opportunities.

But now Intuit was no longer the nimble upstart among behemoths, the radically consumer-focused agent challenging slow incumbents—the company had evolved into a different beast entirely, with heavily staffed business units spanning various lines of work that were unfamiliar with one another.

Tayloe Stansbury, Intuit's chief technology officer and a veteran of the company since 2009, explains how this disconnected status quo within Intuit formed and how the conditions of that company's external environment helped prompt it:

> We started as a software company with separate products on a desktop. There weren't a lot of ways for those products to share work flows or data. . . . Fast-forward, and we've become an on-line and mobile phone [software-centered] company, and guess what? Now there are a lot of opportunities for those various things to happen. Yet we've had fairly entrenched mind-sets that get in the way of that. Part of that is organizational structure by business unit, so that it's harder for things to happen across business-unit boundaries when it requires sharing a lot of technology, or planning user experience or projects that go across their functions.

Stansbury had his finger on the central operational feature not only of companies like Intuit but also Weberian bureaucracies in general that makes them weak in terms of horizontal collaboration: poor lateral connections across teams and silos, which (as Intuit had seen) both lead to *and* reinforce operational and narrative-based gulfs among them.

To those who had the chance to assume different perspectives inside Intuit's hierarchical machine—as I did in the Task Force, moving from leading SEAL platoons to operations-level positions—this problem was abundantly clear.

Brad Smith was one of these individuals—he had joined Intuit in 2003 as a vice president in its Accountant Central division, a functional group devoted to helping facilitate the company's relationships with tax and financial professionals. He transitioned through increasingly high-ranked executive roles in the company—including at its Small Business Group and Consumer Tax Group (which had been formed in the aftermath of Chipsoft's acquisition). Moving through these divisions, it was hard for him to ignore the institutionalized inertia of the company and the growing organizational opacity among swelling business units—which was having a perceivable operational impact on the company.

Like Stansbury, Smith noted that the outside environment had become more favorable to collaboration among Intuit's business units—leveraging "social media, cloud, mobile, and data" technology had emerged over the years as a common opportunity for Intuit's various teams—but had yet to be effectively acted upon.

Soon enough he was in a position to do something about it—Smith raced through the ranks at Intuit, and by 2008 he'd risen to be president and CEO. From this perspective, he could recognize that the company's operationally disconnected state was analogous to those of its peers.

He reflected in 2014, "Legacy technology companies, the big guys, are all worried about the same thing: the small start-up coming out of the dorm room, built on the latest technology, taking huge swipes at us." For Intuit and these "legacies," once insurgents in their own right, it was now a question of "how do you take a company at scale and move it with the speed of a startup?"

It wasn't being asked just by him, either: Matt Rhodes, a current vice president for corporate planning at Intuit, who's been at the company since 2010, knew things were going "fine." In his words, "We weren't doing terribly; we were doing great."

But from team to team, a question remained—one that Rhodes frames simply as "Are we the best that we can be?"

The answer, to many, apparently felt like no. And also, what did he mean by "we"?

THE SOLUTION

This was what began Smith's push to establish what he called "One Intuit"—a slogan that was intended to create a truly united company, break down the echo chambers that existed in its org chart, and guide the strategic alignment of Intuit's separate business units, which he had noticed was lacking.

The communication of this new purpose of "One Intuit" began not long after he assumed the CEO position in 2008—and was intended to be the bedrock of Intuit's equivalent of an aligning narrative, which would end what Smith called Intuit's "six mind-sets" in the business.

But at its inception, and for a while afterward, Smith's "One Intuit" didn't take well—despite its being percolated through conventional, solid-line means and issued in press releases and corporate memos, teams were generally confused and unaware of the significance of the message and what "One Intuit" really meant across the different business units of the company. This is a throwback to a common issue organizations have regarding alignment: oftentimes a top-down, conventional Druckerian approach to strategic alignment can establish solid vertical alignment but conceal horizontal misalignment.

Intuit collected annual feedback from its employees through a third party, and many anonymous responses from across the company's tiers and silos struck a similar note: *we don't feel like one company, and we don't grasp why we should.* Moreover, it wasn't clear to many what exactly the motive of Intuit's leadership was in pushing this agenda—the mandate to "work together" and "unify" being broadcast came across as somewhat vague and confusing. Many felt it was levying *blame* where they'd seen years of perceived success across the company's teams.

And so it was in 2013 that Smith was in a closed-door session with fellow tech executives at Intuit's headquarters in Mountain View, California, talking through their shared experiences in this realm. This is when I first met Brad, as Stan McChrystal and I were in that meeting as well, giving a presentation on operational reformation in the military. After a few back-and-forths with us, Smith asked the McChrystal Group to assist in Intuit's transformation. His direction was clear: to establish better narrative alignment across the many successful but distinct teams within the organization.

At Intuit we would end up using several practices to fully deliver on the final destination Smith intended for the company—ranging from clearer alignment on the desired narrative of "One Intuit" to the use of an interconnecting forum to better communicate and communalize that message and an established operating rhythm to balance the cadence of Intuit's teams. We will detail most of these practices in a later part of this book, but our engagement with Intuit focused initially on clarifying and better communicating through better strategic alignment what was meant by "One Intuit."

It began with developing a way to communicate and contextualize what Smith's strategic leadership envisioned as the practice of One Intuit—and allowing their teams to grasp, with radical transparency, where their efforts fit into it.

This came through the creation and distribution of alignment triangles throughout Intuit's silos, with the contents of Intuit's pinnacle strategic alignment triangle including a mix of traditional Druckerian management by objectives and the behavior expected and encouraged by the preexisting slogan of One Intuit:

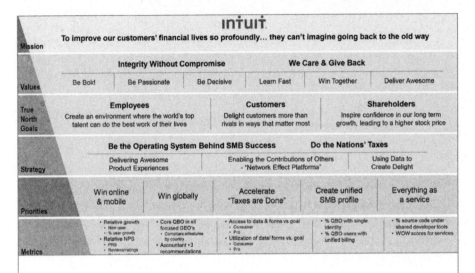

intuit
Mission To improve our customers' financial lives so profoundly... they can't imagine going back to the old way

	Integrity Without Compromise			We Care & Give Back		
Values	Be Bold	Be Passionate	Be Decisive	Learn Fast	Win Together	Deliver Awesome

	Employees	Customers	Shareholders
True North Goals	Create an environment where the world's top talent can do the best work of their lives	Delight customers more than rivals in ways that matter most	Inspire confidence in our long term growth, leading to a higher stock price

	Be the Operating System Behind SMB Success		Do the Nations' Taxes	
Strategy	Delivering Awesome Product Experiences	Enabling the Contributions of Others - "Network Effect Platforms"	Using Data to Create Delight	

	Win online & mobile	Win globally	Accelerate "Taxes are Done"	Create unified SMB profile	Everything as a service
Priorities					

Metrics	• Relative growth • New user • % user growth • Relative NPS • PRS • Reviews/ratings	• Core QBO in all focused GEO's • Compliance/features by country • Accountant +3 recommendations	• Access to data & forms vs goal • Consumer • Pro • Utilization of data/ forms vs. goal • Consumer • Pro	• % QBO with single identity • % QBO users with unified billing	• % source code under shared developer tools • WOW scores for services

Whereas a typical approach to strategic alignment would have placed a tangible event or market-related metric at the pinnacle of its emphasis, the use of the ideological slogan "One Intuit"—with its derivative need for "improving our customers' lives so profoundly they can't imagine going back"—as the primary goal of the company represented a departure from this school of thought, while also not drifting too far into relying only on uncontextualized, open-ended statements (like "One Intuit").

To substantiate this new approach to alignment, the principles and behaviors that informed what "One Intuit" was expected to mean to the company's subordinate teams had to be substantiated as well—the same logic that underlay the Task Force strategic leadership's elaboration on how "defeat Al Qaeda in Iraq" in the form of *Credibility = Proven Competence + Integrity + Relationships*.

So emerged Intuit's "Values," which then themselves cascaded into "True North Goals"—tangible, derivative, stakeholder-centric goals that were to be the focal points of what One Intuit's practice had to center around in each silo. This would theoretically empower Intuit's subordinate teams with a clearer sense of the behavior that One Intuit was expected to entail.

The order in which these True North Goals were presented within Intuit's alignment triangle—employees, customers, and shareholders—was deliberate. The rationale for this was the perceived order of focus each of these stakeholders would take within Intuit's strategic execution.

Intuit					
Mission To improve our customers' financial lives so profoundly... they can't imagine going back to the old way					
Values Integrity Without Compromise			We Care & Give Back		
Be Bold	Be Passionate	Be Decisive	Learn Fast	Win Together	Deliver Awesome
True North Goals **Employees** Create an environment where the world's top talent can do the best work of their lives		**Customers** Delight customers more than rivals in ways that matter most		**Shareholders** Inspire confidence in our long term growth, leading to a higher stock price	

A metaphor often used is that these three are like "air, water, and food," in that order, to the well-being of the company—you die immediately without the first, can make it a little longer without the second, and can survive slightly longer than that without the third. But go without any of the three for an extended period of time, and death (corporate death, in this case) isn't far behind.

These top tiers of Intuit's new alignment triangle were principled, not quantitative—and, interestingly, they were a deliberate throwback to what the company had radically focused on during previous generations of its leadership.

Recall Cook and Proulx's early earnest interest in serving their customers better than any potential competitor or old technology ever could—a narrative they could disseminate well, given the tiny size of Intuit at that point in its history. When Smith and his immediate strategic leadership team began considering how to break down their new aligning narrative, it was this early ideological standard that they wanted One Intuit to deliberately hark back to. And so the company's designated "Mission" (consult the diagram above) was to cater to its customers to the point that "they can't imagine going back to the old way."

Similarly, the very name "True North Goals" came from a series of stakeholder-centric principles that Smith's predecessors had tried to communalize through the organization, through solid line–centric means, with relative success—a management-by-objectives approach. Smith kept this terminology on board, likely to avoid redundancy and confusion.

But Intuit's leaders also knew what they didn't know and where they should stop trying to micromanage the actions of operational or tactical teams—they couldn't feasibly mandate what Stansbury referred to as the "work flows or data" among subordinate silos or force horizontal alignment and interconnection among teams.

"I think the death knell of a company, or a leader in it, is when they think they have more answers than questions," Smith says. "We therefore

	Be the Operating System Behind SMB Success			Do the Nations' Taxes
Strategy	Delivering Awesome Product Experiences	Enabling the Contributions of Others - "Network Effect Platforms"		Using Data to Create Delight
Priorities	Win online & mobile	Win globally	Accelerate "Taxes are Done"	Create unified SMB profile	Everything as a service

Metrics	• Relative growth
	• New user
	• % user growth
	• Relative NPS
	• PRS
	• Reviews/ratings
		• Core QBO in all focused GEO's
		• Compliance/features by country
		• Accountant +3 recommendations
			• Access to data & forms vs goal
			  • Consumer
			  • Pro
			• Utilization of data/ forms vs. goal
			  • Consumer
			  • Pro
				• % QBO with single identity
				• % QBO users with unified billing
					• % source code under shared developer tools
					• WOW scores for services

have to guard against intellectual certainty." In a complex market, and atop the bureaucratic totem pole of a multibillion-dollar company, this is a sound mentality to maintain.

To guard against intellectual certainty, the outputs under each of Intuit's True North Goals were not fixed; Smith left the tactical and operational-level means by which the goals should be "achieved" up to the teams within the company. In turn, these teams—far down Intuit's bureaucratic silos—were encouraged to think diligently and creatively about the means to reach these ends and were afforded the autonomy to create cross-silo connections as needed in order to reach their True North Goals.

This is where more conventional metrics—like relative market share and product performance—could be generated and assigned a place in the triangle by tactical leaders.

Similar to the hybrid structure that the Task Force had adopted, Smith was creating a healthy and natural tension between two systems. Operational- and tactical-level solutions within Intuit were made adaptable based on changing conditions perceived by networks across each business unit, while the higher-level strategic direction of the company was held fixed across the enterprise on a longer time horizon.

Intuit's Vision and Values would remain resistant to change—and communicated in conjunction with the need for the company to act as "one"—so that teams could create cross-boundary solutions and collaborate with autonomy, empowered to do so in line with the steady drumbeat of "One Intuit" coming from the firm's strategic leadership.

So how to set and coordinate this drumbeat?

Recall that when Smith had tried to disperse the "One Intuit" message when he first came up with it—back in 2008—his efforts to contextualize what it actually meant fell short, confusing those on the receiving end of it down the solid-line highways of Intuit's org chart. Further recall that Smith's predecessors had limited success in making their own "True North Values" stick within the company.

The common factor in each of these cases was that conventional means of trying to create narrative alignment across a large enterprise had definite ceilings—they entailed either enlisting different people in a solid-line hierarchy to "pass along the message" or sending out e-mails and company memos that put forth new corporate ethics, approaches that earn only limited buy-in among the dotted-line rank and file.

So for Smith's new initiative a new, better means to communicate the new aligning narrative of One Intuit came through the "One Intuit Forum"—video-supported, mass-participation events that initially occurred biweekly across the company's silos. These forums, first consisting of only Smith and senior staff, would become a means whereby the principles of One Intuit, and the operational state of the company's different teams, could be contextualized firsthand across the company's bureaucracy.

Forums and their associated operating rhythm are major pieces of subject matter that will be explored in this book's following chapters, so we will not dwell too long on the nuances of how Intuit installed and practiced them here. Nevertheless, the company's ability to assemble large numbers of its teams ensured that the newly contextualized principles of One Intuit could be communicated to all influencers and key individuals across the entire company—free from the excess degrees of separation that are endemic to bureaucracies.

As Rhodes recalls, these required heavy investment in technology, as well as consideration as to their frequency, and there was a learning curve about how to best ensure the right type of communication in them.

Rhodes had a firsthand role in helping facilitate the design and assembly of these forums, and during this process he found a few interesting challenges to their implementation, which seemed, at first, straightforward and intuitive.

Rhodes elaborates, "One of the things we did was underestimate how much churn [the One Intuit Forum] would create, even though we told people, *Hey, be vulnerable. Show up. Know your stuff. Facts are friendly. Look at the data.* People still wanted to be really polished and crisp in case Brad [Smith] called on them in that meeting."

In these virtual, participation-dependent realms, Intuit's various teams were expected to both attend and participate in the discussion of their needs, project developments, and potential areas for cross-cooperation across silos—while also being audiences for the communication of One Intuit by Smith and others who worked by its principles. By doing so, the narrative-confined, echo-chamber-esque networks that existed within each of Intuit's silos could be newly exposed to a firsthand experience of One Intuit.

Moreover, when Smith did resort to his "continuing cheerleading, and trying to call out a best practice," he had a greater assembly of participants to pay attention and internalize the type of social learning that would happen throughout the organization.

THE OUTCOMES

So how did this mix of practices, spearheaded by the proper contextualization of One Intuit, change the state of disconnection among the company's siloed business units?

As laid out in Intuit's new strategic alignment triangle in the category of "True North Goals," three demographics were designated to receive the greatest positive takeaway from Intuit's alignment: shareholders, customer populations, and employees.

Regarding communicating the full scale of the company's push for alignment on One Intuit to "people on the street" (i.e., Wall Street), there was a bit of initial hesitation internally within the company's strategic leadership. Rhodes described this debate as centering around a stated concern of "Hey, is this going to really translate externally? Are the nuances of this going to make a lot of sense to these people?"

These concerns were rooted in the idea that the amount of strategic and cultural detail laid out in the One Intuit alignment triangles—which would need to be shared with these stakeholders—would prove overwhelming. Rhodes clarifies, "It is a lot of detail . . . relative to what we have shared in the past about our strategy and what we are all trying to do."

But sharing these outcomes was a success. Intuit's investors appreciated the deluge of strategic detail that Intuit's new alignment narrative offered, versus the relatively clipped lines of dialogue they'd been exposed to before—both from Intuit and from other sources in their line of work.

Rhodes lays this out well: "If I am an investor, I can always go back to see what exactly Intuit is trying to accomplish on one page, but if I want to see the detail on it, it is out there. We've been doing this consistently for two years now."

Intuit's employees, beyond senior directors like Rhodes, also began to see this added value firsthand.

Recall that Intuit regularly used a third party to collect anonymous feedback from its employees on recent initiatives and the status of the company. Smith notes how these changed dramatically within "one or two years" of our initial partnership in 2013: "The write-ins started to say: *One Intuit, it's real,* or *Hey, I can now understand this and see it happen.*"

This also stood in contrast to the state of Intuit's peers in the tech world. "Back when I was at another Silicon Valley company—to remain nameless," says Rhodes, "an investor would ask us, 'What's your strategy?' I'd have to look him in the eyes for five or six seconds and think to myself, *Okay, how do I want to answer this?* Because we didn't have one that we were all aligned on internally." The answer would be specific to both the audience and the member of the organization being asked to elaborate on its strategy.

You may be able to project Rhodes's past predicament onto members of your organization or, alternately, assume that your different teams would be able to pass such a test. A common frame of thinking I often hear when explaining the nuances of an aligning narrative (similar to the concept of One Intuit) goes as follows: *We've already got that here— mission statements hanging on our walls, principles printed in our 10-Q, a knowledge of who our stakeholders are and which goals we're working toward. We've thought these through, and everybody's fine with them.*

If this is your response, then your teams would probably pass the congressional hearing–style test we discussed in chapter 3—but that's insufficient for today's complex environment. Once isolated from one another and pressed for a little more detail in answers to similar questions, different teams' answers on your organization's strategy, and how it relates to their tactical approaches and expected behavior, will start to diverge fairly quickly. Their ability to collaborate and operate with speed and autonomy in a constantly shifting environment, therefore, will also come up short.

Smith remains the CEO of Intuit and today partially credits the firm's success over recent years by conventional metrics, and its business-related decisions, to the clarification and contextualization of One Intuit—as well as the use of forums and an operating rhythm to get this new message out.

"[Through this style of alignment] we rewrote our strategy. We changed our innovation model to . . . [identify] those that we could work with to solve common problem sets. We then changed our values to promote this type of [collaborative] behavior."

This newly contextualized and widely understood state of strategic alignment led to some momentous decisions: in March of 2016, it was announced that Intuit's Quicken brand was being bought by a private equity firm after a long bid-soliciting process.

Smith credits this decision, and the subsequent growth of the company, to the new decision-making apparatus that narrative alignment on One Intuit enabled:

> [Our new alignment] led to a set of decisions where we sold businesses that didn't fit in the ecosystem, they didn't fit in alignment, including the founder's original product, Quicken. We sold [that] last year. The seed core of the company, that work led us to [recognize] . . . does not fit and align. It does not make the whole stronger. As a result, we found those places better homes and it just tightened up our focus and our resource allocation—which in turn got our message clearer to the street, and our market cap went from eighteen to twenty-nine billion [dollars] now.

Intuit seems to be acting as "one" now—in a way both consistent with and distinguished from the vision of its original founders, given the scale of the company. The return to the roots of the organization is not a literal one, then; rather, it's a return to origins in a spiritual sense: a connection with its consumer, a love for its product, and a common, oft-reinforced narrative that makes long nights and difficult quarters as much of a shared experience as the best of times.

For today's Intuit, it is back to a shared sense of ideology and strategy in what is now, in reality, "One Intuit."

CHAPTER 4

INTERCONNECTION

"Remember," McChrystal told me early in my time on his staff, "your position has little formal authority but massive reach. For many of the organizations we interact with, their entire opinion of our organization will be shaped off the tone of *your* e-mails, the courtesy *you* give their staff, and the respect *you* show for their mission." It was eye-opening and important counsel. I'd gone from a leader within a unit to a connector of multiple units in a matter of days. It wasn't me that mattered, but the position I filled, which touched all parts of the Task Force and had the potential to be massively disruptive to their planning and logistics if I mishandled coordination. I had the advantage, at that point, of understanding the aligning narrative of the organization, and I had an appreciation of how critical our credibility was to the mission. What I didn't appreciate, until it was laid out by McChrystal, was how influential my position would be in supporting and strengthening that narrative.

I realized quickly that I was not alone in this space. I began to understand that there were *culture carriers* who connected the organization and shaped our dotted-line connectivity. It was important to recognize who the influencers were in each organization, to empower them to reach across boundaries between teams, and to create an environment that would allow all members of the organization to increase in connectivity. As you move through the process of transforming your team into a hybrid organization, you'll find that the right aligning narrative, targeted at key influencers throughout your small teams, sets conditions for boundary spanners to develop and create connections among silos. Informal relationships and cross-boundary trust can soon follow. The question is *how* to prompt these connections.

INFLUENCERS

When an organization is presenting a new narrative to its teams, it's important to reach out first to the influencers who shape the attitudes and decisions of the organization. Their adoption of a new narrative will ease the organization's transition, so identifying these leaders is crucial. Unfortunately, it's also sometimes difficult.

In networks, individuals with the largest numbers of personal connections to other members of their clustered team are the most "powerful," and this is especially true in the network clusters that spring up within the silos of a solid-line bureaucracy. These people are commonly referred to by network theorists as "hubs" (invoking the image of a spoked wheel), "influencers," or "connectors." It is essential that an aligning narrative be targeted at and communicated to these individuals. Without gaining traction with these influencers, change efforts will stall.

The solid-line org chart does an effective job of depicting the theoretical *authority*-related pecking order among different members of teams in organizations, but it tells little about the practical operational or cultural relevance of them. In reality, it is critical to be able to identify the young logistics specialist as the real center of power when it comes to airfield operations; or to understand that the most respected Ranger in a platoon

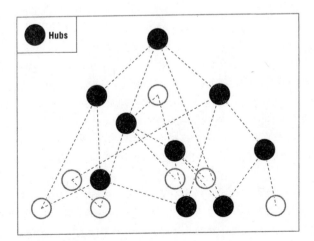

might be a young corporal; or to know that the best summary of up-to-date intelligence might exist within a small analyst lunch group that gathers every afternoon in the chow hall, rather than in a formal intelligence exchange meeting. In a similar way, these individuals should be recognized for their importance to the tribal narratives that exist within small teams.

In his book *Linked,* physicist and network theorist Albert-László Barabási refers to modern-day "opinion leaders," "power users," and "influencers" as great examples of such hubs, given the sheer number of other people who are regularly exposed to their viewpoints (either passively or actively) and feel a valued personal connection to them. In academia, Barabási notes, "the attention to hubs is well deserved. Hubs are special. They dominate the structure of all networks in which they are present, making them look like small worlds."

Barabási elaborates on the potential for social change held by these individuals as well: "Though not necessarily innovators themselves, their conversion is the key to launching an idea or innovation. If the hubs resist a product, they form such an impenetrable and influential wall that the innovation can only fail. If they accept it, they influence a very large number of people."

This truth has already been picked up on across the cutting edge of the marketing industry, in which "influencers" on online social media platforms are increasingly being seen as an effective means of disseminating interest in a brand or product. A 2016 article and platform-by-platform breakdown published by the *Economist* posited that "social media offer brands their best opportunity to reach cord-cutting millennials" and noting the exponentially increasing number of sponsored social media posts being made on these platforms.

These influencers have so much power because of social "contagion," a concept explored in Christakis and Fowler's excellent work *Connected.* Social contagion is the process by which ideas spread through interpersonal relationships and interactions. When people view other people doing something, they are inclined either consciously or subconsciously to mimic it. This is even stronger in the related case of *social learning,* when people are motivated by seeing others being rewarded for a behavior to imitate it.

Social learning and social contagion played a role in creating the narrative of each of our organization's tribes. When influential members of one team demonstrated a willingness to blame other teams for operational miscues or whisper criticisms of leaders in the organization, it set a standard for other members of these units. This formed highly counterproductive strategic and behavioral echo chambers. But when the organization's influencers demonstrated new behavioral standards, this norm began to shift.

Determining who these influencers are can be counterintuitive, because the org chart's leader is often not the influencer in his or her cluster. In military units, especially within the special operations world, it is rarely the young lieutenant on a two-year rotation who has the greatest number of personal dotted-line relationships with those who report to him or her, but rather a subordinate senior enlisted member of the team who's been a part of the organization for many years and could remain for many more. It is these seasoned warhorses, who have seen generations of teammates come and go and who are true mentors to junior members of the unit, who are titans of dotted-line influence in military teams.

Social network analysis has revealed that a similar situation exists in many private-sector organizations. In one convincing example, network theorists Robert Cross and Andrew Parker analyzed the distinction between the solid-line and dotted-line structures of a small executive team in "the exploration and production division of a large petroleum organization." The results were striking, particularly regarding one apparently relatively unimportant member—"Cole," who was, theoretically speaking, operationally connected only to two other teammates. Yet, in dotted-line terms, Cole was the sole connecting hub between eight other individuals in the team's internal network—including the team's solid-line leader. The scale of Cole's significance to the team's operation may have been relatively unknown to his leadership, but his actions and influence were critical to the success of any given project for the team.

In 2010 I was an executive officer overseeing an element of the Task Force based at our U.S. headquarters, while forward deploying to an international location roughly 50 percent of the time. As my home-headquarters responsibilities grew, I was authorized to hire a civilian to be responsible for our budget management, equipment maintenance, travel and training coordination, and a whole host of other solid-line functions.

Our new coworker was exceptionally sharp, but he had no personal experience in the Task Force and had zero dotted-line connectivity to other members of our team. The position he was filling was easy to find on our formal org chart, but he was soon to be immersed in a complex web of long-standing relationships within our team's dotted-line networks.

I knew that if he moved too quickly or aggressively out of the gate, he would burn bridges he didn't even realize he was standing on, do long-term damage to his influence, and thus limit his ability to do his job. To compound this problem, his only strong connection point was me, and I was deploying overseas for several months just a few days after he joined the command.

With an appreciation of our internal relationship dynamics, I took an informed approach to onboarding him—one that friends of mine in the corporate world have since recognized and dubbed a "no-fly zone" model of employee introduction. On his first day, we sat down in front of a large whiteboard, and I gave him a one-hour history lesson on our organization, ranging from where we fell within the military's formal hierarchy to where our tactical units fit within our own. I walked him through our relationships with other military units, how things had evolved post-9/11, and how our current structures were designed to function. He took it all in.

"Now here's the bad news," I said. "It doesn't *actually* work like that. There's a complex web of key personalities and networks that make it function, and your job sits right in the middle of them." He laughed, acknowledging the dual realities. My guidance to him was simple: I would be back in two months and when I got home, I wanted him to explain to me how he thought things *actually* worked, including his take on key personalities, critical relationships they maintained, and any other minutiae to navigating our system. Until then, he was not to engage directly with anyone outside of our team. We would move slowly at first, so that he would be able to move fast in the long run.

In two months I was back at our headquarters, and he walked me through the web of small networks—including key influencers, the relationships they had with one another, where critical decisions were made, and a host of other insights he'd picked up during his eight-week window of learning. His description was close enough, so I congratulated him on how much he'd learned and took the reins off. He was now cleared to engage and interact across the organization's many verticals.

It was an experimental approach, but it paid off. Several months later, he told me that he would have made several missteps in his early weeks had he not been given the time to study our organization, its key influencers, and the dotted-line networks they controlled. Now, he'd found the influencer network that was interwoven in the hierarchical org chart. It would be some time still before he could personally enact change across that network, but he was ready to navigate it effectively.

A friend and technology executive, Chris Hylen, uses a similar approach when hiring new executives. "We call it the no-fly zone," Chris explained to me. "New executives have ninety days to observe and understand before they're cleared to take off." Avoiding early midair collisions greatly increases the odds of team members growing into true network influencers.

Key influencers exist in all effective organizations, but a solid-line org chart will not tell you where they are. Part of a successful transformation is leveraging these personalities where they exist in your small teams. If key, deeply interconnected individuals like these can begin to exemplify the behaviors your solid-line leadership help set out via your aligning narrative, then the rest of your organization will surely follow suit.

FROM INFLUENCERS TO BOUNDARY SPANNERS

Once you identify key influencers in your organization, the next step is to enable them to become what network theorists Rob Cross and Andrew Parker call "boundary spanners," individuals who can "provide critical links between two groups of people that are defined by functional affiliation, physical location, or hierarchical level." In time, these individuals become the backbone of the network portion of a hybrid organizational

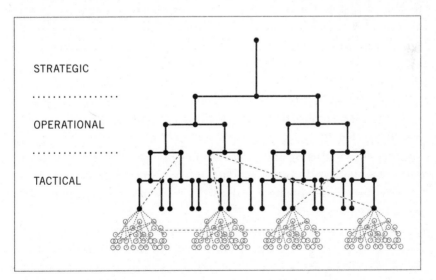

STRATEGIC

OPERATIONAL

TACTICAL

structure, connecting members of their clusters with other clusters and speeding up the adoption of the new narrative through social contagion.

The nature of relationships is such that it is difficult for an organization's strategic leadership to dictate which boundary spanners should connect to one another. You can't expect a solid-line superior to force meaningful interpersonal relationships between individuals. Fortunately, the conditions that can help facilitate the formation of these relationships *can* be arranged, though this can be difficult.

A senior sergeant in a team of operators does not need to be *told* by senior leadership that he needs better intelligence support or additional resources or connections to other groups. He'll recognize those needs long before any planners at headquarters can identify the issue and reallocate resources among teams.

So why should leaders like him, or those of a comparable role in any bureaucratic organization, depend on an increasingly overworked information-pump leader to create the connection between their team and another? The only barrier to influencers seeking to establish boundary-spanning relationships is a traditional org-chart structure that prevents them from meeting and connecting with other teams.

A leader's job, rather than appointing boundary spanners, is to create an environment where any individual in the organization can "connect the dots," and choose to become a boundary spanner themselves. In the Task Force, physical and virtual realms were created to provide potential boundary spanners with the ability to independently familiarize themselves with one another's teams, perceive one another's needs, and identify which of them might be facing a higher-priority issue at any given moment. They could then solve their own issues, well ahead of the pace of distant central planners—and begin to disrupt and deflate the narrative bubbles that had once isolated their tribes from one another.

These interaction-promoting realms not only create a space for boundary spanners to develop and connect but also provide a direct pathway for an organization's strategic leadership to directly communicate and demonstrate their aligning narrative. This allows social learning regarding "best practices" and desired behavior to be more easily encouraged.

An early approach to encouraging this in the Task Force was through the creation of physical spaces in which our organization could colocate influencers from a wide variety of teams. Unlike my deployment to Khowst, where our teams shared a base yet walled ourselves off from one another, these efforts would force individuals from varied specialized teams to work shoulder to shoulder. In doing so, certain members of our respective tribes, acting under divergent narratives, would have no choice but to connect.

The intended benefit of this interaction would be better, more well-informed operational and cultural integration, a belief that Alex Pentland notes has been validated in the private sector. His research shows that "when traders had the right balance and diversity of ideas in their social network, their return on investment increases 30 perfect over individual traders." Similarly, when housing a wide variety of intel specialists directly next to members of operator teams who indirectly depended on their work, information could be communalized, and bureaucratic removals between these tribes could be broken down.

COLOCATION

Face-to-face interaction with others is closely correlated with trust and quality of relationship formation. Social psychologists have identified a human tendency to base interpersonal trust on historical interactions, so when actors have a history of direct interaction, trust is increased and collaboration comes more easily. The greater the level of trust among boundary spanners, the faster and more effective their information sharing and cooperation can become.

The Task Force took action on the recommendation of then–Rear Admiral William "Bill" McRaven to McChrystal in 2004 and established spaces on two Task Force bases in Iraq and Afghanistan where Joint Interagency Task Forces (JIATFs) could work together. These spaces would house and colocate a combination of military, intelligence, and other specialized personnel from across different teams, unit-specific influencers one and all.

The JIATFs were a start point in establishing this level of interteam confidence, and this model of colocation would be helpful for the Task Force's reformation. The intent would remain constant—leverage colocation to produce boundary spanners who transcended the divisions among intelligence collection, analysis, and operations teams. Their members became an influential and captive audience to which the leadership could constantly communicate the aligning narrative of the organization. If these initial teams could overcome tribal boundaries, the behavior could take hold throughout the organization.

The design of these select spaces was, on the surface, unremarkable. Trevor Hough, an army friend of mine from the Task Force (who had helped direct one of the early JIATFs and with whom I coauthored a graduate school thesis on their application), continues to describe them as having "a newsroom format, as you've seen on TV—generally JIATFs were one shared space, arranged in a long, rectangular sort of fashion," which typically hosted up to a couple dozen differently specialized individuals from different teams.

But the seemingly simple concept of JIATFs was revolutionary in the military, where, per Hough, "similar things and similar people are grouped together, so one particular intelligence discipline will be off in its own room, and another will be another room." Literally breaking down physical barriers between these differently specialized teams created space to foster boundary spanners.

Team members would still work closely with their own teams; they just didn't do so behind closed doors. This represented a moderation of the principle of colocation—JIATFs did not separate personnel who were operationally related to one another, but they did remove as many physical barriers to cross-functional communication as possible, in a literal design sense, without compromising the ability of individuals to focus on their task or be distracted by unrelated noise.

This moderation is important to note in an age when "open office spaces" have become exceedingly mainstream in private-sector organizations. Per some estimates, 70 percent of companies today rely (at least in part) on open office space for their employees; a few impose harsh codes of conduct that ban *any* sense of personal space or property, and some have large enough floor plans to accommodate *thousands* of people.

These types of drastic colocation measures are misguided and can even have the opposite of the intended effect. Whereas integrating select members of different teams into a shared work environment is critical, implementers must be careful to maintain these people's ability to focus on "deep work" when they need to, while retaining enough openness to cross-functionally collaborate (which things like loud music on a PA system would prevent). As long as they do so, the creation of physical colocation spaces for teams will become an essential strategy for leaders who want their hybrid structures to develop a healthy network of boundary spanners.

BEYOND PHYSICAL COLOCATION

Physical colocation alone is insufficient to connect teams on the scale required by a large enterprise, and ours was a global entity. The Task Force was made up of thousands of individuals, and despite the benefits that came with operationally cohousing influential members of different small teams, the levels of interconnectivity that these physical spaces offered were still relatively limited. Even when replicated, physical spaces have capacity limits, and there is a point of diminishing returns—an open office space that can fit thousands of individuals (as a building on Facebook's campus is designed to accommodate) can, in practice, reduce the amount of meaningful interaction among new officemates. To scale and incentivize the formation of networks across the Task Force's structure, a different approach was needed to complement the practice of physical colocation.

The depth of relationships and contentualization of information lost across physical and relational distance are significant. As degrees of separation increase between an organization's strategic leadership and teams, it becomes harder to communicate the original intent of a strategy. Consider Christakis and Fowler's framing of a "telephone tree" to better illustrate this:

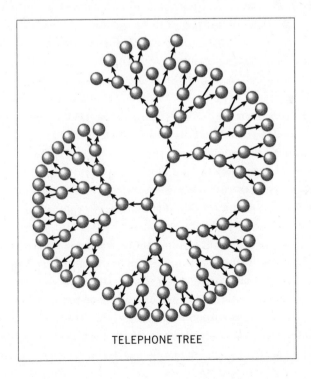

TELEPHONE TREE

In a telephone tree structure, communication among nodes is stretched across many degrees of separation—much as teams are in Weberian bureaucracies. From communication on strategic alignment to coordinating collaboration among different teams to the communalization of desired behaviors, conversations percolate step by step through an organization's complicated structure, inevitably warped along the way.

The effect is a game of *telephone,* where schoolchildren sit side by side, with the first kid whispering a message into the ear of the next, who then passes it in similar fashion around the circle. The final person then announces the message that he or she heard. The lesson to schoolchildren, of course, comes when the final phrase is vastly different from the original—a product of mishearing, jumbled phrasing, or even deliberate twists by deviant players.

As funny as the game can be for children, poorly interconnected organizations face the same challenge. With many degrees of separation between teams, strategy, and intent (even in the case of an aligning narrative) must be communicated across long organizational distances. Honest and unassuming requests for assistance or clarification on a topic can easily be warped into something hostile or disruptive as they make their way through the telephone tree–like series of information pumps.

Many civilian organizations have pursued innovative alternative means of incentivizing rapid social network formation across their clustered teams. Sometimes this has even been through financial compensation, as was seen by Cross and Parker in a large engineering company:

> Senior executives instituted "above and beyond" rewards: Each time someone went out of his or her way to introduce a colleague in trouble to those who could help, that person was nominated for a small cash reward. The reward was paid out quickly, and the good deed was publicly acknowledged, an incentive that rapidly helped create more central connectors in the company.

Well-publicized financial compensation for helping to span boundaries between teams and subject-matter experts is an interesting idea that can assist some private-sector organizations in interconnecting teams. But the Task Force couldn't do this, and any new financial incentive can create its own set of potential pitfalls.

Instead the organization began to deeply leverage a virtual space. As the complex networks we were facing had discovered, virtual connectivity would allow for easier and larger-scale network formation, but uniquely, our organization would implement it while maintaining the order and discipline provided by our bureaucratic hierarchy. By creating virtual decision forums, we were able to limit the telephone effect and create opportunities for boundary spanners to connect with one another even when they were not colocated.

THE O&I

By the time I was deployed as McChrystal's aide-de-camp, he was entering his fifth year of command, and it was clear that *something* was working. As a result, visits to the Task Force's Balad headquarters by external organizations and stakeholders became a regular affair. These visits were always a welcome event from our end as well. We were happy to communicate, *this is working, and here's how* to outsiders and designed these visits to educate, convert, and deepen relationships.

They also improved the likelihood of our reformation's success, if in an indirect way. As in any complex environment, cross-functional knowledge was at a premium—the better our relationships, the more information became available to our teams. Allowing peer organizations to bear witness to the new practices of our organization expanded dotted-line trust and connectivity among our teams.

Every visitor had the potential to walk away as a newly minted boundary spanner. The goal was that every visitor left our Balad base with a true understanding of our team of teams model and, ideally, would become an advocate to drive viral messaging in *their* organization about how our system was functioning.

Not surprisingly, the things we in the Task Force believed were most important for visitors to understand weren't always the same as what interested them the most. Upon arriving to Balad, our visitors often expressed an interest in seeing operators prepare for their missions, watching their helicopters take off from our airfield, or listening in on the radio calls from ongoing missions that bounced around our Joint Operations Center (JOC). And so they were often chagrined when we would tell them that their first stop would be to sit through the Task Force's Operations and Intelligence Forum—abbreviated by us insiders as the "O&I."

This was rarely welcome news to our visitors. We'd walk them across our dusty base in the direction of our Situational Awareness Room (SAR), and they'd see bearded operators in the distance donning body armor and preparing their weapons for a pending raid. They'd see pilots walking to their helicopters for pre-mission checks. They'd see young analysts sprinting across the compound with last-minute intelligence insights. These were the things many wanted to see, the *cool* parts of special operations. They'd want to stop and take in the sights, but our guides would hustle them along.

When we entered the SAR, we would introduce our guests quickly to the concept of the O&I and inform them that they should get comfortable, as they'd be watching it for about ninety minutes. Their disappointment at hearing this was often palpable. *We came all this way*, you could sense them thinking, *and we're back-benching through a conference call?* In their minds they'd just been marched past the things that they'd come all this way to see, and now they were being forced to sit through yet another "death by PowerPoint"–type meeting.

But ninety minutes later, without fail, they would leave that SAR having had a change of heart. They'd not witnessed a traditional report-up, guidance-down meeting; rather, they'd been part of a discussion-focused, relationship-building *forum*. They'd watched as thousands of personnel from around the world connected, shared information, and problem-solved in real time. They'd heard language about trust and relationships that was counterintuitive. They'd seen junior team members solve strategic-level issues in real time and watched as their influence and insights rippled through the thinking of the enterprise. Their attention rarely wavered during the ninety-minute session.

It was only then, after they watched our organization connect through the O&I, that we would take our visitors to meet a team of operators, to examine the latest equipment, and to watch the real-time progress of operations from our JOC. It was only then that these things could be contextualized not as unique capabilities but as part of a holistic system that was grounded in the connection of thousands around the globe.

These visits would often finish with a meal, and our green-tented chow hall was the only option for a bite. During these simple dinners, most visitors talked about what they had seen during the O&I—rather than the other admittedly more glamorous parts of the tour.

I get it now, they'd say. *People were really talking and asking for things from each other, rather than just presenting reports to their bosses and teammates. They were thinking about things strategically, as a group.* They'd pause, then ask, *And you all do that every day?*

They left converted, newly excited to explain what they thought our approach to communication was accomplishing.

If I were forced to provide a procedural description of what the Task Force's O&I was, in one (extended) sentence—it would be as follows:

An O&I is a mass videoconferencing forum involving thousands of participants from different geographically and functionally dispersed teams, who discuss the conditions of their environments, potential opportunities or threats they are observing in them, their intended next steps, and why what their team is observing matters to other teams in the organization.

But on a more conceptual level, a functional description of the O&I would read like this:

An O&I is a virtual space wherein an organization's leadership can create, with the required regularity, conditions for the organic interaction of all of its teams, and reiterate an aligning narrative to the assembled organization. It is a regular reminder of purpose and an opportunity to reconnect with the larger tribe.

During the few years surrounding my tour as McChrystal's aide-de-camp, the world of information technology was subject to especially dramatic changes and upheavals. Video streaming, social media sites, and various adaptable, advanced smartphone software platforms—was becoming exponentially scaled and advanced through public life by the efforts of the private sector.

The Task Force (or, more broadly, the entire battlefield) was feeling the stress of this change. The same virtual space we were leveraging to grow connections between our teams had also been used, before our change efforts, to enhance the operations of AQI's networks.

From posting pro-*jihadi* propaganda on closed chat rooms to using camera-equipped cell phones to detonate an IED on a Coalition convoy, record the aftermath, sync it to music in postproduction, and post it publicly on the Internet, AQI had figured out how to use a blend of new technology and old methodology to enable novel operations by its members. Technology gave our opponents an asymmetrical ability to spread their narrative to as broad an audience as possible, and to recruit an ever-increasing number of sympathizers, supporters, and members.

In our O&I forums, we looked to accomplish something similar. Our aligning narrative, and the creation and nourishment of cross-boundary, trust-based relationships, was revisited daily. And as it did for AQI, virtual reach gave our leadership an expansive presence and an ever-increasing ability to grow the reach of the network.

Operations and intelligence *meetings* had been a fixture of the American military for generations, and they remain a necessity across many commands. Traditional O&Is are treated as opportunities for commanding officers to lecture from their strategic pinnacle on the org chart and bombard junior staff with their views on what has gone well recently, what needs improvement, and the recent performance of different units. At times in my career, I have been immersed in such an environment, as you may have too.

The main difference between the traditional O&I meeting and the Task Force's reinvention of it had to do with the discussion of actions. The traditional version would be a report-focused *meeting* where teams could review actions they'd taken based on the last guidance received, and then be given a new set of directions. The Task Force's take on this model was, instead, a technologically enabled, contextualization-centered *forum,* designed for teams to discuss the independent actions they'd taken since the last forum. It represented an opportunity to exchange newly discovered, and often imperfectly formed, insights with the larger group. Its goal was collective learning to drive autonomous action, not grading one another on completed efforts. It was a forward-looking forum, not a hindsight review.

In addition, traditional meetings typically follow preset behavioral patterns that are strictly followed by attendees—an unwavering series of norms that are virtually identical meeting to meeting, day to day, and month to month. Often included among these is the implicit idea that transmission of intent comes one way, from senior leadership downward; and reporting on progress comes the other way, from the ground up. Multidirectional updates (both from leaders to teams and vice versa) and open-ended discussion among individuals of different rank and specialty have the stigma of being too disruptive to the meeting's agenda. These are all saved for the *meeting after the meeting,* where, as you've likely experienced, things *actually* get done.

A *forum* is inclusive and exists to encourage collaboration and familiarization among participants, rather than to reinforce the solid-line spans of control as defined by an org chart. Rank is respected but is not tolerated as a hindrance to the open exchange of information, analysis, and the proposal of solutions to problem sets.

In contrast to our efforts at colocation, technology-enabled connectivity (like the O&I) offered the potential for scale-free expansion—there was, theoretically speaking, no limit to how many teams they could host, or how many different interactions were possible among their membership. The limiting factors were simply the number of people listening and the bandwidth of the technology used in the O&I. By the time I was serving on McChrystal's staff, this communication process had been evolving for several years, and *thousands* would dial in for ninety minutes every day. Each of these listeners had the opportunity now to be a boundary spanner in some way.

But establishing and maintaining the conditions that would make these forums successful was no small challenge.

A FORUM IN ACTION

Within our Balad headquarters' bullpen-like Situational Awareness Room and above the flat televisions that paneled its front wall, several crimson digital displays hung parallel to one another. These clocks were always reading the current times at various locations around the world—places that were each host to at least one of the Task Force's many teams.

One of the displays was permanently set to the local time of Balad. Every day, when it blinked to read 1600, a crisp, clear voice would be piped in through speakers arranged around the room, filling the open SAR and bringing the soldiers, analysts, and tech specialists occupying it to order.

> "Good Afternoon, and welcome to the Operations
> and Intelligence Forum."

Like colocation, an O&I forum needed to fill two functions: to provide a means for boundary connectors to be created from any individuals in any team and to allow an organization's aligning narrative to be directly recommunicated by strategic leaders to an entire organization. The O&I was purpose-designed to serve these ends.

The first feature of an O&I that allowed for these effects was the breadth and depth of the teams that it was able to assemble, and prompt dialogue between. In order to assemble these teams and facilitate discussion, an O&I depended on someone who could "own" the operation of the forum.

The voice that the Task Force's teams heard open every forum belonged to the O&I's "controller"—a noncommissioned officer (NCO), based at our U.S. headquarters, who was assigned the significant task of enabling discussions and "cross-talk" among the forum's participants. Despite the remote location of this individual from our organization's main realms of operation—Iraq and Afghanistan—their voice boasted a vast, electronically augmented range.

The controller's voice coursed through fiber-optic cables, bounced off distant satellites, carried across nations and oceans, ultimately reaching a globally scattered and diverse audience of thousands. Each participant might have a slightly different picture of our organization's complex external problem set, and each was empowered to address the vast virtual audience with this picture.

The sheer depth and variety of teams whose viewpoints, efforts, and insights could be discussed and publicized using these forums was remarkable. The structure ensured that boundary spanners across the enterprise could be immersed in a virtual environment that made interaction and familiarization among them as likely as possible.

Moreover, unlike contained physical colocation, O&Is allowed for more than a select few influential individuals from each team's small network potentially to be converted into boundary spanners—it allowed for *every* one of them to.

From seemingly run-of-the-mill offices in Florida and Virginia to remote outposts in rural Afghanistan (forward operating bases, or FOBs), teams of civilians and soldiers from vastly different walks of life and work had roused themselves and gathered in front of their own diligently assembled banks of screens, microphones, and video cameras.

As I'd watch the screens on display at the front of the Balad SAR during O&I forums, most of the teams I could see maintained a visibly alert look, for it was indeed morning where they were—the East Coast of the United States, where most of the political, diplomatic, and civilian intelligence partners of our organization were based. Other images showed a few more tired teams from more rugged locales—units that were getting ready for a night of operations.

A great number of individuals from across all functional specialties of the Task Force were always participating in these forums, which allowed for more of them to identify adjacencies and dependencies between their efforts and act on them accordingly.

This massive, deep representation of the Task Force's tactical and operational rank and file provided our strategic leadership with an extremely large audience to which they could communicate their aligning narrative directly.

This leads to the second feature of an O&I: enabling firsthand, person-to-person information distribution or contextualization from any node in the organization to *every other one,* instantly. Participants are empowered to communicate in an unfiltered manner with little restriction on their ability to create dialogue with any other team. In this way an O&I could optimize its functions of both connecting boundary spanners and enabling the recommunication of an aligning narrative to all of an organization's teams.

A telephone tree structure was no longer necessary to distantly align every member of the organization on strategy, nor would degrees of separation (by way of overworked information pumps) be allowed to disrupt the quick distribution of information or resources between two teams. Instead, when a discussion led by a civilian subject-matter expert in Islamabad touched on the actions of a particular insurgent cell in Helmand Province, Afghanistan, an attuned participant from a tactical team might *sense,* based on the analyst's comments, that his team was seeing the consequences of this insurgent cell's actions emerge in their own battle space—a realization he'd then share with the forum's other participants.

The forum was, again, an open-ended discussion, and in an O&I, reaching out to experts for a copy of a report, asking clarifying questions of a senior officer from another branch of service, or even requesting a private off-line discussion was as simple as asking. The new informal relationships that would result, which no solid-line planner could have anticipated the need for, might lead to a tactical team's exponentially faster dismantling of a given cell, or any number of other positive outcomes.

Despite having little to no formal bureaucratic relationship to one another, any collection of individuals in the org chart could now become boundary spanners—able to connect and collaborate in the future, as their different teams required.

The same logic helps inform the contextualization of an aligning narrative to an organization. In the Task Force's case, our commander and

senior staff could reiterate the narrative's quantitatively inspired but ultimately human principles to the entire enterprise, contextualize and clarify them, and highlight demonstrations of their practice by different
teams to every other member of the organization:

Credibility = Proven Competence + Integrity + Relationships

Participants in the forum would gain a better understanding of what
was expected of them and could act accordingly, with that in mind, as
they responded to their complex, ever-changing problem sets.

The pressure on companies to assemble "virtual teams" tasked with
collaborative problem-solving has increased steadily since the early
2000s—a joint product of both globalization and the increasingly available technological means that allow the formation of these cyber-enabled
teams. In their 2012 research paper "Leading Virtual Teams: Hierarchical Leadership, Structural Supports, and Shared Team Leadership," social psychologists Julia Hoch and Steve Kozlowski note that roughly 65
percent of companies believe that their "reliance on virtual teams would
'mushroom' in the future," but that this reliance might result in a degra-
dation in interteam trust.

In the words of Hoch and Kozlowski, "Relative to face-to-face teams,
benefits attributed to the use of virtual teams include the ability to com-
pose a team of experts flung across space and time, increases in staffing
ability to meet market demands, and cost savings from reduced travel,"
they write. "Disadvantages include lower levels of team cohesion, work
satisfaction, trust, cooperative behavior, social control, and commitment
to team goals; all factors that can negatively impact team performance."

Hoch and Kozlowski's summary is a powerful warning to those
thinking that there is magic technology around the corner that would
interpersonally bind an organization's scattered membership to the same
degree as would be seen in a five-person startup. When working with
unfamiliar teammates through e-mail chains and conference calls, much
of the benefit of personalized human-to-human interaction is lost.

The world will undoubtedly continue to see a host of software platforms designed to enable interconnectivity at scale, but no platform can
replace the feeling of strength we all gain through human connection and
the power that comes from trusting that our teammates know and understand us.

Connecting thousands of actors through technology was not the end in itself but simply the means through which our leadership could build relationships, deepen trust, and remind us every day of our aligning narrative. It was true, of course, that the O&I could not overcome all limitations of virtual teamwork, but efforts were made to minimize the impacts. Videoconferencing allows for a degree of face-to-face intimacy, and when participants would take part in a discussion on some subject, they'd be addressed on a *first-name basis* by our senior leadership. They would be recognized as individuals, not only for the work they produced but for who they were and how they contributed to the broader effort. Our leaders would draw out *opinions* and *insights,* not just raw data. And all of us were encouraged and reminded to seek one another off-line to form deeper and stronger relationships.

As a result of these practices, an O&I could overcome the perils of virtual teaming to accomplish its two primary goals: to foster personal relationships between individuals and to allow for the aligning narrative of the organization to be reemphasized by senior leadership.

Moreover, even though an O&I couldn't necessarily match the strength of interpersonal relationships found in small teams, it's possible that the relative weakness of the relationships doesn't weaken the results of having boundary spanners. American sociologist Mark Granovetter has pointed out that even weak, referral-based interpersonal relationships between individuals can have drastic tangible impacts on the lives of those they involve—providing a verifiable counterpoint to other sociologists who prioritize the study of "strong" interpersonal connections.

Granovetter's experiment went as follows:

> In a random sample of recent professional, technical and managerial job changers living in a Boston suburb, I asked those who found a new job through contacts how often they saw the contact around the time that he passed on job information to them. . . .
>
> Of those finding a job through contacts, 16.7% reported that they saw their contact often at the time, 55.6% said occasionally, and 27.8% rarely (N=54). The skew is clearly to the weak end of the continuum.

Rather than be assisted by those they had a strong, frequently reinforced personal relationship with, Granovetter's subjects were more often helped in finding a job by an "acquaintance" or a "friend of a friend" who helped enable their employment where their closer friends could not. This is not unlike the interactions and relationships that the O&I enabled between the Task Force's many differently specialized teams and the influencers inside them.

The Task Force's stand-alone teams of analysts and operators had always been strongly clustered—any given member of these small units naturally possessed dotted-line relationships with immediate teammates. But when one of them needed something outside of the purview of their team—be it resources, personnel assistance, or intelligence—these small clusters of dotted-line relationships might prove useless, depending on whether anyone in that constrained, dense network had a connection with a member of the right external team.

Colocation partially mitigated this problem, but forums allowed weaker ties to be forged at scale and could play host to exponentially larger numbers. These "weak ties" could then be leveraged to provide new resources or information where the long-standing "strong ties" between immediate teammates could not. The daily pattern of the O&I did not guarantee this would happen, but it certainly improved the odds. Every twenty-four hours, there was a new opportunity for cross-boundary ties to emerge, driven by a shared understanding of what was happening on the battlefield and reinforced by our organization's recommunicated aligning narrative.

And real ties, between humans, are at the epicenter of life on the battlefield.

The army of ancient Sparta is a thing of legend. Theirs was warrior culture, and the soldiers who earned the red cloak and shield of the Spartan line sat at the pinnacle of their society. Their tactical use of the phalanx (a layers-deep, shoulder-to-shoulder military formation) was key to their success, and only the finest and most tested warriors could join the line. On an individual level within the phalanx, a soldier's weapon was carried in his right hand and his bronze-and-wooden shield, weighing upward of thirty pounds, in his left. This shield, given the tightness of the arrangement, protected the soldier to the bearer's left as much as it did himself. A phrase seen in Zack Snyder's 2007 film *300*— "Spartan . . . come back with your shield, or on it"—reflects a culture that placed importance on their shields and prided the ability of warriors to protect one another just as much as themselves. It is not a lighthearted narrative, and it shows the depth of commitment that was expected from a member of the line. Plutarch, recounting the customs of the Spartans, recalled a mother handing her son his shield and saying, "Either this, or upon this," and that the Spartans would "deprive of their status those among them who discarded their shields." A Spartan soldier might lose a weapon in battle and survive the shame that followed from his peers, but losing a shield and forfeiting the protection it offered his teammate was unacceptable.

A comparable strength of learned interpersonal trust is incredibly challenging to replicate on an organization-wide scale. But the O&I, where our senior leadership encouraged us all to connect as *humans,* to share insights, and to help others solve their most challenging issues, was our information-age version of the phalanx. When McChrystal—or any leader in our organization—spoke up in this environment, they would be communicating their intent firsthand, instead of relying on others to pass along the message. Moreover, their use of honest dialogue (and praise for others who did the same) would prompt broader social learning and adoption of this behavior by previously narratively isolated teams.

When communicating with thousands, demonstrating transparency was our guidepost. Harming relationships, degrading trust, or concealing insights would have been our equivalent of dropping one's shield and leaving another team exposed to unforeseen dangers. Through all the chaos, churn, and stress the Task Force's different teams were facing, they all knew that they could count on one thing every day: at 1600 hours Balad time, our whole world would be up in our forum, awaiting that the sound of that ever-reliable voice:

"Good afternoon, and welcome to the Operations and Intelligence Forum."

Smith

"We'll begin with the Task Force's leadership in Balad," the controller's voice advised the O&I participants.

"Thanks, Jim," McChrystal spoke into his microphone, replying to the voice's owner back in Fort Bragg, and to the rest of us by extension. "Great to see everyone back there in Bragg. Hope you enjoyed your coffee and doughnuts this morning. . . . We'll just keep fighting the war over here," he said with a smile.

Most of those in Balad's SAR, along with those in other locations around the world, let out a quick laugh. It was common humor in our organization to suggest that everybody else was somehow taking it easy, as everyone knew that this couldn't be further from the truth. "Thanks to everybody for dialing in," McChrystal added, and the forum began in earnest.

An army intelligence officer in our SAR took over, also addressing the virtual crowd. "We'll start with a review of our most critical intelligence updates from the last twenty-four hours. The subject of greatest importance and time sensitivity is that we're aware that Mr. X had a discussion with Mr. Y last night, which we picked up through signals intelligence from a partner agency."*

Though in this case most of us in the forum that day already knew who X and Y were—they were *that* prominent in the insurgency's networks—the scene still had to be set for the O&I's participants, as it would be for other updates. A private-sector equivalent might be a large competitor in a market meeting with another—and just as in any market, it was important for all of our teams to take note of this development and apply it to their own realms.

Participants had to understand *why* it was important that these two had recently held a conversation and find out whether any team, influencer, or subject-matter expert in our org chart could further contextualize or better present on this change in the organization's external environment: Who are Mr. X and Mr. Y connected to, what are their skills, which team is most impacted by this update, and what can be done to respond to this news?

"Fascinating . . . Do we have details or thoughts on why?" McChrystal asked of the intelligence officer and, by extension, a virtually assembled crowd—a question that was on their minds as well. Thousands awaited an answer.

But odd as it may seem, our commander already knew this information—as did several others of us in Balad—and he had asked this very question of the intelligence team that owned this update an hour prior. News of this meeting had been mainlined to our headquarters that morning, so our senior leadership in Balad had already gotten the chance to contextualize the strategic and operational significance of this update.

So why ask this apparently redundant question again?

---

* "Mr. X" and "Mr. Y" are, clearly, pseudonyms.

This forum, again, was designed to prompt organic insights and connections among our different teams—and they needed more than just information; they needed awareness of the larger Task Force's immediate strategy and priorities, on a similar scale that the organization's senior leadership did. Our organization's operational awareness wasn't defined by that of the individual at the top of our org chart; instead, in a complex environment, it had to be set by the broader strategic awareness of all teams throughout the organization.

Offering the rest of the organization the opportunity to discuss this new intelligence and familiarize themselves with subject-matter experts allowed strategic context to be spread throughout our organization, better informing the decisions participants made off-line through their dotted-line networks. Unprompted, a remote intelligence analyst— "Helen"—based at one of the Task Force's remote outstations, chimed in, responding to McChrystal's question.

"Well, direct communication between these individuals is extremely rare, sir—I don't think our team has ever seen it—so I think it appears to indicate some type of significant operation is being coordinated by their cells in the near term. There's no other reason they'd assume this risk, and it syncs with our team's current belief that both of their organizations are under real pressure to produce."

Her voice continued and her image streamed across the network. "But I spoke with the original analysis team this morning, and they don't have any other definitive information at this point. X and Y's next steps and time line are unknowns to us. Our intel shop has been in tight coordination regarding this with the operator units on the ground in the key locations where these guys are known to operate, so I'd like to hear from Lieutenant Colonel Smith, who probably has a better perspective right now."

An adjacent video screen at the front of the Balad SAR then filled up with the image of a special operations officer—Lieutenant Colonel "Smith"—and another intelligence specialist by his side. Their faces showed steely focus, drawn with the fatigue that comes from extensive, repeated deployments, and consistent eighteen-hour days. Yet there was real opportunity in front of them, and neither would rest until it was exploited.

Smith started, his voice coming in clear from his team's remote operating base. "Afternoon, sir and everyone—and thanks, Helen. Happy to pitch in. As many of you know, we've made some pretty aggressive moves up here recently, and we believe that's what's forcing these guys to come to the surface. We're confident that some of our recent operations have decimated their communication networks to the point that they need to pop up and talk directly with one another. They know it's high risk, but they have no other choice currently. But the intel we're seeing isn't as precise as we'd like, so we don't know exactly why they're talking."

He paused. "If I were them, I'm thinking: *We need to do something big soon and regain momentum, or both of our groups are in a lot of trouble.* A big attack is the best way to demonstrate strength. That's our assumption at this point, and what we're focused on disrupting." At this moment Smith was evaluating and making sense of his immediate environment for the rest of the organization—his contextualization of the evidence arrayed before him helping to prepare all participants for some unforeseen eventuality.

"We don't know" and "If I were them"—Smith's word choice was important and reflective of the united culture that O&Is helped maintain. He wasn't trying to look good, nor was he dwelling in (or apologizing for) his uncertainty. The environment was complex and opaque. It produced uncertainty, and we had to be comfortable acknowledging that fact. Not knowing was acceptable; not *thinking* wasn't—a norm that, once demonstrated by one influential member of a small team (i.e., Smith), could be easily encouraged and made contagious across different tribes.

Honest, raw, ground-level truth is invaluable in a networked age, and so the slightest effort to clean up the data or round a sharp edge can quickly cover up some overlooked detail. Information does not retain its full value forever. In chemistry, the amount of time it takes for a radioactive isotope to decay to half of its radioactivity is referred to as its half-life. Similarly, the half-life of information is very short in a complex age. Any lack of transparency through omission of personal perspective was discouraged. Our senior leadership had created the environment for this sort of exchange, and the best leaders in the organization, like Smith, were given space to publicly demonstrate it.

"Okay, that all makes sense to me," McChrystal responded. "If anyone sees this differently or has a follow-up point, please jump in," he looked around the room and then up at the screens in front of us, inviting teams from around the world to offer comment, input, or follow-up questions for Helen, Smith, or anyone else present.

Moments like these, in a traditional *meeting,* would be extremely intimidating. Interacting in a very frank manner with superiors, and asking questions from an acknowledged point of uncertainty in front of them, would typically quiet even the most contrarian or inquisitive participant. This is especially the case in traditional military settings, where conventional ideas of rank, and the ever-present enlisted/officer divide, risk discouraging clarifying dialogue or information exchange.

Someone in the room raised a question about another ongoing mission in another part of the country, and Smith's operations team responded with its opinion that the risks were manageable. An outstation asked whether they should anticipate impacts to a major resupply effort taking place in the next forty-eight hours, and a head logistics officer responded that there were no immediate impacts, but he'd monitor closely. One or two others commented, and the global network resettled.

The nuances of this update were now as clear as they possibly could be to everyone. After a pause, McChrystal began again. "Smitty, what else can we do to support you right now?"

Smith was the authority on this issue and was to likely take the lead in response to this intelligence update. But he still might need assistance of some kind from other teams. His leadership and the forum combined to provide an avenue for him to pull what he needed from the rest of the organization. The O&I was a means to an end, not an end in and of itself.

"Right now we're good, sir. No immediate requirements," Smith responded. "This might have been a one-time event. But if we see any additional activity in the next twenty-four hours, my team will need to flood the area—and we may need some additional people and ISR [intelligence, surveillance, and reconnaissance] to go after several targets."

To translate, Smith's team would continue to watch the situation closely, and if they identified increased activity between these objectives, or anyone else they believed connected, they would need to pull additional intelligence capabilities and resources from other teams so that they could increase their mission tempo. Other teams were being put on notice: *We might need to respond to this at some point in the next few hours.*

This conversation was syncing thousands of us around the globe on Smith's view of a key part of the fight. We were realigning our perspectives on an emerging issue, making resource plans, and thinking through prioritization around the world. Smith's team was empowered and enabled to exploit an opportunity, and the organization would be ready to support. Importantly, all of the organization was now aware that his team might need more help, and quickly, should the situation change on the ground.

A nod from McChrystal. "Okay then. Let us know what you need if anything changes," he said. "Wrapping up either of these guys would be significant. Great work, everybody."

I looked up at the red time displays at the very top of our screen bank—the one for Balad now read 1605. We were just a few minutes into the O&I, and our teams already had a clear sense on what one of our organization's top priorities would be in the immediate future, at least until tomorrow's forum.

Most important, hours of telephone-tree debate and discussion had been cut to mere minutes. Dozens of people and several ancillary units that could be involved in supporting Smith's effort had been informed on the situation and were postured to help. Hours of follow-on meetings or bureaucratic delays had been avoided. Smith's team would monitor the situation, and if any further developments took place in the next twenty-four hours, others around the country would be ready to flock the necessary assets over to his team.

We moved to the next topic for discussion.

BUILDING YOUR FORUM

This all comes back to the question *How do you create a forum?* You've now been shown how dialogue can be created or fostered and how controllers can help facilitate discussion, but the next-most-important element is how to divide time usage and schedule the presentation of subject matter.

The answer to this came in the form of an agenda—designed and digitally distributed by the forum's controller, these agendas were laid out in a manner that synced with the functions that the O&I would need to fill.

The agendas for the Task Force's O&I forums would appear as follows and were made readily available through e-mail and intranet portals. Anyone anywhere in the world connected to the organization could access them.

They could have been designed as a simple table of contents, but in

Business unit	Division	Time	Topic/Links	Briefer with contact info
SALES	Northeast sales	1620–1625	Upcoming sales conference www._____.com	Bob Smith, VP xxx, (___) ___-___ Bob.Smith@_____.com
SALES	Southwest sales	1625–1635	. . .	. . .
MARKETING	Product launch review	1635–1650	. . .	. . .
MARKETING	Marketing trends in northeast	. . .	. . .	. . .
ETC.	. . .	. . .	. . .	. . .

our case agendas had to include means by which our teams could better understand the significance of the information presented by the briefers *ahead* of the forum and be empowered to interact with the presenter offline, outside the context of the forum.

The layout, as shown in the example above, would include hyperlinks to the briefer's supporting documents, so that an individual following a briefer could, at her leisure, access a stream of additional data. The briefer, meanwhile, was free and encouraged to keep the discussion at the "here's why this matters" level, rather than diving too deeply into the hard data.

For example, a two-minute briefing on the status of air assets for a single twenty-four-hour period might also include a hyperlink to the six-month equipment rotation plan. The 1 percent of the organization that might want that level of detail, therefore, didn't have to unnecessarily interrupt or sideline the two-minute brief.

In addition, the name and detailed contact information for each subject-matter briefer was provided in the agenda. A popular way of further emphasizing this, and making connections as easy as possible, was displaying it on-screen during forums, next to the live image of a briefer and their presentation.

This accomplished a variety of things. First, others from around the world could address briefers by name, helping add to the personal feeling normally missing from virtual teamwork. When senior leaders would reach out and address people around the organization on a first-name basis, it helped reinforce a sense of familiarity and ease to all present on the forum—helping mitigate the potential downsides of virtual team interaction that Hoch and Kozlowski discussed. It was a good feeling for briefers to be referred to by name, and it sent a clear message to participants that *individuals* mattered in our organization.

Second, in line with the previous point, people in our organization started to feel like they now *knew* "Karen," that once-faceless young analyst in a distant corner of the fight whom few had previously heard of, let alone actually met. When complex problems arose that might require Karen's expertise, someone in another pocket of the organization could feel confident reaching out to her across conventional team boundaries. The O&I process was a means to enable the formation of relationships; others could connect with Karen, create connections, and quickly become boundary spanners themselves.

With this extremely public level of visibility, briefers learned to welcome a flood of new information, e-mails, calls, and even visits from fellow participants, off-line and after their update to the organization. Whenever Karen said, "I believe this is similar to a trend we saw in this region during the election cycle a few years ago," a senior leader who had led a team in that region in previous years could quickly send Karen a study he'd overseen during an earlier election cycle that either supported or contradicted her thesis. Her team on the ground could learn and adjust accordingly, and a new dotted-line relationship would form. A junior member, given the environment and platform to hypothesize, similarly gained quick access to the collective knowledge of the group.

This free sharing of information took place constantly during the forums. But in order to prevent information overload and chaos, an alternate channel of communication—that of live chat rooms—was critical.

Recall that Smith had mentioned the possibility of help being needed by his team. Having heard this presented in the forum, individuals at multiple levels began to independently parse through what he had mentioned as possibly being needed—ISR equipment and potentially extra personnel—and they began working off-line to ensure that Smith's team could be provided with whatever it needed, should one of a million potential contingencies arise in the hours ahead.

As individuals from around the world continued to listen closely to

the exchange going on between Smith and McChrystal, my laptop pinged
with an open chat room window:

Karen: Fuss, u have that intel report?

    I took my eyes away from the video screen at the front of my SAR
and typed out a quick reply.

Chris: No, let me connect you w/ Smitty's analyst

             Chris has added Mark to the chat room.

Chris: Mark, this is Karen. She's back in the states, and looking for
the intel report Smitty just ref'd. Can u share?

Mark: Roger, here ya go. Good to meet you Karen, happy to talk
off-line.

             Mark has shared an attachment.

Karen: Thx. Who knows the details best? There are overlaps with a
target we're watching.

Mark: That'd be Rashad and Sarah, I can pull them in . . .

Mark then added two other people to our thread while Karen pulled
in three from her side. The chat room ballooned to seventeen people in
less than a minute. I minimized the chat on my laptop's screen, returning
my focus to the O&I. I was no longer needed as a boundary spanner between these tribes, and they were now talking at a depth of detail that
exceeded my relatively shallow understanding of the topic.

    In real time, both in front of my eyes and out of my sight, connections
and networks among teams germinated, developing and operationalizing
on what Smith and McChrystal were talking through in real time in front
of them. Other networks similar to these, some that I wasn't privy to and
others that I was, also returned to life—communicating out of the immediate supervision or direction of our solid-line leaders. Karen would soon
connect with Mark without my help—another series of teams had been
familiarized, echo chambers had been disrupted, and a now-and-future
social network between them had been formed.

But boundary spanning was only one of the critical functions of the forum. This was also the senior leadership's opportunity to recommunicate our aligning narrative.

SIGNING OFF AND REALIGNING

Ninety minutes, as always, flew by. The O&I forum was about to draw to a close—the last discussion on the agenda had wrapped up, right on schedule. The controller shifted to our senior leadership for closing comments.

"Team, thanks very much for what you're doing here," McChrystal said, addressing the forum's thousands of participants.

"I know this is hard, and that every day each of you needs to wake up and recommit to the fight. We've been at this for years now, and each of you is giving an incredible amount of energy to this effort. But we're starting to do the little things right every time. As we always say, there will be a winner and a loser in this war, and while it's far from over, we're definitely on the winning side of the equation. Remember . . . credibility gives us freedom to maneuver, and our credibility comes from our competence, our integrity, and our relationships. That's our differentiator, and everyone on this team plays a critical part in managing that balance. All of your actions matter. Your commitment to this team *matters*.

"What I mean is this: Each of you is critical to ensuring we remain committed to our relationships *with one another.* Without that, we're just a big organization with no trust. So thanks for the incredible work you're each bringing to this effort and the commitment you make to each other every day. Any one of you could be someplace else right now, doing something easier, but instead you're choosing to be part of this team. Thanks for what you're doing."

And with that, the forum concluded. I watched the screens at the front of the SAR with interest, right up until they turned off—taking it in as every team on them stood up in their own respective bases and went about their work off-line.

Every day, there was this type of sign-off from our senior leadership, a reminder about what mattered within our organization's aligning narrative: that we were each a part of something larger, a global team with a collective mission that mattered more than any of our personal or tribal biases. Some days were better than others, and some days you wanted nothing more than to retreat to the comfort of your own tribe.

But every twenty-four hours (the cadence of our O&I), there was a steady reminder that reverting to that safety would come with a real cost. Losing a war was something that none of us could live with. And every member of the organization had a choice to make every day. They could default to their small-team, tribal norms and risk losing the fight, or they could recommit to the aligning narrative of the organization and force themselves to think as a cross-functional whole.

Even today, when I ask people who were also involved in that period of the Task Force's fight to describe what it felt like, the responses I hear always have one underlying universal commonality: *We felt like such a close team.* We were one extended unit with one culture—whose actions were influenced not by the identity or narrative of a single unit but by the aligning narrative that was constantly recommunicated and transcended our previously festering cultural divisions. This allowed us to truly cooperate and collaborate with one another against the complex problem sets that our teams regularly encountered. In practice, we were like any other large, global organization, with countless activities happening at any one time within our different silos. But in feel, *we were such a close team.*

While the world we lived in was full of ever-changing life-and-death issues, we committed ninety minutes every day to a *conversation.* In time, this felt to many of us like a group sitting around a table, small-team dynamics on a global scale. Sustaining that reality took constant and unrelenting discipline—but the other option was to lose, and that was unacceptable.

SHARED CONSCIOUSNESS AND
ACTION OUTSIDE OF FORUMS

So the realms discussed in this section—both physical and virtual—when executed correctly, help create interpersonal connections that transcend bureaucracies, help break down small-team narratives, and allow an aligning narrative to be recommunicated throughout an organization.

When this is completed, a state of *shared consciousness* is established, which we described in *Team of Teams* as a "state of emergent, adaptive organizational intelligence" brought about through transparency and information sharing. In this moment everyone is brought onto the aligning narrative and aware of the state of the organization. The goal was to reach this state at the end of every forum.

But an organization's teams must also be given the space to act on these connections, this aligning narrative, and their reestablished shared consciousness. They must be allowed to move, to take action.

This prompts a natural follow-up question: what happens in the gaps between realignments?

QUESTIONS TO CONSIDER:

♦ How does your organization currently communicate and contextualize information or strategic guidance, or news of the organization's current state, to its teams? Do you feel that it is often warped or misinterpreted by those who hear it through a telephone tree style of communication?

♦ Could your organization leverage both physical and virtual spaces to drive cross-silo coordination and improve communication on strategy?

CASE STUDY:

OKLAHOMA OFFICE OF MANAGEMENT
AND ENTERPRISE SERVICES (OMES)

PREFACE

As you read the following story of the Oklahoma Office of Management and Enterprise Services (OMES), consider how the organization used interconnecting technology to create a virtual forum for the operational and cultural interconnection of its dispersed teams. Notice how this interconnection created space for influencers and deepened relationships among disparate tribes.

In particular, note how the leadership of this organization did not necessarily practice both physical and virtual means of interconnecting teams but blended physical design considerations into their virtual ones.

Moreover, consider how careful OMES was in scaling its forum and "staffing" it accordingly, not only limiting initial participants but also actively considering their interests in designing the content of each session.

Finally, note how pressure was taken off bureaucratic leaders in the reduction of their traditional "meeting" functions, while the operational efficiency of the organization was improved—as well as that the technological issues of OMES's forum remain a challenge.

THE SETUP

The building is trim and plain—a tan, glass-and-concrete cuboid, built in 2009 to protect a resource of increasing value and utility in the twenty-first century.

Placed behind seemingly decorative flower beds and sloping green lawns, containing multiple lines of concentric walls and with entire floors designed to shear off in the event of an F5 tornado, the structure is designed with survivability in mind. Unforeseen eventualities are further controlled for deep in the building's interior—four thousand-kilowatt generators, stocked with six days' worth of fuel, will activate should the facility somehow become cut off from the public power grid.

As I move deeper into the bowels of this complex, passing through an electronic security gate, the hairs on my arm bristle at the change in temperature, a result of the air-conditioning working hard to keep the product cool.

So what is it that lies behind these checkpoints and paranoid-seeming safeguards? Military technology? Emergency petroleum reserves? Maybe even water?

Actually, it's none of the above—as I walk into the cavernous space at the middle of the building, all that I can see around me are rows upon rows of tall metal, plastic, and glass closets: these are data banks, whirring across a space of about nine thousand square feet. Through here the daily lives of nearly four million Americans are maintained: from bill paying to e-mail systems to the issuing of report cards to the operation of traffic lights, a host of complicated functions that maintain order for an entire state are conducted through this facility.

"See this?" My intrepid guide, Dustin, a senior technologist in the facility, spreads his hands until they're about a foot apart and holds them in front of a couple of slim black rectangles, which look not too dissimilar from the cable boxes or gaming consoles that might sit under your television. "Those are the phone systems of fifty thousand people, right there."

I take a slight step back, trying not to touch anything.

I'm about three blocks from the State Capitol in Oklahoma City, in the heart of an organization that makes government services in the state tick: the Oklahoma Office of Management and Enterprise Services (OMES). The still-growing result of a years-long effort by the state to consolidate IT resources and personnel from a horde of disparate agencies, OMES is a unique entity in the world of public service: the average employee at its data center struts around in a button-down and slacks and is likely to hold a master's degree or two, in fields most of us would struggle to comprehend.

This atmosphere, and the nature of their work, might contribute to the shared sense that OMES is more like a tech start-up than a government agency in the Midwest. Its employees strike you as a real family—jokes fly around their offices and down the green corridors that line their headquarters. (One good one I overheard when walking to a meeting: "How can you tell if an IT guy is extroverted? When he's talking to you, he's looking at *your* shoes.")

OMES is young. In 2011, IT personnel geographically and bureaucratically segregated from one another, often having been embedded in specific Oklahoma agencies for a good part of their careers, were at once told that they now belonged in, or would soon be integrated into, an entirely new enterprise—which ended up being OMES.

The new organization essentially had to occupy two roles: first, continue to consolidate new resources, and personnel that were being handed to OMES regularly. By mid-2016 about fifty-six Oklahoma agencies had been brought into OMES, out of seventy-seven that would eventually have to follow this path. As new employees, systems, and individuals were being integrated into the OMES family, the transition process had to be smooth, with as little friction as possible for resources being moved from different agencies into the relatively new organization.

Second, OMES had to continue providing service to its "clients"—the scores of agencies it had just stripped IT resources from—and accomplish the delivery of these services in a way better than what was being done before. Between sudden technical issues ("incidents") and demand for new IT products ("projects"), the work pushed on OMES by its clients varied hugely, from data hang-ups to cybersecurity breaches to hardware installation to chronic technical issues to correcting the faulty repair of an entire IT system. These needed to be kept within specific time constraints.

This didn't work out so well at first.

THE PROBLEM

In the beginning, OMES's consolidation had been predictably nightmarish: as one survivor of the transition put it, it "felt like a dictatorship." Technically now unified but still narratively disparate groups of personnel were scattered across the org chart, often based out of agencies that they were no longer a part of, while having to work remotely for personnel they'd never met before and had no opportunity to interact with. This cultural divide eventually led to operational ones.

Unresolved incidents piled up, project delays were routine, and there were never any "lessons learned"—an issue experienced by one client, and solved by one team, would often be seen again in a separate case, but the solution would have to be scrounged up from scratch once more, as the personnel had no opportunity to pool their knowledge.

Moreover, what IT specialists inside the organization deemed "cowboy IT" reigned: rogue IT specialists implanted in locations outside

OMES headquarters would regularly jury-rig a solution to a problem, without documenting what they did or informing their parent organization that the issue had ever come up. This only added to the confusion the broader organization encountered when something else went wrong with the same client.

For Matt Singleton, the COO of OMES, the missteps of his organization were no secret, with the firing of his old boss indicating that OMES's operational and cultural problems were well known to decision makers above his pay grade. He has intense eyes and is tall—something that was apparent even as he sat behind a wooden desk in OMES's modern pristine headquarters.

It wasn't impossible that he might be the next to go, which was vexing on a personal level—Singleton was born and raised in Oklahoma and had transitioned into an IT career after building financial models for the University of Oklahoma (his alma mater). By this point in his career, as a senior director in the state government's IT apparatus, he felt duty bound to do right by his home state.

From his perch near the strategic levels of his organization, he could recognize why his employees felt the way they did, given their unfamiliarity with one another and their past experience as government employees, cogs within vast bureaucracies. "Creating common urgency—it's tough when you're in public service," Singleton explained to me during my visit to Oklahoma City.

"But it was exactly what we needed—because before all of this, we were just a black hole for our clients." Multitudes of projects and incidents were being thrown in to OMES's wheelhouse, and nothing was coming out the other end—a situation that was a product of disconnects between teams. Worse, the demands being put on the organization were getting larger: the state government of Oklahoma was continuing to prioritize cheaper, automated IT systems—and guess who was going to be tasked with building and installing those?

OMES's black hole looked like it would keep on growing.

A potential answer to these issues came in a chance podcast that Singleton was listening to as he drove to work one morning. "I read *Team of Teams* and thought it was a great read—and then, whaddaya know, I was listening to the *Unmistakable Creative* podcast a few weeks later and you came on."

Singleton wasn't misremembering: back in late 2015, I did indeed go on the show and got a chance to talk about some of the ideas expressed in *Team of Teams,* as well as my experiences since. "That made me go straight to Bo [Reese, Oklahoma's CIO]," Singleton said, "and think over everything some more. We agreed that it was worth trying to build our own O&I."

THE SOLUTION

OMES didn't have a defined equivalent of an aligning narrative that we can compare with that of the Task Force or Smith's "One Intuit"—an important detail that limits the way we can examine its case as a holistic demonstration of all of the practices this book discusses.

Nevertheless, OMES's practice of, and outcomes derived by, O&I forums is useful for readers to appreciate.

Singleton knew he wanted a forum-type environment, where a sense of shared consciousness could be established across OMES's different teams on a set cadence, and they could better interact and become familiar with one another. This was what would help end the organization's black hole and create a better space for these scattered teams to be exposed, firsthand, to the strategy that Singleton and Reese wanted to distribute.

So where should he start?

Singleton's initial approach to selling the idea began through his solid lines of authority: after getting clearance from Reese to attempt this, Singleton started a book club for the senior IT directors—the heads of OMES's ten functional silos—who formed his leadership council.

When asked about this, Singleton's response is cavalier—"Yeah, we wanted to get people thinking in the right way, and to do that, we had to show them what we thought would be a great end state." Assembling the necessary solid-line decision makers around a table was a natural way to do this.

The first book assigned to the OMES book club? *Team of Teams.*

After their initial read-through and discussion, Singleton went around and met with his directors one on one. The team members remember these meetings pretty distinctly, as exemplified by one female director recalling his casual approach as very unassuming. "He'd come find us and just start like: 'So . . . I was thinking . . .'"

Apparently there were occasionally frosty receptions—for valid reasons, from the perspective of these directors. As one put it: "The elephant in the room was that I was extremely skeptical. I'd been through so many of these things before—a big organizational idea with buzzwords that hadn't really changed anything in the long run."

Another was a little more explicit about what she and her peers were mostly thinking when Singleton first brought the idea of an O&I up to them: "We thought it was going to be a colossal waste of time—a meeting from ten to twelve every day, on top of all of the other ones we've got. We were all like: *Do you know how much this is going to cost us in other work we could be doing?*"

A significant portion of Singleton's leadership team had the same belief: that their boss's idea was going to be an unwelcome overload of dead time. One director explained this quandary articulately: "We already had change-management meetings every Thursday, incident reports every day at nine fifteen, problem case updates every Friday—and in every single one, there was only maybe five minutes of useful information coming out of the whole meeting. Our reaction to Matt [Singleton] was: *How in the world would this, another meeting, make our jobs any easier?*"

To the directors, it seemed that they were listening to their boss describe the death knell for what remained of their productivity—another meeting to crowd their limited time to sort through OMES's "black hole."

As a side note, their instincts ended up being wrong—but we'll get to that later. What's more important is that Singleton got a critical initial veneer of cooperation—as forced by solid-line authority, per OMES's impersonal order.

The question then became how to best utilize this hard-won time, with an eye to the interest of these directors, whom he had only barely convinced to participate: What would prove to his team that an O&I forum was a good idea, and which of their concerns could he try to mitigate?

Robert Page, a young, energetic senior assistant in OMES, helped out on this front: at Singleton's direction, Page went from director to director, armed with a specially drafted list of questions aimed at determining exactly what they'd want to see reflected in the O&I. After these interviews, Page drafted a "word cloud" that displayed the different key terms he had heard repeated by the IT directors.

The most heavily emphasized takeaway from Page's responding directors? *Transparency,* they seemed to be communicating, *is what we'd need to get from this.* With this Singleton deciphered how he could design

OMES's forum to match the interests of his desired participants and thus use their buy-in to extend enthusiasm for greater participation.

OMES's O&I then needed a "controller"—similar to that used in the Task Force—who could act as an agenda setter and corral the stakeholders whom Singleton had selected to be included in the forum. In addition, Singleton needed this person to have enough of a personal touch to encourage the right behaviors among participants while discouraging perceived "negative" conduct. Moreover, because the central objective of the O&I was transparency, this figure had to be able to sufficiently challenge participants and presenters to be fully honest and up front about the state or needs of their work and their appraisal of whether they needed any assistance on an issue they or their team were encountering in their work.

Singleton started an interview process, searching for a full-time forum controller through the recommendations of his director team: "We had great, cool candidates. We had the directors nominate people. . . . [We wanted] people that embodied our core values, with bias towards action and an aggressive nature."

This is where a clearly articulated strategy and sense of internal values—like those that an aligning narrative would offer—could help guide the selection of controller-type individuals. Nevertheless, Matt's sense of strategy, and his vision for the discussion that would happen through OMES's O&I, was sufficient for him to know the personal qualities to look for in his controller.

Enter Carissa Terry—a former project manager at the Oklahoma Department of Education, a client of OMES. Her background, on the surface, seemed not quite ideal for the role—she was a young outsider who would be expected to help lead an overhaul of OMES and facilitate the dialogue of its senior officers. But when Matt and Bo interviewed her for the position, her simultaneous candor and command showed through. Per Singleton, "We knew she was who we wanted."

Terry was Singleton's new controller, charged with stewardship of the forum. Despite her optimistic intentions, the skepticism held by those she'd soon be trying to corral was palpable and initially got to her. "I was all gung-ho about it . . . until I met with the directors for the first time. Once I'd heard out all of their doubts, I was like: *They don't even want to be here—how am I supposed to make them [participate]?*"

The solid-line endorsement of Singleton and her experience in each early session would help change her level of confidence. After Singleton had selected Terry, together they moved on to thinking through the means by which forums would be operated, starting with design considerations.

The location from which Singleton and Terry chose to direct the forum was, of all things, a tornado shelter in the basement of the data center, only one wall removed from the ranks of data banks that were the epicenter of OMES.

It was a fitting setting: the huge room had an open floor plan—much like the Task Force's SAR—and was interrupted only by the odd concrete pillar, and there was plenty of space for the installation of TV monitors, cameras, and microphones to facilitate the smooth functioning of the forum.

The shelter, like other aspects of the forum, was chosen very deliberately from alternatives that were evaluated.

A boardroom on the second floor? Said Singleton: "No—too ivory tower-y."

What about if everyone dialed in from their desks to a virtual conference room, like a mass Skype session? "No—sure, it'd be cheap, but that'd probably be harder for Terry to control, and the visual is important."

So the tornado shelter it was. Whenever remote participants would join the forum virtually, from computer or phone, their screens would show a large, nearly empty space, occupied only by a U-shaped central table and neat lines of chairs behind, within which OMES's senior leadership all sat, bound on all sides by thick gray walls. This wasn't uncontroversial, as a good number of OMES employees (both directors and other participants) felt that there might be a bit of overthinking happening behind the symbolism being projected. Moreover, it might even be counterproductive to the purpose of the O&I—acoustically speaking, a tornado shelter is not exactly ideal for communication.

But it's a glaring scene to lead from, by design: Singleton and his team were trying to project a utilitarian image of leadership, to which an open concrete floor space was well suited. Dispersed participants in the call, joining it from various locations around the state, would have few visual distractions to draw their attention from the content of the forum.

During each session, the only things filling their screens would be the slides being shared by the presenter, a feed of the presenter talking, another video feed of OMES's senior leadership in the tornado shelter, and a public chat room.

Singleton, Terry, and Page also had to design the agenda of the forum with an eye to what participants had demonstrated (in Page's fact-finding) an interest in hearing: transparency, between all wings of OMES. They whittled down the topics to fulfill this criterion: "project spotlights" (case reviews of recent project for clients), "project updates" (day-by-day run-downs on how existing projects were progressing), and change-management updates (presentations on what new resources had just been or would be rolled into OMES), as well as "escalated cases" and "ad hocs" (pressing issues that required urgent resolution).

Presenters on these topics (ranging from external IT strategists to directors themselves) were all subject to guidance from Terry, assisted by Singleton, on how the topics would best be presented. Ahead of the first O&I in early 2016, the following guidelines were provided to OMES's original directors by Terry and Singleton, to set a behavioral standard in advance:

- **Be there.**
  Attendance of these briefings is mandatory for our service directors—unless they are on leave. Our administrative support team has spent time today attempting to clear conflicts on the directors' calendars. We are willing to make some exceptions, but any absences once staff are attending will be very visible and will undermine the importance of these sessions.

- **Be on time.**
  We will start the O&Is at 10 a.m. Tardiness will undermine the importance of these sessions.

- **Be engaged.**
  O&Is are device-free sessions. Instruct your staff to come get you from the ITOCC if there is an emergency. Using your devices during the briefings will undermine the importance of these sessions.

- **Be prepared.**
  As we get more mature in the itineraries and supporting processes, documentation will be available for each agenda item. Review those materials and come prepared to help our staff be successful. For active incidents on your team, ensure you either know what is going on or have a team member in attendance who does. Not being pre-pared or saying "I'll have to look into it" will undermine the impor-tance of these sessions.

As more OMES staff were gradually added to later forums, for their individual project spotlights—recently completed IT assignments with positive takeaways—Terry would ask the presenters ahead of time to make sure they focused on communicating a few key topics, including:

- The project's time line

- The actions of key stakeholders along that time line

- Lessons that were learned from the project, as well as the client's subsequent experience with the new product

Moreover, Terry made sure that the presenters knew what types of behavior it would be helpful to follow up their discussion with, with an eye to building cross-organization relationships and developing familiarity among different subject-matter experts.

In order for this to occur, she repeatedly reminded them—both on the forum and through private communication—to ensure they:

- Verbally highlighted the people who helped them get this project get done.

- Openly asked of the participants how this project might be applied to other clients or existing incidents.

From there, Terry would step into the discussion and try to draw a tangible connection between the project and the work of other participants in the forum, regardless of what client they were implanted in. During this time Singleton would sit back, allowing Terry to dictate and control the flow of conversation—interjecting only every now and then to highlight desired behavior or results.

Each project spotlight would last for five minutes, per Terry's agenda, and would involve both a recap of what was important to a specific issue being faced by a team in the organization and an attempt to determine how that work could benefit or be benefited by another team.

Interspersed with project spotlights were to be a discussion of other subjects that Singleton and Terry decided needed less frequent dialogue but were nevertheless important for participants to be made aware of at times. This category included sessions for the introduction of new employees, the reporting of client feedback surveys (which, according to an internal briefing, had to "include the good, the bad, and the ugly") and the highlighting of well-performing individual employees. These subjects were to be included on a bimonthly basis.

To complement the live oral discussion of projects and issues on the forum, OMES's O&Is were also designed by Singleton, Terry, and Page to maintain a public online chat room, which displayed in literal parallel to the main video feeds of the forum. Participants joining from their remote devices would have a live chat box running at the bottom right hand of their screens as they watched the forum progress.

So how did all of these efforts turn out?

THE OUTCOMES

The operational and cultural improvements OMES's O&I efforts have achieved are most on display during the forums, one of which I managed to catch while watching an online, multicamera-captured recording of an OMES O&I forum a month after my visit.

At 10:00 a.m. the giant screen at the front of OMES's tornado shelter turned on, and the public chat room it displayed lit up with greetings and salutations from geographically distributed participants: morning everybody! Argh, it's a Monday! :D and morning all :) were among a string of typed greetings I read.

Starting, Terry spoke up. "Welcome, everyone. Good morning and thanks for dialing in to the O&I. We're going to start with an Action Items review." She promptly plowed into a summary of the displayed agenda for that morning, her seated image fully visible against the gray concrete of the shelter to the hundreds of OMES employees who had tuned in from their locations across the state.

Singleton, in contrast, sat back in his chair, to Terry's left—looking on as his employees autonomously interacted in real time and asking only one clarifying question of Terry as she spoke. In doing so, Singleton was making a choice to observe the scene, rather than interfering in dialogue and demanding a front-and-center role in the forum.

During a later presentation on the same forum, a question suddenly popped up in the chat room from a remote viewer. An IT director for OMES situated in the tornado shelter looked up and saw it, then vocalized what he was reading, interrupting the presenter: "Hey, Jeff had a question—aren't we at forty-seven left to migrate in IS?"

To translate, some employees had yet to transition to a new e-mail system that OMES was trying to standardize across its employee base, and it seemed that Jeff wanted to bring this to everyone's attention. Everyone's eyes around the table, and those of people on display at the front of the SAR, turned to watch the chat room. The presenter cleared his throat and clarified, his voice filling the audio feed:

"Hmm, yeah, forty-seven—actually, I think we have actually added a few contractors in since we began that move, so that's probably up to fifty-two now." Another line of dialogue, apparently from a different division officer in OMES ("Michael") then appeared in the chat room's window.

Terry, monitoring both the presentation and the chat room intently, took note and spoke up: "All right, it looks like Michael will make sure his office knows that too. Thanks, Michael!" Another message came up in the chat room from Jeff: thank you!

I wondered at that point how long this type of communication among these different individuals would have taken before the introduction of the O&I. I figured it would have depended how well Jeff, Michael, and the presenter knew one another, information that I wasn't privy to. If they were acquainted, I suppose a direct person-to-person e-mail chain would have distributed this logistical update effectively—although the time taken for this to happen through that method could have ranged from being a few minutes to a few hours to never. If these three weren't acquainted, then information pump–type leaders would have needed to work across OMES's structure to pass this simple question from one narratively isolated silo to another, possibly distorting the innocently framed message into something more harsh sounding along the way.

In contrast, within this forum, teams could interact freely, visually, with one another at a rate limited by only the speed of light and sound—and form personal relationships that might lead to better information exchange and collaboration in the future.

Ten minutes later, a recent project review was being shared with the forum—and its "lessons learned" were pretty impressive, the project having wrapped up with apparently terrific results and with follow-on actions already being taken by its team with others across the organization, as was now being reported to the O&I.

The presenter—"Ayana"—had clearly taken Terry's pre-distributed guidelines on presentation to heart, not only discussing what the broader organization could take away from the project but also thanking the other teams that had helped hers get the job done.

After her presentation, the chat room filled with messages: great job, Ayana, FANTASTIC!, and excellent job Ayana were submitted by various virtual participants—even though some of them had never met her before. Ayana, now smiling behind the U-shaped table in the tornado shelter, retook her original seat off to the side.

Watching this forum remotely, it was clear that its participants had developed and been encouraged to participate in inclusive, honest communication with one another—partially through the efforts of Terry, Page, and Singleton to prepare them for what was expected from them in an O&I and also clearly through social learning. By watching their peers get publicly praised and seeing operational benefits derived from information sharing across silos, OMES's employees learned to adapt their behavior accordingly—which Ayana had just demonstrated.

Yet the outcomes wrought by OMES's use of an O&I forum defied the typical drawbacks associated with the use of virtual teams. With no demographic was this more apparent than with the remote IT strategists of the organization, each of whom was physically emplaced at a client site full time, away from any other member of the organization.

One strategist I spoke with put the change she'd been a part of in stark terms. Before the implementation of the O&I, she said, "I felt like so much of an outsider"—culturally alienated from the rest of the company and unsure of what others needed to know from her to accomplish their jobs.

Now, as a member of the forum?

Says the same strategist, "It's been a godsend."

A challenge I often find when trying to explain the benefits of a team of teams model is empirically demonstrating how a qualitative cultural change across teams inherently leads to tangible operational ones. The behavioral and (per my terminology) narrative-related shift that OMES underwent is a good demonstration of this.

There are a few anecdotes OMES employees referred to when I asked them how this narrative unification had impacted their operations—essentially, I wanted to know, had any of this impacted OMES's "black hole"?

Fortunately, Singleton is a stickler for quantifying results, and the impact of the O&I forum was no exception—in the time since the forum's introduction, the number of IT incidents open past their completion date in Oklahoma has dropped considerably, despite the relatively steady number of total incidents being thrown in OMES's direction.

Internal metrics at OMES help corroborate this:

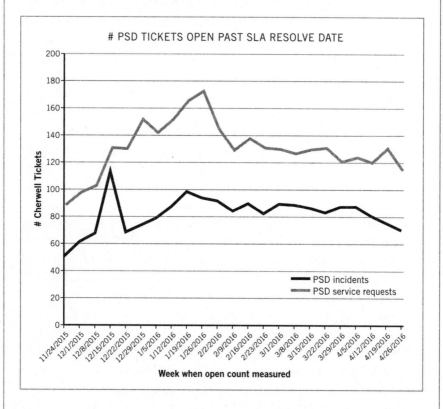

The above figure charts the number of service requests and incidents that exceed OMES's "SLA Resolve Date" within a specific service team on a week-by-week basis—essentially, how many IT service teams had been presented with or missed the deadline on resolving for this type of problem. On this diagram a line indicates when Singleton, Terry, and Page began implementing O&I forums, in January 2016.

Both figures dropped, with the ability of O&I forums to distribute "lessons learned" much better throughout the organization and a crackdown on "cowboy IT" helping proactively prevent future incidents from occurring, even as new clients were added to OMES's portfolio. Moreover, whenever incidents did arise, they could be quickly adapted to and addressed within the context of O&I forums—resulting in the decrease in time taken for the organization to respond to them.

The diagram on the previous page is just one of many data-based presentations that OMES showed me to demonstrate their results, but unfortunately I just don't have the room to present all of these and properly contextualize them as they so deserve.

Today, though, OMES's leaders regularly use diagrams and quantitative figures like this, in addition to their qualitative testimony, as a means for substantiating the returns of their O&I. During the O&I I attended on my visit, one of these was displayed at the front of the room, and Singleton piped up, pointing out excitedly: "See? Look at that, everybody!" Most in the room laughed—apparently they'd come to expect this exuberance.

Recall that there was a concern among Singleton's immediate subordinates that O&Is would end up being an example of yet another stressful time-suck to add to their calendars. This is not unusual and is a common complaint I've heard thrown around when discussing the scheduling of these forums (which we will discuss in the next chapter).

But so far these fears have been reversed.

Though OMES's O&Is were initially set to be two hours long, in practice they began to organically wrap up within roughly forty-five minutes.

Take the long-standing change-management meeting, for example: every Thursday at 1:00 p.m., over the years since it began integrating IT personnel from other government agencies, OMES had held weekly updates on the creation of new IT resources for these new clients, including updates on which projects were being prioritized, what work had to be done on them, and the risk levels associated with each.

On paper these change-management meetings required the attendance (physical or virtual) of all directors in OMES—but in reality, before long, those organizing the meeting would be lucky if even three directors tuned in, a good indication of how, without solid-line buy-in, these initiatives are often for naught.

Despite the importance of the information being shared during these meetings—with some new projects possibly causing system failures if they were executed incorrectly—there was nevertheless minimal interest or perceived urgency in attendance by OMES's senior leadership, which set a social norm for subordinates to take their cues from.

Now, as is readily admitted by the Service Quality team (those in charge of operating change management), the content of the meeting has become organically merged and streamlined into the daily O&I, leading to its being indefinitely canceled.

As for why, there seem to be at least a couple of reasons for those involved. First off, according to a member of the Service Quality team, "cowboy IT" has declined drastically—"discernment seems to have started to take place" among personnel as issues and standard practices advocated through the O&I started to take root and employees began to become more comfortable admitting to judgment lapses in a public setting, knowing they'll be free from blame. It was this behavior that helped drop the number of PSD incidents and time-extended projects, which we displayed earlier.

But more important, content-wise the O&I forums developed to include change-management updates from individual members of the Service Quality team: the growth in the number of participants in the forum had made it a tempting platform for the team to broadcast the information they had wanted to talk about on Thursday. Now, every day, the team could update the entire organization on their work and whom it would impact (directly or otherwise).

Emotions remain mixed in some corners—admittedly, the new reactivity and access offered by the forum have been a blessing to OMES's work. Per an IT director: "Now we can respond to any issue presented to us, with everyone listening and on the same page, in real time." But as for the extinction of the old way they did things? John Santos, the director of Service Quality, seems a little rueful that they could never get the dedicated change-management meeting off the ground.

Singleton, on the other hand, has no reservations. "We've been looking, for a long time, to do cross-pollination across teams and to break down silos. We'd [always] been talking about it, and after a while these things become buzzwords. . . . It wasn't until we brought Carissa [Terry] on . . . and until [the O&I] happened that we were able to realize some of the things that we've been promising for a while."

But technological concerns also represent a front where OMES has room to grow, even as it further expands the attendance of its forums.

As put by one director who became an enthusiastic supporter of the O&I, "the biggest complaints from those who report to me about the O&I, far and away, are about the technical issues." Even from my perspective as a visitor, it's clear why—whenever person-to-person cross talk picked up in the tornado shelter, or there was dialogue from one of the staff sitting behind the U-shaped table, the chat box in the corner of the display screens came alive with comments from various virtual participants: "can't hear," "speak up please," and "turn up your mic" were common among these.

Dustin, my technologist tour guide, hit the nail on the head about why this was ironic in OMES's case. "We're a tech organization that can't get the tech part of this figured out."

According to Singleton, it all really came down to external pressures in the midst of repeated "bad budget years." In Singleton's words, "I think our O&I infrastructure has held up remarkably well considering the financial constraints put on it." I make sure to ask one of my guides when the last "good budget year" was. His assistant grimaces. "Maybe eight years ago?" Technological factors are key to ensuring that O&Is are scalable, run smoothly, and create effective personal familiarization between attendees—and if not implemented appropriately, they risk undermining the purpose of the forum.

Yet since my visit to Oklahoma City, Singleton has shared news that OMES's expansion in operational purview—and in O&I attendance—has gone according to plan, and that recent investments in better technology would by early 2017 allow for total daily attendance to be raised to 150 employees, with 46 percent of OMES's 700 staff attending at least one forum a week.

As I leave, Singleton tells me a line that I've caught him using frequently around OMES's data center headquarters.

"This is how we're transforming government." It's a big ask, but the efforts of OMES offer a sign of hope in turbulent waters.

CHAPTER 5

OPERATING RHYTHM

Football has long been thought of as a sport defined primarily by strength. A line attributed to former Green Bay Packers coach Vince Lombardi captures the intensely physical nature of the game: "Football isn't a contact sport, it's a collision sport. Dancing is a contact sport."

This line of thinking continues to a certain extent in today's National Football League, wherein a prospective player's height, weight, and sprinting speed are detailed and discussed by commentators extensively as leading metrics indicating their ability to hit hard and, thus, their playing potential.

But in 1899 John Heisman, the Cleveland-born namesake of college football's highly sought-after Heisman Trophy, was entering his final year as the head coach of the Auburn University football team—the Tigers. At the start of the season, Heisman looked on, likely with mild disappointment, at what was possibly the physically smallest collection of players he'd ever coached.

This was a presumptive death sentence for the season ahead. But as a student of the game, Heisman wouldn't give up so easily. Instead he turned a thoughtful eye toward the norms of play. Specifically, he considered ways to leverage his team's relative strengths—speed and endurance—against their burlier opponents.

What if, he asked himself, his players could adapt their play of the game in order to utilize these advantages?

The beginning of any play in a football game is defined by two things—the play clock and the offense putting the ball into motion. Once one play ends, the offense has forty seconds to either initiate the next snap of the ball or face a delay-of-game penalty. Typically, teams take full advantage of those seconds to catch their breath, communicate with coaches on their sideline, and plan the next play—but there is nothing in the sport's rulebooks *requiring* the offense to use all of these seconds. Yet where most teams had long grown comfortable with the traditionally plodding rhythm of the game, Heisman saw the possibility for disruption.

If his team were to minimize its use of the traditional offensive huddle and push immediately into the next play, Heisman theorized that he could win with the 1899 Tigers. In short order, he believed, the larger opposing players on defense would fatigue, and the endurance of his smaller players would become a decisive advantage.

Heisman began to run what would eventually be called the "hurry-up offense." Following the end of each play, Auburn's offense would forgo the presnap huddle and instead head straight to the line of scrimmage and begin the next play—well shy of the allotted time on the play clock, forcing the defense to rush back to their positions.

The results were dramatic, as Heisman himself testified:

> The team of '99—my last at Auburn—was a great one. It only weighed about 160 (pounds per player), but its speed and team work were something truly wonderful. I do not think I have ever seen so fast a team as that was. It would line up and get the ball in play at times before the opposing players were up off the ground. . . . That Auburn team of '99 was the first to show what could be done with speedy play.

Heisman's smaller players were vanguards, disrupting the game's traditional balance between planning and execution, and they quickly reaped the benefits. They could exhaust the stronger and larger competition, catch slow-to-recover defensive players offsides, gain penalty yardage from their forced errors, and create a dynamic environment where endurance and adaptability became defining competitive advantages.

Auburn's 1899 team would outscore its opponents 148–11 over the course of that season, having harnessed a new cadence of operation that defied previous iterations of the game and allowed it to adapt quickly based on the conditions on the field.

The concept has seen surges in popularity over the years, from Jim Kelly leading the Buffalo Bills' "K-Gun" offense in the 1990s to Peyton Manning using it to help set the NFL record for most touchdown passes in a game, and in a season, in 2014. The use of Heisman's "hurry-up" approach allows a team to determine the correct balance between centralized control and decentralized execution, based on the team's perception of its immediate environment.

Heisman's no-huddle offense is strongly analogous to finding and refining an *operating rhythm*, which truly unleashed the capability of individual teams within the Task Force. Large windows of empowered execution, where teams freely react to the situation in front of them, were offset by periodic syncs via O&I forums to ensure that the organization was still aligned.

Our operating rhythm allowed us to proactively dominate the environment, not live in a constant state of reaction. Our O&I was the access point for key data, strategic conversations, and the creation of cross-boundary relationships in support of complex operations. This well-tuned balance between reestablishing alignment and empowering decentralized action, our operating rhythm, allowed tactical units to move with a speed, precision, and autonomy that far exceeded the norms of a traditional bureaucratic system and, more important, established a pace that our competition in Al Qaeda, despite its completely decentralized model, could not maintain.

BALANCE AND RATIOS

Thus far we've discussed the problems that face traditional organizational models when they try to compete with networks in the information age. I've offered a view of the evolution of the Task Force, explained how the organization transitioned into a hybrid model, and suggested why organizations in other sectors should emulate the approach. We've considered methods of interconnecting isolated leaders and teams in the organization, both physically and remotely, and talked about the importance of an aligning narrative to overcome compartmentalization.

All of this raises, of course, the next critical consideration—the balance between creating shared consciousness and opening windows of highly decentralized decision making (which *Team of Teams* dubbed "empowered execution"). This balance is what we'll refer to as an organization's *operating rhythm*.

Though Heisman likely didn't describe it as such, his no-huddle approach was analogous to an effective operating rhythm: in his new play style, there essentially existed large windows for empowered execution, where his team was free to read and react to the situation in front of it (when the offense went into "hurry-up" mode), and periodic longer syncs when conditions demonstrated the need for it.

A series of different stand-alone but preset weekly *meetings* at different tiers of the organization might be the closest equivalent many enterprises have to this—tactical teams have a "sales call," operational-level leaders have biweekly updates on division performance, and strategic leaders have quarterly reviews of entire business units. Most organizations are far too comfortable with a traditional, bureaucratically limited cadence and, as we found on the battlefield, can be quickly disrupted by a threat that challenges their rate of operation in ways previously unseen.

A team of teams model creates decentralization and empowerment, but personnel in the system still need to be regularly resynchronized on key insights and strategic intent if their actions are to sit within risk thresholds. Finding this balance—between synchronization and action—will become one of two major practices to control for risk within a team of teams model (the other being the establishment of *decision space*, to which we'll devote a later chapter).

Establishing an effective and appropriate operating rhythm must be the result of, not the antecedent to, understanding the speed with which your organization's external environment is changing and creating new problems.

Balancing strategy with execution is not new. What has changed is the type of *pacing item* you should be comparing your organization against. It is no longer sufficient for an organization to look at its traditional competition only; it also has to consider the rate of churn in its external environment, and match that with equal or greater rates of adaptation—to the point of becoming disruptive.

Whereas empowered execution can create rapid action at the small-team level, each move toward decentralization adds nonlinear levels of risk that decisions could be made that are misaligned with the strategy or aligning narrative of the organization. In other words, missteps at a tactical level can cascade to far larger problems with cumulative consequences. A thoughtful operating rhythm is designed to mitigate this risk, to the greatest extent possible, by balancing decentralization with realignment, balancing centralized control and autonomous action.

The logic of empowered execution, partially advanced in *Team of Teams,* is easy to digest: when teams are given access to key data, invited to relevant strategic conversations, and are encouraged to independently leverage relationships to enable cross-boundary collaboration, their ability to problem-solve and take effective action can quickly exceed the pace and quality possible within a strict bureaucratic system.

Too much talk, of course, can mean perfect narrative and strategic alignment with insufficient action upon this understanding—and many organizational leaders will recognize how frustrating this status quo can be. Prussian general Otto von Bismarck verbalized this gnawing impatience well, once reminding the debate-prone legislators in the North German Reichstag that "a conquering army on the border will not be stopped by eloquence."

Similarly, it is easy to give in to the opposite type of behavior and act too presumptuously, without proper forethought. Statistical mathematician Persi Diaconis argued that more dangerous than overthinking a problem is "getting involved in the minutiae of a partially baked idea and believing that pursuing it is the same as making progress on the original problem." Action might feel good, but all energy and no strategy can be just as dangerous for an organization's interests as excessive dialogue.

A well-struck operating rhythm allows the senior leadership to determine a balance between these critical elements, between stability and fluidity, hierarchy and network—connecting, at a cadence of their choice, the dotted- and solid-line parts of the organization's hybrid model.

OPERATING RHYTHM

The critical early question for an organization looking to assess its operating rhythm is *How fast is our environment changing?* Then a second: *In its current state, how fast can our organization adapt to change?* The delta between these two is the gap your operating rhythm should aim to close.

When looking externally, an organization's leaders shouldn't constrain themselves to looking only at the obvious institutional competitors that have always been competitively evaluated for strategy. Consider, in addition, broader extra-institutional factors; the changes being driven in the market by new technology; the speed at which small competitors are acquiring new market share or accumulating positive consumer feedback; and how an interconnected client base can outpace marketing efforts or the ability to address their concerns. These are the types of organic networked problem sets that an organization needs to pace itself against.

Any organization struggles with addressing these considerations, of course, and the Task Force was no exception. On the ground, our teams were seeing what appeared to be isolated problems in our external environment but were actually individual nodes of the same complex, interconnected problem set—that of extremist networks scattered across our various realms of operation. Much as any large organization's frontline elements are biased to see *their* part of the process as unique and isolated, so too were our teams programmed by their narratives and experience to look at their immediate problem, or node, as the organization's top priority. In large part these biases contributed to the tribal mentality that existed at the level of our small teams.

But our senior leaders were positioned to see the fight across small-team boundaries and realized that individual wins at the small-team level weren't adding up to collective success. Through thoughtful deliberation on an ever-growing intelligence picture, they began to visualize the interconnected nature of our threats, realizing that one action by the enemy in an isolated pocket of the fight could have near-immediate impacts across our organization's different fronts. In simple terms, the structure of the network we were fighting changed every day, based on the interactions of its members, the operations we were conducting, and countless other variables.

Our teams needed to be equally interconnected, be given the autonomy to move quickly based on emerging insights and new data, and realign themselves at the same pace as the network we were fighting. Therefore, a *twenty-four-hour* operating rhythm was established, allowing for the most consistent, well-adjusted balance between windows of empowered execution and the reestablishment of shared consciousness for our organization. As a result, our leadership didn't really choose a twenty-four-hour rhythm; our environment demanded it.

So too should you thoughtfully consider the speed of your environment as you search for an appropriate operating rhythm.

But bureaucracies without designed spaces for shared consciousness and empowered execution will have a limit to their operating rhythm. Let's step back and consider how normal bureaucratic structure imposes a ceiling on an organization's operating rhythm, simply by default.

RIGID DELAY

Bureaucratic systems are purpose-built to pass information in an approved fashion, and to ensure that official process (per an impersonal order) is followed.

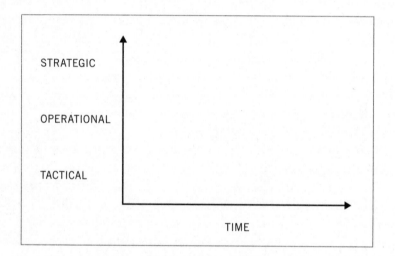

The y-axis on the graph above divides the different leadership levels of a bureaucratic organization—tactical, operational, and strategic—whereas the x-axis represents time. These leadership tiers, by design, must make decisions at different frequencies and time sensitivities.

For example, tactical leaders and teams (in both military and business) generally undergo a quicker decision-making cycle than those at operational or strategic levels—they're constantly making sales, servicing clients, responding to calls, or going after insurgent fighters. Their tempo can vary widely depending on the precise task at hand and the organization in question—from the frenetic pace of a call center to the disciplined approach of an accounting firm to the stochastic nature of a hospital emergency room, the junior levels of every organization fall into a natural but high-frequency decision rhythm based on their industry. A junior analyst in an investment bank is expected to rapidly assemble numerous financial models for their solid-line superior to interpret and act upon, while ground units in the Task Force were expected to launch multiple direct-action raids within short time frames.

Sales happen in the field, with prospective clients. Missions happen on the ground, against an enemy. Surgery happens in a hospital's operating rooms, on patients. These tactical leaders and teams make countless incremental choices and judgment calls on any given day—collecting new data, formulating a marketing pitch, preparing for a raid; they must execute on small dilemmas rapidly and repeatedly.

These high-cadence actions are, in many organizations, what truly defines the business. Decision-making frequencies at the tactical level of organizations will therefore occur at a very rapid rate—we can represent this as follows:

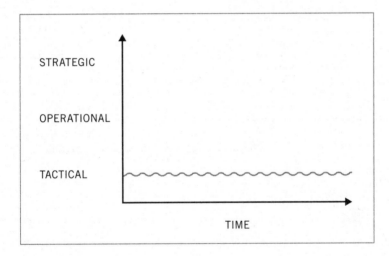

The individual setting or context of these cases is not necessarily significant—what matters is that these teams or individuals largely face the external environment and are constantly interacting with it.

One tier up, at the operational level of the organization, coordination, actions, and decisions occur at a slightly slower frequency than on the tactical level, but generally at a much wider breadth. At meetings between information pump–type heads of different teams and across functional silos, this level of the organization is dedicated to keeping an organization moving as it has been bureaucratically designed to.

The natural tension in a position like this can be oppressive, so its occupants try to remain impartial in their decision making. At this operational level, their days are filled with moments of multidirectional pressure for a variety of reasons: a single critical tactical error can be attributed to them not effectively communicating the intent of senior leaders' views on strategy; providing resources to one team means that someone else doesn't get what they need; a surprised senior leader means they didn't get the right information up the chain of command quick enough.

As a result, their decision-making frequency is slower than those at the tactical levels beneath them, as they're necessarily held back by the need to filter requests from and coordinate with multiple internal stakeholders—both above and beneath them in the hierarchy.

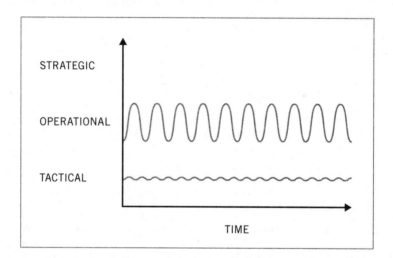

From here we enter the strategic realm. This is the home of the C-suite, the executive team, the commanding generals. Here, in theory, minds are concerned not necessarily with as much information pump–type coordination but rather with long-term strategic thinking. Decisions are framed around 10-Ks, the actions of subordinate divisions or silos, public disclosures, quarterly board meetings, C-suite committees and annual shareholder meetings, and a litany of other concerns tied to the future rather than the tyranny of the here and now.

This, of course, is the family of problem sets that many proven young tactical leaders hope to one day concern themselves with, assuming they perform well within the rapid cycles of tactical life, then do equally well performing a middle manager's information pump function.

Strategic leaders are therefore traditionally living on the lengthiest periodicity of decision making of any bureaucratic tier:

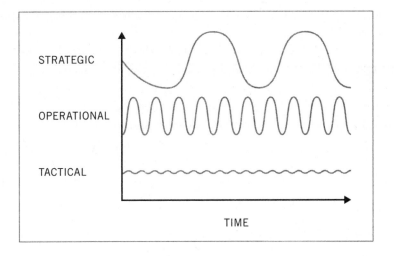

The above model is, admittedly, a simplistic way of categorizing and visualizing the different decision-making cadences of leadership tiers in an organization. Nevertheless, this diagram will help us as we dive deeper into visualizing the balance between shared consciousness and empowered execution needed in an effective operating rhythm.

Yet the strategic leadership tier is, more and more frequently in today's increasingly complex world, where many difficult decisions land after being kicked up through the operational and tactical tiers of the organization.

The observation that strategic-level leaders are becoming increasingly subject to deeper-scale strategic evaluation in their enterprises has been noted—just one example of this, a 2009 article published in the *Economist* assessing corporate strategic management, observes that corporate strategy formulation has "evolved into a [newly] continuous process, not (as it had been) a discrete half-yearly or annual coven attended by a select few."

Again, the Task Force's operating rhythm eventually navigated toward a 24-hour cadence—a cadence set to match Al Qaeda's rate of change. These 24-hour windows were defined by 90 minutes dedicated to reestablishing broad shared consciousness via our O&I, followed by 22.5-hour windows of empowered execution.

The short, intense length of this cycle is naturally intimidating, and far too aggressive for most private-sector organizations. As we'll see in our upcoming case study of how Under Armour's supply chain altered its operating rhythm, the cycle that seemed most suited to that organization was a weekly cadence, with supplemental opportunities for individual teams to synchronize between different forums. Alternatively, however, as we saw with OMES, some organizations are better suited to a daily rhythm and can maintain it effectively. The critical question, again, is examining how fast an environment is changing, then setting your operating rhythm to move faster than the disruptions around you.

Let's return to this diagram to discuss how a traditional bureaucratic cycle of decision making would prevent an appropriate pace of organizational reactivity from happening:

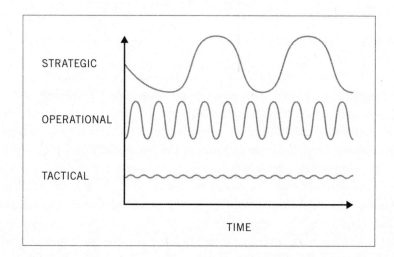

Let's say you're a tactical-level leader in a large organization. Your team is working in the field every day, constantly exploring and responding to your environment, operating at a high decision-making cadence while regularly feeding new insights up into the higher levels of the organization.

In that vein, ground units within the Task Force would venture out against insurgent cells, gather new intelligence about the current state of the enemy's network, and report back to senior leadership with near-real-time information about the state of the insurgent network. *Go out, find new intelligence, come back to base and hand it over, await new permission to act on it, then go out again.* This cycle, conceptually the same as in many large organizations in the civilian world, is constantly repeated.

But what happens if the speed of your external environment's change suddenly outpaces the speed of this procedural decision-making flow within your organization? Imagine that you or your team discover a valuable piece of information, and you believe it's relevant to other teams in your organization. Your intuition tells you that it is time-sensitive data, and you sense that your organization may need to realign in response to these updates. What pathway would you use to disseminate that information across your organization's teams?

If you're like many organizations, the most likely available path is your solid-line hierarchy. Sure, *theoretically* you can walk into the CEO's office or send a mass e-mail across the enterprise, and if your instinct is correct, you'll be rewarded as a perceptive leader. But practically speaking, what if you're wrong? How many times can you alert your superiors to your hunches or concerns before they stop listening and your reputation suffers? The conventional frame of organizational thinking looks down on bypassing one's immediate supervisor as "more companies than not still view the act as insubordination," per an article in the *Wall Street Journal*.

The safer, standard route is instead to speak with those directly above you—whose job it is to consider your perspectives and face the same decision you've just wrestled with, albeit with a slightly broader horizon of authority. They're similarly incentivized to pass the information up to another member of the solid-line leadership. Resembling Christakis and Fowler's telephone tree, discussed previously, this pattern of information transmission continues, and the request for a decision (or clarification on action) moves rung by rung up the hierarchy, with each rung interpreting, filtering, and telling its own version of the original information to those higher up the ladder.

You can imagine this new data gradually filtering its way up, then across, then back down the organization's solid-line highways as quickly as it possibly can. People in this system might move with a sense of urgency, but with even the best of intentions, the limiting factor of solid-line authority is always at play. Without a strong, immediate dotted-line conduit to the necessary teams or leaders—or clarification on whether one team can independently act on this information—the organization must settle for bureaucratic patterns of coordination, communication, and permission.

A response from senior leadership based on fleeting information is either difficult to get or, if it does happen, pulls senior leaders into an operations- or tactical-level issue and away from their long-term thinking and strategic planning. Either solution pathway has negative outcomes.

Imagine again that you're the team that first discovered these insights and pushed them up the chain of command. Meanwhile, you wait patiently for a response but then watch in frustration as, once again, things start to evolve on the ground. The pertinence of your initial information begins to fade, and the external environment shifts. Too much time, you realize, is being spent delivering your insights to the *right* people in your organization's hierarchy; too many others have weighed in at each tier of the organization.

This can occur even when each person in this chain is doing their job to the best of their ability and with good intentions. There is often no *one* at fault in these situations, no evil actors. It is simply an outdated structure trying to apply a predictability-based playbook to a highly complex environment.

Meanwhile, your more agile competitors may have identified and leveraged the fleeting opportunity. The social media post went viral. Someone else got the sale. The target changed locations. By the time approvals arrive, the opportunity is gone. Maybe you execute the next step, and maybe you don't; but you know that it no longer matters. Your well-resourced, powerful enterprise was simply too slow; the half-life of the information passed.

FROM X_1 TO X_2

In the Task Force's early days of the conflict in Iraq and Afghanistan, the cycle described above would repeat itself often. Tactical teams would find and evaluate a significant piece of actionable intelligence, pass it up to their next point of contact in the bureaucratic command chain, and wait for them to do the same. By the time the team would receive clearance or guidance on how to best move upon that information, it usually would be just too dated to have the desired impact. The insurgent network had evolved, the target had become less actionable, the environment had changed, or a combination of all three.

It was a painfully common pattern and even more frustrating given that everyone, from the tactical to the strategic level, was doing what they were supposed to be doing. Our machine's different pieces were working *very well,* just as the system had been designed, but that simply wasn't good enough in a complex, rapidly changing environment. We had to iterate quicker—just as all organizations today need to.

To make this possible, an organization must close the time gap between "X_1" (when an actionable piece of information is identified by a tactical team) and "X_2" (when it is finally acted upon)—yet the traditional difficulties with doing this effectively in a bureaucracy can be best represented by the diagram below.

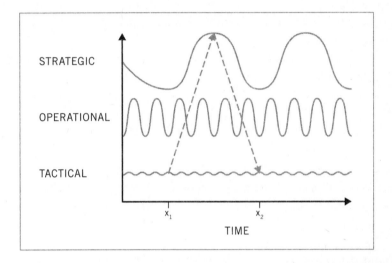

Worse than the tangible delay between X_1 and X_2 is the hidden opportunity cost that comes with accepting this action gap—subsequent additional environmental intelligence that would have been reaped had X_2 come sooner, allowing information collection and execution at moments of X_3, X_4, and beyond. As the half-life of information grows increasingly short, the opportunity cost of not moving when the time is right continues to rise.

You certainly have similar patterns across your enterprise. Consider the gap between identifying a prospect and closing a sale, between a customer complaint and a resolution, or between new market research and integration of these findings into your product design; the list could go on.

If you believe optimizing your existing bureaucratic processes will close the gap between X_1 and X_2, you're doubling down on a dated organizational process at the risk of sinking the enterprise. Solving this issue through the preexisting rule book requires speeding up the processes that move information up and down the rungs of the ladder, but there is a point of diminishing return with this approach.

Admittedly, the Task Force took that approach at first; and as with any large organization trying to be more adaptable to constant change, it meant less sleep, more work, and unsustainable levels of stress on people and the system itself. If your organization is going down this path, you'll quickly find in-boxes growing too crowded, equipment and personnel being pushed to the edge, and the problems around you continuing to expand. You'll find that this approach quickly hits a point where the human element becomes a limiting factor, and there are simply no more hours left in the day.

The solid-line system alone can be optimized only to a certain point—a hybrid approach can offer exponentially better returns.

FINDING RHYTHM

To recontextualize an earlier question we suggested organizations must ask themselves—and delving a bit deeper—an enterprise's leadership must also ask itself, *What is the fastest that our teams can currently move from X_1 to X_2?*

Disciplined windows for the reestablishment of shared consciousness, as demonstrated by an O&I forum, create an opportunity for vertical realignment, inter-team cooperation, and cross-silo and cross-level information exchange. The forum allows decision makers at every level to act together, eliminating time loss. With realignment established, teams can be empowered to move from X_1 to X_2 (then X_3 and beyond) without reverting to the too-slow bureaucratic decision loop. And they're empowered to move like this until the operating rhythm dictates it is time to resynchronize.

It is an elegantly simple approach but one that is made possible only through discipline at every level of the organization. In this model an organization's senior leadership can no longer simply focus on the optimization of bureaucratic solid-line *processes* that push information—instead, information at X_1 can be organically shared with an entire organization instantaneously by the team that discovered it within periods of shared consciousness, which then shortens response times to X_2.

In this model, within spaces for shared consciousness, an enterprise's

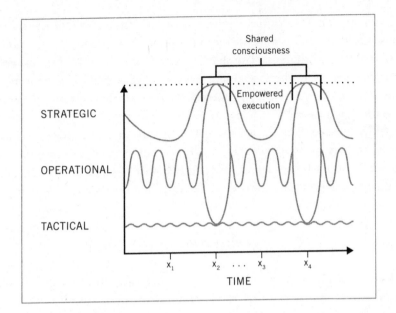

strategic leadership must focus on providing the services that only *they* can effectively provide—reiterating an aligning narrative, articulating an understanding of the speed of the organization's external environment, helping foster interconnections among teams, highlighting and praising positive results and cross-functional relationships.

In time, and with the transparency offered by a suitable operating rhythm, senior leaders will find themselves increasingly freed from "firefighting" or information-pump duties during periods of empowered execution, as they decentralize the decision-making authority for these issues lower into the organization (which we will elaborate on in chapter 7). With shared consciousness consistently refreshed, teams on the ground can collaborate with one another, gather new data, index those insights against their understanding of strategy, then execute again, and again, and again.

During phases of empowered execution, teams are largely subject to their *own* approval process and information networks to quickly move from X_1 to X_2 and beyond—while the role of strategic leadership during phases of empowered execution becomes primarily about monitoring actions, noting the impact they're having on the environment, and shoring up relationships with outside partners to maintain and deepen the credibility of the enterprise.

Yet for the Task Force, at the end of any given cycle, windows of empowered execution were meant to pause (or slow down) as the organization took time to reestablish shared consciousness in O&I forums. For a brief period every day, the global enterprise was virtually reconnected, and took on the feel of a small, narratively aligned team solving problems around a table.

Ninety minutes later, the organization would again be unleashed into a state of empowered execution. A simple but elegant ratio was maintained. Yet not unlike a healthy diet and exercise regimen prescribed by a physician, the solution is obvious once stated but is easier said than done.

AR-RAMADI

My senior leadership was attuned to balancing our phases long before I could conceptualize the real power and intent of our twenty-four-hour operating rhythm. I remember clearly a moment in 2006, well into the transformation of the Task Force, when I saw in vivid terms the risk of unbalancing this.

At that point in my career, I was a cog in our bureaucratic machine, but its overall function was still opaque to me.

I was on an operations-level deployment to Iraq—a coordinator rather than a doer. That day I was watching, through a live drone feed, one of our tactical teams finish a successful midday raid in a heavily populated part of Ar-Ramadi—a city to the west of Baghdad that had become a hotbed of the country's insurgency. It was an X_2 moment—environmental cues that had been collected, analyzed, and disseminated off-line throughout our organization, via the connections an O&I forum fostered, had now been acted on by an operator team.

Daytime raids on insurgent strongholds like this one were outside the norm for us, if only because such visibility made it easier for other fighters in the target area to perceive and respond to an operation. Our forces owned the night; daytime operations held exponentially more risk. Teams working under these conditions would need to get in and out especially quickly, as additional time spent on the ground increased the risks posed to our forces and the local population. This operation had gone as near textbook as possible; with no snags encountered, it was time for the operators to come back to base.

As the team smoothly withdrew from the target location, boarding their extraction helicopters and flying back to our compound, the drone I was watching the scene through remained on station—continuing to observe the target building as the helicopters pulled away. It slowly circled above the compound, unseen and unheard by the inhabitants of the city block below.

I sat a good many miles away, watching the drone's feed, most of my teammates sharing our small operations center had begun moving on to other matters now that this mission seemed complete. It seemed as though it was time to contextualize what had just happened, analyze any new data that had come as a result, and plan the next cycle of operations.

My intelligence officer and I remained staring at the grainy live image of the target location.

"It'll be interesting to see who shows up," I'd said to her.

"Yeah," she'd replied. "That rattled their cages."

Often members of an insurgent network would visit a target site after one of our operations, understandably curious to piece together what had just happened, after the Coalition's forces had left. My intelligence officer and I wanted to watch for this activity in the aftermath of the operation, which would indicate how our opponents were handling the fresh damage inflicted on their network.

I peered at the image, waiting for someone—anyone—to show up.

Seen through the drone's camera, the target site was remarkably still: it was a nondescript compound on a crowded block, with a layout that was relatively standard in the area. My intelligence officer and I could pick out the finer details of the property, consisting of a main building and two smaller structures, a now-empty courtyard, and a high cinderblock wall preventing anyone on the street from seeing in.

As we looked on, rubbernecking pedestrians began to crowd the narrow street in front of the compound, curious about what had just taken place—just as we had expected. But within a few minutes, we watched as a vehicle trundled down the busy street, breaking through the crowd and pulling into the compound's empty courtyard—soon followed by another, and then a third. The ordered convoy of unmarked vehicles formed a ring within the property's outer wall.

This was what my intelligence officer and I were on the lookout for.

Then a flurry of activity as their doors seemed to swing open from above: three figures quickly exited the lead vehicle and ran into one of the buildings. Two more got out of the second vehicle, while a fourth vehicle arrived just before the first departed, having left one of its passengers apparently standing guard in the courtyard.

This rapid pattern of departures and arrivals repeated itself again and again, all picked up by our drone's camera and beamed to our operations center. Cars pulled in, people got out, frenzied activity followed, and then people left once more—for thirty minutes, the compound was a picture of chaos.

This was a real-time feed of our enemy network restructuring. Suddenly missing a few key hubs and influencers they'd had before our raid, this cell was in the midst of organically redrawing itself, adapting to the structural damage it had just been dealt.

Yet our most attuned personnel, the members of the tactical team that had just been on that target site, were being forced to unplug from their phase of execution and deliver their insights and intelligence into the Task Force's solid-line machine. They had to report up, present intelligence, and wait for a full understanding to permeate through our organization's bureaucracy—rather than be enabled to keep moving, leverage dotted-line connections, and fully take advantage of the liberties of empowered execution.

As an information pump in that system, watching as the environment changed in real time, I began to realize that I had misunderstood the intent of the Task Force's operating rhythm. I was thinking of this like a football game, in the spirit of Heisman's opponents: when a play concludes, immediately return to the huddle.

But while I worked to enforce that cadence, the networks around us still ran amok, free to adapt to our most recent action. Our most informed tactical team was flying back to base to report the results of their raid up the impersonal command chain, but as I watched the screen, I realized that their insights were becoming dated right before our eyes.

As we huddled, AQI's local cell would have luxurious hours, perhaps days, to react to the events of the team's operation—destroying intelligence, evacuating sites in the area, breaking off communication between key actors. Potential follow-up events at X_3 and X_4 would be lost to us, as AQI's networked structure would adapt and avoid any further damage from subsequent operations.

As I watched the drone feed, the enemy network my organization was trying to understand was morphing. An hour after our team was off the ground, its structure would be fundamentally different.

And so, watching that feed, I thought to myself: *Am I helping this team move faster against these threats or slowing them down by forcing them to realign with my solid-line perspective?* During this window of empowered execution, I was displaying counterproductive bureaucratic behavior.

Yet my role during these windows of empowered execution was clear. I was there to help facilitate effective action at the small-team level, not to slow things down. With our team en route to our compound, and the problem changing in front of my eyes, I considered what else I could have done to help that team execute one more successful action. If the answer was "nothing," then how should I have been redistributing our resources to help other parts of the organization *immediately,* once I knew that they were no longer required in our corner of the fight?

I looked to my right, at my intelligence officer, and shook my head.

"They're moving too fast," I said, pointing to the swarms of actors who had now moved in and out of the screen in front of us. She nodded.

I didn't voice my next thought.

Right now, I'm part of the problem.

I would later realize that our senior leadership had already spelled out the solution. Our Task Force's operating rhythm offered an easy answer for how to control my behavior as a solid-line leader: every twenty-four hours, I was accountable to push information up and into critical forums like the O&I, playing my part in the creation of shared consciousness. But in the gaps, during windows of empowered execution, my job was to enable the autonomous action of our teams by connecting them with information, getting them the assets, and coordinating with adjacent units to ensure they maintained freedom of maneuver throughout that part of the cycle.

The basic components are simple, but their execution, I realized, was a mind-set change. It took all of us time to realize this, and some understood quicker than others. You'll see similar patterns in your own organization. As a leader, talking about this fact with your organization will help everyone face this reality faster than they might on their own.

QUESTIONS TO CONSIDER:

♦ How quickly does it seem that your external environment is changing relative to five years ago? Ten years ago?

♦ At full efficiency, how fast can your organization hypothetically react to important new information presented to *any* of its teams? Is that faster than the rate at which threats and opportunities emerge organically in your environment, or only faster than the speed of traditional competitors?

♦ When your organization misses opportunities, how often is it true that the information was there, but it was not connected fast enough with the appropriate team?

CASE STUDY:
UNDER ARMOUR

PREFACE

As you read the following case study of Under Armour's supply chain division, keep in mind how the unit's experiences managing different product pipelines across various functional groups was improved through the use of an effective operating rhythm.

In particular, note how this functional group of the organization was being repeatedly surprised by X_1-type events that would emerge across different silos, how its leadership had historically pushed solutions through solid-line channels, and how that approach was losing effectiveness as the company's rapid growth and success brought with it new levels of complexity.

Consider how different forums, each structured to meet specific ends, were created. Note how key actors from the relevant functional groups were brought into this new cycle and how that shift improved the organization's reaction time to X_2. Additionally, take in how behavioral norms and relationships among these siloed teams began to shift as a result of this new approach.

THE SETUP

"Wow . . . well—it's like being parachuted into a tropical jungle . . . with no compass . . . or GPS . . . or any bearings . . . and then being asked to find your way out of there."

So answers the corporate officer when he is asked to summarize the challenges of managing a global supply chain—a function he helps fill for a multibillion-dollar company whose logistics have had to adapt to the organization's external complexity. As the chief of staff for its chief supply chain officer—Jim Hardy—this source has borne close witness to how this entrepreneurial company has had to adapt its traditional culture and ethos in the face of success and subsequent growth.

They both work for Under Armour, a sports apparel firm recognized around the world today—and its efficient logistical operations are an example of the practice of operating rhythm being used to great effect.

The company's sizable status in its field belies its humble roots. It all began in 1996 when Kevin Plank, a fullback for the University of Maryland's football team and the self-described "sweatiest guy on the field," found himself repeatedly forced to play in soaked T-shirts—a result of their clingy cotton fabric. Frustrated, Plank conversely noticed that under the same conditions his compression shorts always stayed dry, no matter how much of a sweat he managed to work up on the field.

Thus inspired, Plank started a business manufacturing breathable-fabric athletic undershirts. Starting out by distributing prototypes to his friends on Maryland's varsity teams, he would see it grow to a multibillion-dollar organization.

But as the company grew into the enterprise it is today, its people retained an entrepreneurial, athletically derived spirit intertwined with its initial success. The company's equivalent to the Task Force's aligning narrative remained strong, even after its dramatic internal and external transformation: in its 2010 10-K filing, Under Armour announced that it had passed the billion-dollar net revenue mark for the first time in its history, having increased net revenue 24 percent over the previous year's figure. But the tone the company used in announcing this milestone was not one of boastful adulation or fulfillment. It was one of *hunger:* "We are 14 years into this thing," the report reads, ". . . and it feels like we are just getting started."

Even after the firm's growth, Plank's initial entrepreneurial emphasis on improvisation and grit—the need to *find a way*—held in the company. Teams and leaders within Under Armour still felt like they were a part of Under Armour's original start-up story and acted in accordance with it, often inventing spontaneous, ad hoc responses to their problem sets—which, when combined with the newly global scale of the company, brought both advantages *and* leadership challenges, which were most apparent to a select few.

Kip Fulks was one of these. The cofounder of Under Armour, Fulks is a high-energy being who was a two-time All American lacrosse player at Maryland while Plank was on the university's football team. He was one of the early samplers of Plank's undershirt prototypes and has been with the company since day one—eventually serving as Under Armour's chief operating officer, to whom Hardy reported as the chief supply chain officer. Fulks's strategic-level perspective at the top of Under Armour's bureaucratic lattice, at the head of various information highways, made its teams' lack of operational interconnectivity clear to him.

I first met Fulks in 2014, when he and another Under Armour executive attended a leadership forum in Alexandria, Virginia. Hosted by the McChrystal Group, it was designed to assemble leaders from various backgrounds for a daylong discussion about the challenges of contemporary organizational leadership.

After a long opening conversation, we all took a brief break from the confines of our conference room setting. We drove to the National Mall in Washington, D.C., for a run, and Fulks and I took off on it together. Passing Capitol Hill, the Washington Monument, and the White House, we talked about the earlier discussions of the day.

I wasn't familiar with the nuances of Under Armour's business at the time and had no awareness of the pressures the company's supply chain division was coming under. But I tried to use my experiences in the Task Force in answering Fulks's questions, which started to come quickly: *How did your units synchronize timelines across silos? What role did senior leadership take in helping that happen? How did you push ownership of decisions onto younger leaders?* On and on, running the whole time, I was both being asked about my experiences and educated about Under Armour's state.

We finally started a slow recovery walk up the steps of the Lincoln Memorial. Fulks looked over at me and spoke. "Look, Under Armour's awesome," he said. "We've got good products, people, all the things we used to dream about when we started. And we're still super aggressive, which is awesome but can sometimes be a problem, now that we're getting bigger and scaling up is harder. Our ethos is to *find a way,* and our teams all take that to heart.

"We're solid. But getting our teams to stay synced and communicate while each *finds a way* is getting challenging," he continued. "Come to Baltimore when you can, and we can talk it through further."

A few weeks later, on an early Chesapeake morning, I pulled up to Under Armour's harborside headquarters. A repurposed Procter & Gamble soap-manufacturing facility, the campus's redbrick buildings were still emblazoned with names like "Dial" and "Ivory," marking these products' past points of manufacture. By 6:00 a.m., employees had already filled the property's waterfront athletic field. Looking on, I watched as a crowd of them completed group fitness classes, flipped tractor tires, and worked out with in-house personal trainers.

By midmorning I found myself going back and forth on a whiteboard with Fulks as we talked through the state of Under Armour's logistics. "I hate consultants," he said, opening our discussion with a laugh. "Don't take that the wrong way, but I hate paying someone to tell me what I already know. I need to know that your team can help us actually solve something."

I couldn't argue with that—it's a common viewpoint—and I appreciated his direct nature. We settled on a middle ground. Fulks would give me a few weeks to spend time with his teams, attend meetings, and get a general sense of how their operations ran. "Then," he said, "come back to this whiteboard and explain how you think your model can help. We can both decide from there if it makes sense."

A few weeks later we were back in that office, facing a whiteboard. Much as Fulks had said early on, the various stakeholder elements in Under Armour's supply chain division apparently needed synchronization. Also in the room was retired U.S. Army general Billy Don Farris, who would work on-site with these teams for the following year.

With all of us present, I owned up to how hard this issue would be to change. "There's no magic button to solve this immediately. It's about leadership. Your senior folks will need to drive this."

Fulks smiled. He was fine with that.

THE PROBLEM

So what *exactly* were the symptoms being presented among Fulks's subordinate teams? As Under Armour had grown, introduced increasingly diverse types of product, and entered unfamiliar markets, its pseudo-aligning narrative, *find a way*, gradually proved to be insufficient to guide appropriate, scalable responses to the complex problem sets that percolated through the company's teams.

Nowhere was this more clear than within the company's supply chain division. This functional group of the firm, according to a senior source within it, is unique in that it is "affected by every aspect of the organization: from design concept, all the way to grabbing that piece of apparel, or footwear, or accessory off the shelf and going up to the cash register." Its silo was a unique bridge among the peer product design, marketing, customer service, and sales divisions and was thus subject to the shortfalls and miscommunications among these.

The status quo of the early 2010s in the supply chain division—a period marked by record conventional financial success for the broader company—has been described by some as being riddled with "stovepiped" communications and a "lack of visibility" among these peer divisions. None of them was necessarily at fault; the organization's structure had simply become a victim of its own exponential growth.

Denny Ward, a younger member of the supply chain team who currently works in more senior levels of product sourcing, has a clear memory of the former downstream and upstream interdependency weaknesses of these different functional groups. "Our Supply Chain logic is that we will go place POs [product orders] at factories to service those buys. . . . Then, as the factory is accepting that order, they'll provide visibility in terms of what they can hit . . . and then, through the likes of production, they will give updated dates, in terms of any delays that they're working through." These distinctly negative X_1-type events were often held up by "timing and lack of visibility" among necessary functional groups.

Sometimes, though, these sudden developments were potentially positive—for example, as Ward puts it, "if product is selling extremely well—better than planned—often we'd have to react to that market trend by creating a slightly newer, different design." But one thing was consistent among negative and positive environmental changes: "Time is of the essence."

A critical metric long used to evaluate the success of Hardy's division was the ability to meet the "buy-ready date" for products—the deadline by which the technical specifications, or "techpacks," of product orders had to be delivered to manufacturers. Yet whenever unexpected problems did arise from peer divisions—like delays in design specifics or an issue with product quality or a need for new products (X_1)—they took too long to emerge and were dealt with too late, often in non-scalable ways (X_2). These "bottom-of-the-ninth," last-ditch scrambles to hit buy-ready dates were common and highly frustrating to the teams involved, which all too often fell short. They were, indeed, "finding a way," but it wasn't enough—which was especially galling and clear to Hardy's more tactical teams.

Hardy—an experienced logistician from the consumer goods industry—could only look on as Under Armour's buy-readys "kept on slipping past" due to steadily increasing bureaucratic disconnects among the supply chain division and other silos. Each slip was limited in its consequences, but in total the problem was costing the company dearly. Strict *deadlines* became flexible *guidelines*, but whenever Hardy would raise these issues with his higher-ups, the reply given to him was that he "couldn't control for those variables."

Yet as logistics-related problems and delays associated with meeting buy-readys became more and more complex, Hardy found himself *personally* bogged down in resolving them for junior-level subordinates in his solid-line bureaucracy—reducing his bandwidth for dealing with strategic-level considerations for the division.

The forms that X_1 events took were becoming more complex over time, exacerbated by corporate growth. As put by Peter Gilmore, an Under Armour officer who has floated between product design and other divisions of the company, "four years ago, we couldn't make a Black Tech tee, our number-one-selling SKU, in more than one location." This was a reality shaped by Under Armour's historical focus on the North American market, but now the demands of international markets had started to outstrip the existing model, which had begun to rely heavily on "bottom-of-the-ninth" responses in line with having to "find a way." It was a good problem to have, but a problem nonetheless.

And so at the center of supply chain's challenge was a need to overhaul what Hardy thought of as the "cadence and communication" issues that would implicate any divisions involved with Under Armour's supply chain.

Hardy uses a powerful metric to summarize the scale of this problem supply chain faced just a few years ago, and how effective and critical the eventual changes in their operating rhythm were to solving it. "In 2012," he commented, "we were a one-billion-dollar company . . . that was servicing our customers at a 50 percent on-time rate. Today we're a five-billion-dollar company, servicing our customers with at least an 85 percent on-time rate."

But this didn't happen from pure luck. To achieve this, a few steps would need to be implemented simultaneously—the most important of which was a new operating rhythm.

THE SOLUTION

Under Armour's supply chain division would implement not only a series of O&I-esque forums but also set a cadence on which they would be synchronized with one another—as well as a separate, unique one for clarifying the decision-making rights of tactical leaders and teams.

After we first met in 2014, Fulks returned to Under Armour's headquarters with what Hardy later described as "a thirty-page binder" that summarized the Task Force's reinvention and how its teams had been networked. Fulks chose to issue this reading material to the various solid-line leaders who reported to him in Under Armour's bureaucracy and asking them to think through "what this approach would look like" if they were to apply it to their teams—implicitly sending a signal to Hardy that reform propositions were welcome and had the critical strategic endorsement needed to succeed.

It wasn't as though Hardy hadn't tried to create a "shared consciousness"–esque space among his teams already—although he hadn't referred to it by this term before. The supply chain had long held a gathering among themselves every Friday called the "war room," during which informal but in-depth information exchanges would take place among various members of the supply chain teams.

These had actually begun under previous iterations of the supply chain and were invented during a previous period of upstream/downstream crisis in the company between 2012 and 2013. Ward remembers this as follows: "[That initial War Room] went on for about six to eight months when we were at crisis mode." Once that passed, there was a recognition of the need for a regular briefing of "outlining the game plan of what needs to be executed, cross-functionally, with a few different partners." Representatives from across the functional group's leadership tiers would gather on a conference call where Hardy and his teams could discuss emerging problems from around their global arena of operations.

These War Rooms were certainly forums—very much in the spirit of the Task Force's O&I—but they operated on a far smaller, informal scale and lacked video feeds of presenters. Ward remembers these as simple setups that occurred "on the fourth floor of our Cascade building. . . . We kind of grabbed the conference room in the back corner, where no one ever had meetings." They were small and physical presence–centric, and informal to the point that their "locations jumped around a bit." Nevertheless, these War Rooms were structured around key briefers, created space for discussion of issues, and encouraged off-forum networking.

Ward voices a real fondness for the informality of these stages of the War Room, wherein a small, clustered group of representatives could "print out their slides" and get together under their own power when needed. For these early iterations of War Rooms, pressing issues of note would be addressed through a mix of qualitative and quantitative dialogue, and their progress would be charted by "a red, yellow, green stop-light approach."

But the limitation of these early forums was the *scale* of shared consciousness that could emerge from each forum—whereas attendees of these forums did share close bonds with one another, the lack of formality changed over time as new needs of Under Armour's supply chain division were addressed. Other divisions impacted the company's logistical operations and had key perspectives on external and internal developments that would impact the supply chain's ability to hit buy-readys, but they and their senior decision makers were nevertheless absent from the first generation of War Room forums. Naturally, the absence of these senior voices from other divisions that were implicated in the supply chain's operation easily created conditions for distrust and raised the potential for finger-pointing among these elements down the road.

Hardy read through the binder Fulks provided "from cover to cover" and saw a chance to fully optimize Under Armour's now-global supply chain—a goal he'd been pursuing for "three and a half years, by that point." Writing in the binder's page margins, he returned it to Fulks with a plan for how Under Armour could finally create communication and cooperation across its different functional groups, at which its supply chain was the heart.

The regular use of War Rooms wasn't abandoned—they remained a helpful tool by which individuals *within* Under Armour's supply chain division could exchange best practices with one another. But in order to provide truly cross-functional information sharing and collaboration, a similar space was needed to achieve the same end state for *all* functional groups whose near-term decisions had longer-term impacts on the supply chain.

This new forum, one that could be expanded to include members from design, marketing, and sales, became known as "Win at the Shelf." Its purpose, recalls Hardy, was to ensure "right product, right place, right time, right cost." Simple goals, clearly stated; but attaining them would depend on the inclusion of other silos, as ensured by Fulks's strategic-level endorsement—and the mutual need to *find a way.*

Between the continued use of War Rooms and the gradual introduction of Win at the Shelf forums, Under Armour's teams would have regularly timed spaces for the creation of shared consciousness and establishment of empowered execution, on a set cadence. War Rooms would continue to be hosted every Friday, and Win at the Shelf forums would take place every Wednesday. War Rooms would last sixty minutes, and Win at the Shelf forums would be strictly held at two hours—accounting for the increased participation and discussion expected from this latter forum.

So how was this cadence determined?

Hardy's ideal end result was a series of proactive and transparent dotted-line networks *across* the company's different silos that could forecast issues well in advance of their manifesting as costly impacts on the supply chain—and thus move as fast as possible in relation to the change in Under Armour's external environment. Hardy needed to balance this with a respect for each division's particular cadence of operation and market complexities—and so a weekly cadence was set, as a compromise between the speed of external environment change and the interests of the desired participants.

Hardy's chief of staff was the designated controller for Win at the Shelf forums and thus was ultimately responsible for managing dialogue in them and ensuring that the forums themselves were designed to provoke the right behavior among participants. Instructions issued at the beginning of every forum relisted the rules for participation and, critically, set the conditions by which empowered execution would occur "off-line" outside these spaces. Prime among these were directives like:

- "Look for opportunities to network in order to tackle problems."

- "Know your own data, and provide appropriate analysis."

- "If you don't know, then don't guess; it is better to tell the team you will follow up with the right answer."

Hardy's chief of staff also took the time to carefully divide the forums by subject matter—every Win at the Shelf would include not only explanations of recent decisions made by different teams, Regional Updates, and "6 Month Rolling Calendar Highlights" but also a section set aside for designated "Special Topics": issues of particular merit or scale that were deemed worthy of discussion across the multiple divisions represented.

Not surprisingly, it started up slowly—Hardy's chief of staff remembers sitting down with Farris in front of Under Armour's org chart and "identifying all of the key leaders from different parts of the organization," with the intention of extending an invitation to some of their teams to participate. Slowly these invitations were accepted, and participants from product design and sales teams joined over time. This was a joint result of Fulks's solid-line influence and perseverance on the part of Hardy's staff.

As the discussions in these forums among functional silos picked up, so too did transparency and honest exchanges among them—not always to positive effect. Strong personalities and interpersonal residue from disputes long past meant that some negative behavioral norms had to be worked through. Hardy recalls one discussion in a Win at the Shelf over a missed buy-ready date resulting from a previously undisclosed holdup in another functional group. Addressing the presenter, and with his patience severely tested, Hardy barked, "When are you guys going to stop being [expletive] surprised by deadlines?"

After that forum concluded, he took the time to reflect with Farris on this testy exchange. "I really kicked that guy's ass, huh?" Farris nodded. "Yeah, sure you did—but keep winning battles like that, and you'll lose the war. How transparent do you think other participants are going to be, after watching you blow up on that guy for being honest with a problem his team is having?"

Hardy took the lesson to heart. Building forums is one thing; exemplifying the right behavior within those forums is another, and it must be done, lest the wrong behaviors become communalized across functional groups.

But these behavioral hang-ups eventually were worked out, and transparency led to understanding: in Hardy's words, he gradually developed "not quite sympathy, but empathy" for the internal processes and stresses of his peers across these different silos. These slow reconciliations, tempered by patience and non-emotional accountability, helped foster truly meaningful discussions within these forums, ultimately driving the creation of shared consciousness for those involved.

Yet if Under Armour's supply chain division was to be better integrated, it was going to happen not through the forums themselves but rather through the networking of teams outside them. The critical question was how to balance the strategic awareness created in these spaces with similar ones for action, through networks of teams.

Hardy's chief of staff, as discussed, ensured that the briefings provided in each Win at the Shelf forum emphasized that "participants were expected to network with each other," so agendas were structured accordingly. Gradually, networking began to happen not just as a result of dialogue occurring within the forums but also by cooperative off-line behavior—the eventual results of which are detailed in the "Outcome" section below.

At the same time, there were certain issues that these networks of teams couldn't resolve for themselves. Their space for empowered execution was encouraged and respected, but some problems remained too complex or strategically relevant for cross-functional networks to execute upon on their own.

As a result, in order to complement the space provided for empowered execution, Hardy created "decision-making forums." Set to occur every Thursday, the supply chain's decision-making forums allowed for the division's teams to present especially time-sensitive challenges or disputes they'd recently encountered and didn't feel empowered to solve.

Yet there was a clear danger in establishing spaces for Hardy to continue making decisions on behalf of the supply chain's tactical-level teams. Using a decision-making forum might take away from the ability of these lower-level individuals to exercise empowered execution—defeating the purpose of the supply chain's reformation. But the supply chain's leadership were made aware of this threat and today describe the decision-making forum as a means not to exert greater control over decisions in Under Armour's logistical teams, but rather to reinforce the types of decisions that lower-level leaders are empowered to solve themselves through their network.

A senior officer in the supply chain says that the benefits of the decision-making forum were multiple: not only was his boss's bandwidth increased by establishing a normalized cadence for highest-level decisions, but also "for the VPs and SVPs that reported to Hardy, they felt empowered and began to understand which decisions had to be owned by them. It made everything else more efficient."

THE OUTCOME

The positive change in Under Armour's supply chain division had several contributing factors, all of which were derived from the practice of various forums and the spacing of them through an operating rhythm. The ability of the supply chain to meet buy-readys and react to sudden crises improved due to better communication across silos; lower-level teams and leaders gaining a greater grasp of the decentralized decision making expected of them; and the provision of a new structure by which Under Armour's organizational ethos could be expanded.

The tangible, quantifiable evidence for this improvement rested in the change in Under Armour's buy-ready metrics. Hardy is quick to rattle off the improvement Under Armour has seen in its ability to deliver techpacks on time—and the "50 percent to 85 percent" figure might well be one of his favorites.

But it is the qualitative personal testimony of members of the supply chain division that may resonate the most. "I can't remember the last buy-ready debate [the supply chain] had" with product teams, Hardy says, noting that the improved "accountability and awareness" among different functional groups on the importance of achieving these numbers has given the organization a common purpose to achieve. "It's treated as a deadline." Hardy's chief of staff corroborates this change in expectations, noting that these regular periods of vertical communication created "a level of accountability we hadn't been used to."

This was augmented by a perceptible recognition among supply chain's operational and tactical teams of what behavior was expected of them during phases of empowered execution.

Hardy remembers watching this develop as follows: "In the old days, people would bring data to forums, but then they'd wait on someone else to make the decision. People like me." As a solid-line leader, Hardy had historically controlled all of the decision-making authority in Under Armour's supply chain division—even though the War Room had been a fixture among his teams, their lack of connections to other functional silos meant they leaned on him to make decisions or communicate across Under Armour's org chart.

Creating a new space for inter-silo shared consciousness in Win at the Shelf forums, communicating in them the need for decentralized decision-making, and further clarifying which decisions had to be owned in decision-making forums, Hardy noticed a gradual change take place. "Indexing what happened back then to today, junior people are now bringing their *decisions* to the War Room and Win at the Shelfs, to make sure folks understand the *decision* they've made and the *implications* of that for others."

At the same time, his decision-making forum became increasingly cleared up—the results of networks forming, solving problems proactively, and describing *what they'd done,* not presenting data and asking for permission.

So Hardy started getting his time back. Similar to the experience of directors at OMES, Hardy found his days less crowded with resolving tactical issues and making decisions for his teams. Through forums like the War Room, Win at the Shelf, and the decision-making forum, the scale and expectations for the empowerment of teams and junior leaders were constantly reiterated, allowing them to own these decisions, rather than overload Hardy as an information pump. From correcting an IT system issue within a new distribution center in Canada to setting up a third-party logistics agreement in Korea in record time, this empowerment has seen numerous instances of paying off operationally.

Nevertheless, a question implied by these practices was whether this set operating rhythm in Under Armour's supply chain division would fly in the face of Under Armour's long-standing pseudo–aligning narrative—"find a way." This common creed, core to the organization's identity, emphasized the value of entrepreneurship and creative, improvised solutions above all things—and its widespread acceptance had long allowed the company to rapidly invade new markets and aggressively overthrow competitors since those early days in Baltimore. If a disciplined operating rhythm ran counter to these principles, then the potential for narrative and cultural conflict would be heightened.

Gilmore hasn't seen these risks manifest. In fact, he believes using a well-balanced method of creating forums allowed the opposite to occur. "I think this help[ed] scale what Under Armour's all about—Under Armour can't continue to operate the way it has so successfully in the past as the ten-billion-dollar global company it will be soon." Rather than limit, formalize, and strictly define how the supply chain teams might be able to work, the thoughtful implementation of forums according to an operating rhythm has, in Gilmore's eyes, provided a lattice to expand the organization's ability to act upon the original ethos—in effect, the aligning narrative—of its founder.

"We're very different from other places I've seen," Gilmore continues, "and a lot of our competitors have cultures where it's more about one superstar than the team—but Under Armour has always been a very blue-collar place, and it still is. People aren't associates; they're teammates. Meetings don't exist, but now huddles do."

Its supply chain division has demonstrated a greater ability to scale this aligning narrative and provide a stronger structure across participants to War Room, Win at the Shelf, and decision-making forums. They were scaling more than process—they were scaling culture and narrative, multiple times a week, across globally dispersed teams.

These factors have combined to inform supply chain's capability to rapidly react to unexpected crises when they inevitably arise and increase the ability of supply chain to hit buy-ready deadlines for its stakeholders— there have been a number of documented instances where a new development in supply chain's environment is identified (X_1) and acted upon (X_2) at a far greater rate than would have been possible under the previous, bureaucratic system.

One favorite story involves a "pinnacle product" that was found to have issues with fit and performance when it had already reached an extremely late stage in its manufacturing process and inventory was already beginning to be built. Supply chain's response was to "bring it up at the next Win at the Shelf forum," says the source. "And with all of the key leaders being there, we were able to take immediate action on that issue. We were able to execute on the strategy created through the forum within a week. In the past it would have taken a couple of weeks to make decisions about a response [to this crisis]."

In a similar instance, in early-to-mid-2015, the Port of Los Angeles— among the largest commercial ports in the world, handling nearly 180 million tons of cargo that fiscal year—was racked by a large-scale labor strike that effectively shut it down for the foreseeable future. For Under Armour and the broader apparel industry, this was a true disaster, as a great deal of their product bound for the North American market would be delayed indefinitely.

Under Armour's teams had little advance notice of the strike. They knew that some critical contracts were about to expire and that the labor negotiations were not going well, so they prepared to react autonomously should things at the L.A. port be disrupted. In short order, the team reconfigured major portions of Under Armour's global logistics pipeline to be routed through Vancouver, New Jersey, and New York, softening the blow of the strike and impressing their customers with levels of adaptability that did not go unnoticed. The bottom-line result of this response? "Millions of dollars saved," estimates Hardy, while other major competitors were seemingly stuck with the realities of the strike.

Under Armour has since come up against fresh challenges, as is the norm for any growing enterprise. As of early 2017, Wall Street analysts and external onlookers were openly noting that the firm had misread market trends and was struggling to maintain a connection with its core consumer demographic. But Under Armour is a natural underdog, dangerous when cornered. It has faced challenges throughout its existence, and if anything has proven true, it's that the company's constant drive to *find a way* has surprised the market more than once.

And throughout any recent rough seas, supply chain's operating rhythm and discipline to the mission have allowed its teams to consistently meet Hardy's simply stated goal of "right product, right place, right cost, right time."

Much as the Task Force experienced on the battlefield, a unified team with a disciplined approach to communication and decision making can prevail through the fog of war and demonstrate a resilience that few competitors can match.

CHAPTER 6

DECISION SPACE

Popular science icon Carl Sagan once said, "All inquiries carry with them some element of risk." Similarly, with any loosening of control, the decentralization afforded by a team of teams model requires an up-front investment of confidence in subordinate teams by an organization's leader, with a delayed payoff.

By bookending periods of empowered execution with designated spaces for shared consciousness, an operating rhythm offers an organization the first of two major ways to control for potential risk in decision making in a team of teams.

Any given phase of empowered execution must see action-oriented decisions being undertaken by those who are closest to the problem. But just as a water molecule requires two parts hydrogen and one part oxygen, a proper proportion of realignment is critical to creating the desired outcomes of empowered execution. A team of teams model's component parts—creating an aligning narrative, building communication forums, and driving shared consciousness at an appropriate operating rhythm—are critical considerations. But the grand combination of these elements is for naught if an organization's frontline teams either can't or won't act with autonomy during windows of empowered execution.

The last piece of the equation, then, is to clearly articulate, as specifically as possible, what actions any given team is expected to have autonomy over, accountability for, and limitations to which the team is subjected. Whereas periodic resynchronization is the first way to control risk in this model, the thoughtful application of *decision space* provides a second control lever.

Simply put, decision space is the breadth and depth of responsibilities that an individual leader or team in an organization is responsible for *doing* during periods of empowered execution and for *discussing* during the reestablishment of shared consciousness. It is the equivalent of senior leadership saying, *Here are the authorities and decision-making rights that I am giving you. Use them creatively to achieve our mission. You've been provided the communication structures and operating rhythm necessary to maintain shared consciousness, and I will advise on actions that fall outside of your decision space; your job is to move as an interconnected team, leveraging your decision space to its fullest capacity, during periods of empowered execution.*

It is easy to say in a forum, "Okay everyone, we're moving into a phase of empowered execution now, so go act on everything you've just heard," but far harder to translate that sentiment into a culture of autonomous action. Individuals in the organization need to understand what exactly they're allowed to do during periods of decentralized action, and they must feel truly obligated to pursue such activity.

HESITANCE AND DEVIANCE

There are two opposite forms of decision-making behavior that can take place during phases of empowered execution, in my experience—*hesitance* and *deviance*. One can think of hesitance as the reluctance to take action; it can stem from anxiety over either the potential to make an operational mistake or overstepping one's bounds.

In contrast, deviance is what hesitant decision makers are afraid of demonstrating—stepping beyond convention or the norms of the organization in ways that could be either positive (resulting in practical innovation or improvement) or negative (to the detriment of the organization's state).

Oddly enough, both hesitance and deviance can occur simultaneously among networks of teams. Anyone who earns new decision-making rights has the potential to fall into one of these patterns—and hesitance may be the more common.

A popularly known but widely misconstrued quote from eighteenth-century Irish political philosopher Edmund Burke's extended essay "Thoughts on the Cause of the Present Discontents" goes as follows: "When bad men combine, the good must associate; else they will fall, one by one, an unpitied sacrifice in a contemptible struggle."

Political scholar David Bromwich charts with contempt how this line became twisted by popular culture into today's far more recognizable version of Burke's statement: "The only thing necessary for the triumph of evil is for good men to do nothing." According to Bromwich, "the sentiment extractable from the [latter] corrupt version is pompous, canting, and demonstrably false."

But the line can be further modified to capture the dangers of hesitance among empowered teams to fully practice their authority: *the only thing necessary for organizations to fail is for informed and empowered individuals to neglect their expanded responsibilities.*

In his 2004 book *The Paradox of Choice: Why More Is Less,* psychologist Barry Schwartz makes the case that when one is given more choice, it can easily overwhelm and lower overall performance:

> As the number of available choices increases, as it has in our consumer culture, the autonomy, control, and liberation this variety brings are powerful and positive. But as the number of choices keeps growing, negative aspects of having a multitude of options begin to appear. As the number of choices grows further, the negatives escalate until we become overloaded. At this point, choice no longer liberates, but debilitates.

Having additional pathway options for decision makers naturally prompts a desire in them to research further and creates a sense of being more responsible for the ultimate outcome—feelings that can easily be compounded when multiple decisions need to be made in a short period. Using a consumer market example, Schwartz writes that "in order to solve the problem of choosing among 200 brands of cereal or 5,000 mutual funds, we must first solve the problem of choosing from 10,000 web sites offering to make us informed consumers."

One can see how being granted too many options or too much room to make decisions can lead someone to hesitate in resolving them. Similarly, granting decision-making authority and shared consciousness to subordinate teams can create this hesitance-inducing effect—even when these things come at the request of the teams. "Everyone likes to be empowered," I'll often tell groups of business leaders, "until they're actually empowered."

Real empowerment, when supported with the correct access to information and the necessary authority to make decisions, can be a lonely place. Properly empowered leaders and teams no longer have the bureau-cratic excuse matrix to fall back upon, a luxury most will not realize they depend on until it's gone.

Many teams in your organization are likely frustrated with the bu-reaucracy while also subconsciously comfortable with their solid-line leaders filtering and contextualizing relevant information, despite the eas-ily offered complaints. Bureaucracy can be frustrating to individuals in the system, of course, but their complaints are overlain by a sense of se-curity as they look to the information pumps of the centrally ordered system for guidance and ownership of outcomes.

In a complex environment, such a safety valve must be removed, but unless teams know clearly what they are expected to do autonomously and what they cannot do without the permission of their solid-line supe-riors, they'll be unable to contextualize against their own line of work the large amounts of information they will be exposed to in O&I forums. As a result, shared consciousness could naturally lead to information over-load if teams aren't clearly informed regarding their authority and limita-tions.

The need to ensure a balance between the quality and quantity of information exposure to employees was captured well by several IT ex-perts in an article published in the *Financial Times* in 2012—one source, a director at Accenture Analytics, describes the abundant risks associated with companies overproviding information to decision makers, "creating multiple business intelligence dashboards . . . to satisfy a handful of exec-utives."

In the military and national security worlds, contemporary chal-lenges have been similar. As one former intelligence analyst said of the general issues surrounding modern intel collection and analysis, "Pieces [of information] fall from the sky and add to the pile the analyst already has. . . . There is no picture, no edge pieces. And not all of the pieces fit in the puzzle."

When presented with such a wide medley of "puzzle pieces," if a leader doesn't understand his or her decision space, information can quickly overwhelm and confuse. When combined with large spaces for decentralized decision making (during windows of empowered execu-tion), this overload can create demoralization and stress, as well as a *hesitance* in some leaders to fully embrace their newfound authority.

Hesitance is heavily informed by personal desires for safety and security—this is why employees are often reluctant to fully embrace decentralization. They don't want to take this mandate too far, are unsure of where to begin, and would rather not be accountable for problems when they do inevitably make a mistake.

This point was made in a 2004 article in the *Journal of Applied Psychology* in which Claus Langfred and Neta Moye assess the relationship between autonomy and performance. Somewhat counterintuitively, they note, "it has been suggested that autonomy can be a subtle form of control, in that individual employees become more accountable and responsible for their own performance . . . and, therefore, to the extent to which individuals do not want accountability, autonomy can lead to negative outcomes."

But a pervasive hesitance to take independent action is the quickest way to ensure that a decentralized approach *doesn't* have the intended impact. Taking the safe route of seeking permission in the moment misses the short-half-life opportunities or threats that come and go in today's fast-changing environment. In an overly cautious culture, your teams may have amazing access to insights from across the organization but still remain myopically focused on their own priorities, tacitly refusing to problem-solve across silos.

Rather than *remove* accountability, the Task Force's transparent communication model and well-designed operating rhythm was designed to *increase* accountability for taking autonomous action. The senior leadership of the organization built the model, but the onus ultimately fell to the operational- and tactical-level teams to proactively interconnect and collaborate. Our leadership reminded us about this every day, reiterating that there was no more excuse matrix for hesitant behavior.

But hesitance is only one type of behavior to watch out for—leaders should also be aware of the opposite type of decision-making behavior: *deviance*.

Importantly, whereas hesitance is not desirable in any sense, some types of deviance can be very valuable.

Simon Sinek's recent work *Leaders Eat Last* offers a compelling example of the positive effects of deviance. In it, Sinek details a time-sensitive situation when the cabin of a Florida-bound commercial flight began to fill with smoke. The pilot immediately began requesting clearance from the controller for an emergency landing. But under Federal Aviation Administration (FAA) rules, in-flight aircraft may not come within five miles of each other—and there was another plane, also trying to land, just two thousand feet below the malfunctioning aircraft.

This was clearly a major dilemma, one that tested the controller's personal read of the rapidly changing situation. Should he delay taking action, adhere to the conventional rule book, and ask the flight to keep circling until the aircraft below had landed? Or should the controller exercise his own judgment, based on limited information, in defiance of conventional regulations?

He chose the latter route.

> The air traffic controller replied to the pilot's request to descend immediately, "KH209, turn fifteen degrees right and descend." . . . He radioed the pilot of the other aircraft and spoke in very clear, plain English. "AG1446, there is an airplane flying above you. He has declared an emergency. He is going to descend through your altitude at approximately two miles off your right front."

Acting against regulations, the controller successfully guided the aircraft to a safe landing. His decisions on that day in 2013 potentially saved hundreds of lives yet went in defiance of the decision-making route the controller had been taught to follow. Had he retreated to the norm of "asking permission," who knows whether the situation might have turned out more tragically?

This is the type of independent decision-making leaders wish their employees demonstrated. Decision makers who are willing to push traditional boundaries and norms in an organization are not a new phenomenon, of course. These types of people, labeled *deviants* by social science in the late twentieth century, are those among us who are prone to find new solutions despite what formal doctrine or accepted norms might dictate—a critical behavioral phenomenon that predates modernity.

Under previous norms of organizational leadership, these individuals might have been perceived as troublemakers (which, technically speaking, they are). But as our leaders in the Task Force often said when presented with the solutions of a positive deviant or high-performance team that was pushing the boundaries, "If it's broke and it works, it's not broke."

Such individuals, rarely satisfied with the status quo, can be critical to an organization's constant advancement. The term "positive deviant" is heavily explored in and foundational to the field of positive organizational studies (POS). POS thinkers Gretchen Spreitzer and Scott Sonenshein have framed a definition of it as "intentional behaviors that depart from the norms of a referent group in honorable ways." Their use of the term "honorable," I would argue, maps closely to behaviors that are unconventional but respect the strategic intent and aligning narrative of an organization.

In their book *The Power of Positive Deviance: How Unlikely Innovators Solve the World's Toughest Problems,* Richard Pascale, Jerry Sternin, and Monique Sternin elaborate on positive deviance: "The concept is simple: look for outliers who succeed against all odds." Positive deviance, they write, "is founded on the premise that at least one person in a community, working with the same resources as everyone else, has already licked the problem that confounds others," often through unconventional means that their peers fail to recognize. Importantly, this individual's outcome "deviates in a positive way from the norm."

The authors elaborate on examples of this type of behavior: they credit the identification of positive deviant behaviors among impoverished parents with a "65 to 80 percent reduction in childhood malnutrition in twenty-two Vietnamese provinces," once some of these parents' unconventional practices (like feeding their children several small meals a day) were communalized. Similarly, the unprompted initiative shown by sales staff at pharmaceutical firm Genentech in educating health-care professionals on the administration of an antiasthma medication was shown to result in "modest improvement in market penetration," despite concern from their superiors that this was a step too far outside their established roles.

This is what strategic leaders practicing a team of teams model typically aspire for their employees to demonstrate—a willingness and capability to make constant, small breaks against the historically restricted operational norms of the organization. Positive deviants, a critical asset to any enterprise, are empowered in the team of teams model to favor judgment and emerging insights from dotted-line networks in order to solve time-sensitive, complex problem sets. The transparency of the communication structures, of course, allows these new findings to be quickly validated by senior leadership and shared with others in the organization.

Patterns like this surely exist in your own organization. But during most attempts to practice decentralized decision making, it is often unclear to teams and their leaders *which* rules and norms in an organization are permissible to challenge and which must *always* be respected.

"The 'positive' aspect of 'deviant' behavior," Pascale, Sternin, and

Sternin posit, "is all in the eyes of the beholder." This is critical to consider when thinking about how to distinguish between your organization's conceptions of positive and negative deviance. Not all leaders in an organization may act with the same level of judgment as that air traffic controller. The result of this can be *negative* deviance by newly empowered decision makers, of which real-life examples are—often tragically—abundant.

Take, for example, the massive loss Société Générale, one of Europe's largest banks, suffered in 2008—a year widely beset by poorly guided decision making in the financial world. A junior derivatives trader with Société Générale, Jérôme Kerviel, specialized in arbitrage trading—when two securities are meant to have the same price but temporarily don't, the idea is to buy the cheaper one and sell the more expensive one, then wait for their prices to meet, pocketing the brief price disparity.

However, Kerviel discovered how to bypass Société Générale's risk software and conduct only half of the trade—offsetting long positions with nonexistent short ones. As a result, he was making riskier bets instead of what appeared to be safer trades. With little transparency existing among the bank's traders, this deviant activity went unnoticed. By the time Kerviel's actions were discovered and settled, Société Générale had lost $7.2 billion as a result of his actions.

Deviance is therefore a double-edged sword. The challenge associated with this type of behavior is in identifying the difference between positive and negative variations of it, and subsequently either promoting or mitigating them accordingly.

This was a lesson I learned all too well, once I was in a more senior position within the Task Force's hierarchy.

NEGLECT

"So . . . why aren't you guys moving?" The familiar voice on the other end of the line sounded calm, but the light southern drawl I heard was underlain by a detectably frustrated tone. There was a new edge to my solid-line superior's voice.

It was eighteen months prior to my aide-de-camp tour, and I was filling an operations-level seat responsible for coordinating direct-action efforts in Al Anbar Province, a large western region of Iraq. Ours was one of several similarly specialized headquarters around the country, each overseeing the actions of multiple units from different branches of service assigned to its region.

It was a "stretch" position for me, my first leadership role that required a deeper sense of how our enterprise truly functioned. At the time of this call, I had been in the position for only a few weeks. My thinking remained hesitantly "down and in"—diligently focused on the teams within my immediate span of bureaucratic control and optimizing their operations; not realizing at the time that I was nowhere close to looking "up and out"—in accordance with our broader aligning narrative—into the networks that were becoming the real drivers of our most complex actions and through which lateral cooperation among our silos was enabled.

I was, like many people when they move up a hierarchy, still focused on doing what I'd done in my previous position, despite having inherited new responsibilities and authority. I remained set on facilitating the needs of our tactical teams, fighting to get the resources necessary for them to accomplish their missions, and concentrating on targets in our immediate region of responsibility. I was implicitly aware of, but passively neglecting, the priorities of peer units and leaders across the Task Force.

Though I'd yet to realize it, I wasn't demonstrating the necessary behavior that our organization needed. I was *taking advantage of* the autonomy our model offered but was hesitant and neglectful in delivering its benefits back to others.

On the surface, my approach seemed to work well for those immediately around me, and the teams in my silo seemed satisfied with how things were running every night. After a few weeks in the seat, my confidence began to rise—a good sign that it was due to be knocked down a peg or two.

The voice I was hearing from that night belonged to "Steve," a talented army officer three years my senior whom I'd known for several years by that point. He oversaw the Task Force's operations among multiple subcomponent commands around the country, including mine. I reported to him every day as his junior officer, but he was also a mentor who had given me great advice to this point in our relationship. The clear frustration in his voice woke me up.

Steve had been keeping tabs that night, as he always did, on the different operations the Task Force was launching across the country. Like most in our organization, he had been afforded the ability to see everything happening (or not happening) around the battlefield, in many isolated corners of our org chart—a reality of the technology-enabled battlefield and our regular O&I forums. His experience and capability, coupled with the transparency of our operating model, allowed him to reallocate resources to the needs of others on the field.

Hearing him over the phone that night, his voice sounded different than it had on courtesy calls we'd previously placed to each other. He was, I realized, *annoyed.*

"Why aren't we moving? Well, it's a quiet night here," I answered to Steve's sharp line of questioning, still not quite sure why he was agitated.

I knew he was asking why we didn't have teams currently going out on operations, but this was due to a lack of actionable intelligence on our priority targets, something we'd shared during the last O&I. Like him, I could see that there was plenty of activity happening around the rest of Iraq, which I assumed would be more worthy of his attention. Our element's battle space certainly covered a large swath of territory, but there were several other units spread around the country that were more active than ours at that point in time.

Each of these peer commands had the same operational approaches that mine did in their respective regions of responsibility: they generated internal lists of insurgent and terrorist cells active in their immediate areas of responsibility, learned who was particularly influential in these networks, and directed their efforts toward dismantling these networks accordingly.

Our operating rhythm set the cadence at which this activity occurred across our commands—twenty-four-hour cycles, seven days per week. The operational tempo that tied our teams together would be slowed down only by weather contingencies, resource shortages, or the occasional lull in actionable information. The night of Steve's call was just one such night for the teams in our region: again there was a lack of actionable intelligence worthy of executing upon. Key Al Qaeda personnel in our region were lying low, so our tactical teams were doing the same.

"Well, if you're not planning to launch, then you're not paying close enough attention to what's happening across our fight," Steve replied. His subtle annoyance with me had shifted quickly to open frustration.

As it turned out, Steve had thought I was deliberately ignoring a key piece of information that he had previously flagged to others across our organization's networks. As we spoke, and I demonstrated my broader ignorance, he calmed down *slightly.*

He reminded me that an individual in Al Qaeda's network had disappeared from another team's area of operations. This target's cousin had recently been spotted drifting into my unit's battle space: they were occasionally known to move together, but the cousin was considered insignificant on his own. Steve asked whether I was aware of this.

"Yeah, I know of the guy, but he's not on our priority list over here," I explained. "He's not connected to any of the cells our guys are tracking. And his cousin is a nobody."

I thought Steve was confused. The person he was referencing had nothing to do with the fight in our sector. There was no indication that he was ever in our region, and the cousin seemed to be of tangential significance at best. In my myopic view, this individual wasn't a priority for our teams.

I was swiftly corrected, and the phone came alive in response to my brush-off.

"First, you're wrong, and I'm going to tell you why in a minute. But second, you already know he's important to someone else. Since he's in your neighborhood, he's your priority now," Steve said. "Just think about that for a second—we talk about this all the time, Chris. We don't win unless you think about the needs of other teams."

It was a coaching moment.

Steve, I realized, was more interested in our *inactivity* than he was in the active hustle around the rest of Iraq—to the point that he felt the need to talk with me about it and shake me out of my apathy. Tonight I was his specific issue. Because of our inaction in this moment, he had to shift from an *eyes on, hands off* mode of monitoring to a *hands-on* one of direct guidance.

Steve then went on to explain his first reason why I was wrong in my interpretation of the significance of this individual: sure, this guy wasn't a fighter; he didn't hold a formal leadership position, have unique skills, or have the charisma to star in propaganda videos. But he *knew people*— he was a classic hub, an enabler who brought out the best in those he was connected to.

In a high-tempo networked environment, actors like him are not easy to focus on, and his actions might have seemed insignificant on paper. However, when he moved around the country, it was an early indicator of larger attacks about to emerge through other, previously unrelated actors down the road. Alone, he couldn't impact our operations—but when given space to interact with like-minded others, he could catalyze a tremendous amount of disruption.

Now he had potentially moved into our region of the fight.

This was the context that I'd missed as I remained focused *down and in* on my solid-line chain of command. Though I had been exposed to the thinking and priorities of other teams, I was still focusing on local threats to my own teams, despite occupying a different type of leadership role from what I once had.

An imported nonfighter, non-leader, non–IED builder from a different corner of the war? And another command had a *suspicion* that he might be with his cousin, who was himself a nobody? Surely that wasn't something I was expected to connect the dots on, let alone act upon?

But this coaching by Steve, a leader whom I knew and respected, highlighted the type of thinking that leaders in our hybrid model were required to practice. It was my job to consider the priorities of our broader organization and act upon them accordingly.

As Steve wrapped up, I was eager to correct my error.

"Got it. We're moving." I hurriedly spoke into the phone before moving to place it down on the receiver, already thinking about the moves we would need to make. Before I could hang up, I heard Steve's voice emerge from the phone in my outstretched hand. "Hey, hold on," he said.

I paused and pressed the receiver back up against my ear.

"Listen," he said, "all of the information is at your fingertips. If it isn't, let me know what else you need. Connect the dots, make the decisions, and execute. You have the authority, and you're expected to use it. From my level, I can explain strategic priorities and ensure we're all still talking and sharing information. Then it's up to you to put that all in context and move out."

I took the interaction as a proverbial shot across the bow. And I got it—in theory, if not quite yet in practice.

DECISION SPACE AND FINDING POSITIVE DEVIANTS

Decision space, to recap, is the explicitly communicated lane of decision authorities owned by critical leaders and teams within an organization. When wide decision space is granted to all leaders and decision makers in an organization, both hesitant and deviant behavior can be identified and adjusted for among the rank and file.

Historically, when similarly built armies or enterprises met, they could mirror each other's structure and efforts across the field of battle or market. This approach afforded a relatively straightforward approach to centralized command, with opposing leaders positioned on a literal or virtual distant hill, reading the situation and directing actions. It was akin to a game of chess: masterful thinkers on either side could read the gradually developing moves of their opponents, analyze the opportunities presented by each shift in the position of units on the field, and adjust their forces accordingly.

In such *symmetric warfare,* as this approach is known, senior leaders set strategy, cascade that to the execution arm of the organization, and constrain decision space to the minimum amount of deviation required to accomplish the job. Granting additional authority runs the risk of adding uncertainty to a senior leader's view of the chessboard. Passing simple, short-term directives through the solid lines is a more manageable alternative: *Take the starred objectives. Stay clear of the teams on your left and right. Wait at the objective for new guidance.*

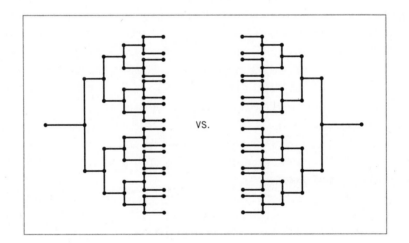

But many of an organization's biggest threats today aren't structured in a traditional fashion. They are networked; fast and ever changing, with which the centralized controls of a traditional model cannot keep pace. Organizations must adapt their approach to decision making accordingly.

A hybrid team of teams model enables an organization's frontline elements to react quickly to networked, varied threats in its external environment—bypassing previously overworked information-pump leadership and reducing the degrees of separation clustered small teams and leaders have between one another.

But in practice this can only benefit an organization if individuals in the system demonstrate the right behavior and initiative as they encounter new external developments. Strategic leaders can design and implement the necessary practices to create a team of teams model, as detailed in this book—including creating and communicating an aligning narrative, building an O&I forum, and setting an operating rhythm—but unless rank-and-file members of the organization make full use of the opportunities they are provided, its utility is limited.

Instead of straight-line guidance, as in symmetric conflict described earlier, today's teams need broad lanes of general direction. Instead of saying, *Do these steps to accomplish X,* a team of teams model tells units, *Accomplish X, given the following authorities and constraints that are invested in you.* Constraints are not to be broken independently by teams or leaders, but authorities are to be combined in whatever creative fashion is necessary (in their opinion) to advance toward X.

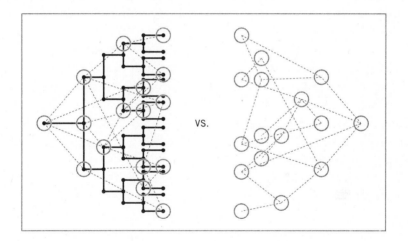

Within the Task Force, senior leaders delineated decision space across teams and leaders through the responsibilities vested in them, as well as the explicitly communicated *limitations* imposed on them. Whenever a network of individuals or teams came across a problem set in the external environment that required them to "break" one of those constraints, they'd need to check back in with their solid-line superiors, who could then either approve or deny the request during periods of empowered execution.

This significantly expanded the bandwidth that our teams could operate within—no longer were they limited by the question *What am I being told to do and how am I expected to accomplish that objective?* Rather, they were asking, *What is within the realm of the possible, given our decision-making authority and the strategic direction of our organization?* Beginning to be encouraged to think in this manner in our transparent system quickly highlighted both deviant and hesitant behavior when it occurred.

In their 2015 book *Simple Rules: How to Thrive in a Complex World,* management theorists Donald Sull and Kathleen Eisenhardt propose using easily comprehended guidelines for decision making in a complex external environment. Their overarching thesis is that as complexity increases, organizations are biased toward creating increasingly complex solutions, which are both very difficult to scale and challenging to repeat with consistency. "Simple rules," on the other hand, create an easily scalable and understandable framework to operate within. These rules, in the words of Sull and Eisenhardt, work for decision makers "because they focus on key aspects of a decision while ignoring peripheral considerations."

Our recommended method of delineating decision space follows similar logic—particularly that of Sull and Eisenhardt's proposal for "boundary rules," which help decision makers narrow down action alternatives by clearly communicating which conditions must be met for action. Creating decision space is a recognition that shared consciousness *alone* is limited in how much it can inform free action and networking during phases of empowered execution.

Moreover, the decision space must be kept *variable.* This variation should depend upon the proven competence of specific teams or their leaders, as well as changes in the environment. In the Task Force, proven competence, demonstrated integrity, and good relationship management translated into broader decision space for a team.

Newer teams or leaders should, of course, be placed under tighter operational constraints. This will likely be to their relief, as they are forced to "check in" for permission from solid-line superiors far more often than their more experienced peers. As leaders demonstrate greater competence in the decision space they own, and push for more autonomy, they are subsequently rewarded with a reduction of constraints.

There are a few alternative methods of presenting and communicating decision space to leaders in an enterprise. For example, in the case of

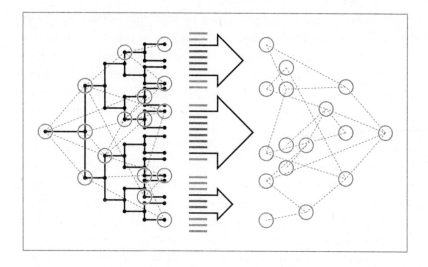

a multibillion-dollar consumer goods corporation that the McChrystal Group partnered with, the senior leadership team found that distributing physical decision-space "place mats" for product-supply leaders to keep on their desks was the best means to clarify the current state of different leaders' individual lanes.

In contrast, in the case of the Task Force's decision space, lanes were communicated through traditional firsthand verbal reinforcement by leaders, combined with social pressure from same-rank peers. What was key to the success of both of these methods (and to that of others that fall between the two examples) was that the decision space of all was extremely *visible*—both to the person who was the subject of it and to the supporting cast of individuals in their immediate function of work.

But returning to hesitant versus deviant behavior, the creation of decision space encourages those who are naturally hesitant to fully and independently leverage their authority, while simultaneously constraining those who might push their deviance beyond acceptable risk levels. Coupled with the transparency of the O&I forum, leaders are able to witness and learn from one another's experiences at a pace that *far* surpasses what bureaucracy alone could ever accomplish. Almost all leaders, upon first receiving unconventionally generous lanes of autonomy like this, naturally find their new freedom intimidating.

Initially reluctant to act within the open bounds they are expected to operate in, leaders like me acted, at first, in pattern with dated methodology—checking in with their superiors to ask permission. We would ask, *I'm going to let one of our intel partners take a look at our intercepts. Is that all right?* You might hear, *Can I share our projections for sales with a person in market research?* This is natural hesitance to embrace true empowerment. Leaders will need to see that this is more than words before they're truly ready to commit and assume the risk at their level.

But a transparent hybrid model allows multidirectional mentoring and social pressure to discourage the instinct to cede ownership of a decision and reinforce positive behaviors across the enterprise. As a result, the collective learning of an organization can be scaled exponentially.

This happens directly and indirectly. For example, the coaching I received from Steve was direct. But the behaviors that other leaders demonstrated, which I needed to learn from and mirror, were visible to me every day through our communication structures. I, and countless others, could see what "right" looked like every day, and we were held to that standard.

The entire purpose of these practices is to enshrine the personality type of the positive deviant—a leader respectfully aware of their decision space but willing to push against the line and challenge the system.

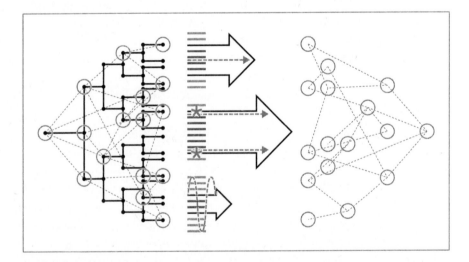

Inevitably, not every leader will emerge as a positive deviant in this model. Any organization practicing team of teams will discover a mix of different personality types among its ranks, including positive deviants that push against the limits of their decision space (indicated by the middle arrow), individuals hesitant to use all the autonomy they have been granted (shown by the top arrow), and negative deviants, who regularly exceed their decision space (reflected in the bottom arrow). Hesitant leaders and negative deviants are drags and risks, respectively, on the operational efficacy of the organization and will need greater individual attention and decision-space variability if they are to survive in this fluid system.

This is where the merits of a well-defined operating rhythm set in—where communication structures ensure that relevant environmental developments are shared and contextualized, positive behaviors highlighted and reinforced, and negative deviant or hesitant behavior eradicated in real time. Rather than quarterly or annual reviews, our rhythm ensured, for us, a daily understanding of leader performance across the enterprise.

The identification of positive deviants among our ranks was the most important result of the Task Force's allocation of decision space. These leaders would consistently test the bounds of their decision space: they understood the game and were willing to follow the rules, but constantly sought better ways to play. They grasped the complexity of the fight and were comfortable walking on the edge of their authority.

Organizations are well served to identify and protect these leaders, but they are difficult to identify in a traditional org chart, where younger leaders are typically highly restrained in their autonomy. Bureaucracies are built to constrain, or even punish, positive deviants. A team of teams approach flips this tradition on its head, highlighting and rewarding the efforts of your best and most adaptable leaders.

PUSHING BOUNDARIES

A month after Steve's wake-up call, I saw a demonstration of positive deviant behavior, firsthand, in my own ranks.

"What are they doing?" I heard my assistant operations officer ask from his seat next to me in our JOC.

I had been focused on coordinating two other missions that were getting ready to launch. Looking up from my laptop, I followed his eyes to the screens on the JOC's front wall. One of them, displaying a live video feed from one of our drones, was filled by the image of a convoy of six Strykers—heavily armored wheeled vehicles that serve as personnel carriers in various NATO militaries.

The single file of hulking machines was moving, seemingly in the direction of the Euphrates River—likely toward a cement bridge that our forces frequently used. The physical structure was just one of a few entry points our forces used to enter Ar-Ramadi, a city then at the height of a peak in violence that would give it a deservedly grim reputation throughout the conflict.

I recognized those Strykers. They belonged to a team of Army Rangers who were attached to our command, a subordinate element in our solid-line org chart. They were, based on what my operations officer and I could perceive, spoiling for a fight.

The selection process for Rangers—similar to that of many other elements in the Task Force—is arduous. The U.S. Army's Ranger School course in Fort Benning, Georgia, is a thing of legend and has an attrition rate of roughly 50 percent. For their troubles, soldiers who eventually make it into the regiment are presented with a small tab to wear on their left shoulder reading RANGER, to signify their ascension into this elite tribe of soldiers. Much like the golden trident of the SEALs and the green beret worn by Army Special Forces, this physical totem is emblematic of a tribal narrative that those who wear it take to heart.

But since the inception of the Task Force, practices like an aligning narrative, forums, and an operating rhythm had enabled the operational and cultural meshing of our tribes into a *one mission* mentality. This ensured that whereas senses of unit loyalty did continue to exist, they did not usurp or corrupt the interactions or common purpose that our teams valued holding with one another. This allowed me (as a SEAL officer) to effectively manage the operations of different cultures of Rangers, SEALs, and others at once, just as SEAL elements around the battlefield were similarly managed by army unit leadership. The tribes were respected, but the mission came first.

Having been responsible for the coordination of past Ranger operations throughout Al Anbar Province, I'd watched that same Stryker convoy move into the city on numerous occasions. The platoon of Rangers who used them had conducted high-intensity operations in various parts of the city, day and night, over the last few weeks—demonstrating a level of competence and willingness to network with others that allowed them a relatively wide lane of decision space.

The outskirts of the city were relatively under control, but crossing the bridge into the city, as they were clearly planning to do, meant entering an entirely different realm of danger that could implicate many of our other units. Of late, nearly every convoy from our command that entered Ar-Ramadi's dense urban jungle was being ambushed—struck by an improvised explosive device, engaged in a small-arms gunfight, or a combination of both.

As we watched the Strykers trundle steadily toward the city, I turned to my deputy operations officer, trying to make sense of what I was watching.

"Do they have air coverage?" I asked him, pointing to the screen in front of us. I'd just been working on several other things and assumed I'd missed this critical detail.

"Not yet," he replied. "I'll call Balad and see if we can get some."

This was a problem—going into Ar-Ramadi without air support was outside of this team's decision space. The prohibition was one of this team's "boundary rules"—a requirement that absolutely *had* to be met for action.

Like many resources our organization possessed, overhead air support— like an attack helicopter or fixed-wing fighter jet—was always in short supply on busy nights like these. When present, these assets offered teams much additional firepower if needed. Crossing that bridge, as this Ranger unit was doing, practically guaranteed some sort of heavy engagement with insurgents, so it was deemed too risky to send teams in without overhead firepower (even for a team as well thought of as this one).

The decision-space constraint on these Rangers was our solid-line leadership's way of saying, *Move as fast as you can against the enemy, but we've assessed the risk in this case and believe you need additional firepower when operating. This rule is inviolable.* In creating this limitation, our leadership could control for negative deviant behavior that might be demonstrated by this team, which would create nonlinear consequences for the entire enterprise, and (through having to be consulted for air support) be kept aware of the activity of these Rangers.

As a result, our solid-line leaders didn't need to spend a lot of effort trying to look "down and in" at the efforts of subordinate teams. Instead, teams would actively inform them when they were beginning to brush up against their established constraints.

Yet I'd received no request by the Ranger officer to launch without air assets. This was uncharacteristic—I knew him as one of our command's most experienced leaders, who had earned his team a large lane of decision space. But now, he was apparently planning to disregard one of the few established constraints he operated under—not unlike Société Générale's rogue trader Kerviel, the officer seemed at risk of giving in to his eagerness to accomplish his mission; he would be breaking rules without thought of the risks his actions posed to the broader organization.

Worse yet, what he needed was not something that I directly controlled as an operations-level leader: air support was a centralized asset that I typically had to request of *my* solid-line superior on behalf of our teams. Why this Ranger officer might be taking this course of action with his team was beyond my comprehension.

"Any update on their air coverage yet?" I asked my assistant operations officer, hoping that our command had somehow already acted on the request we'd put in only a minute earlier.

"Not yet. Apparently the assets are stuck over Baghdad," he replied. "No estimate on when they'll be able to get here."

Now standing, I reached for my headset and radio. My assumption now was that there'd been a miscommunication in our command chain and that the Ranger officer had been misinformed about the status of his air support. I *had* to turn him around quickly, before his team was pinned down with no assistance in the insurgent-seeded city.

But just before I keyed up my radio to connect with him, all Strykers in the column came to an abrupt stop. I held my thumb back from the radio's call button and stared at the screen. The aperture of the drone's camera shifted, and now I could see where exactly he'd stopped his vehicles. The lead Stryker was a few yards from the bridge.

The convoy idled, poised on the edge of Ar-Ramadi proper.

The radio I was holding then spoke: "Requesting ETA on air support." It was the Ranger officer, calling in from his Stryker.

I laughed, uncharacteristically, given the situation.

There was no miscommunication, and the leader on the ground *hadn't* disregarded his decision space—he'd just taken his authority to its extreme limit. One of his team's few restrictions was that they couldn't *enter the city* without overhead support—but nothing constrained him from talking to analyst teams, briefing his Rangers, loading his vehicles, driving through the few miles of relatively safe terrain that came before the bridge, and stopping just *outside* of the dangers of the city to ask for a spare helicopter.

His team was sitting, quite literally, on the edge of their decision space, pushing our bureaucratic boundaries firmly. The officer had done everything in his power to move his desired next action forward as quickly as possible, and at the same time was sending a clear message to our system that we were the limiting factor in this case.

"All right, I'll call Balad again," I said to my assistant operations officer, and picked up the secure phone line on the desk in front of me. I wanted to see whether I could expedite the air-support request that had already been lodged.

Steve, the army officer who had given me the pep talk a few weeks earlier, picked up the phone.

"I've got a platoon outside Ramadi that are ready to go. Can we get some air coverage?" I asked.

"Yeah, I can see that," Steve laughed. He'd been watching the same footage from Balad. "Point taken. We'll get the air over there soon."

There was a pause, and I could hear him chatting with some folks around him, no doubt confirming that Steve could get the Rangers what they needed. He came back to the phone. "An asset is headed your way. They'll be over Ramadi in four minutes. Have a good night."

We made a quick radio call to the team on the ground to confirm that they would soon have the coverage they needed. Five minutes later, the last Stryker in their convoy crossed into the hostile territory of inner Ar-Ramadi, and their mission was properly under way.

The constraining requirement of air coverage would never be removed from that Ranger officer's decision space for the remainder of his deployment, but his creative approach to pushing against his decision space helped reinforce the importance of this type of behavior among his peer teams.

Moving forward, other teams would even emulate his actions—through networked dialogue and contextualization on our O&Is, it became "best practice" for teams to regularly prep their vehicles and launch toward the city prior to receiving all of their required assets for a mission, forcing us at the operations level to work diligently to get the coverage in place. It became a forcing function for all of us in our organization's bureaucratic leadership to move as quickly as possible and would shave critical minutes off our time lines in the endless game of cat and mouse we played with the insurgency.

It was an ideal demonstration of Spreitzer and Sonenshein's framing of positive deviance. The Ranger officer departed from norms in a way that respected our strategic intent and aligning narrative while also challenging his prescribed constraints. Moreover, it would have a cascading effect on the behavior that peer leaders in our organization would soon demonstrate. Finally, the events of that night and the subsequent adoption of this behavior provoked a question in the minds of our solid-line bureaucratic leadership: *Should we relax our restraints and give our tactical units more autonomy in the future?*

Controlling decision space allows leaders to better mitigate excessive risk but also gives the best leaders in their ranks the ability to walk right up to the edge of their authority—and then push for more. These positive deviants and their high-performing teams were a consistent pressure test on our system, challenging everyone involved to move faster, do more, and never let rules or traditional thinking stifle our ability to solve complex problems.

But inevitably, decision space has its limitations—a point past which lanes cannot be widened any further and the intervention of senior leadership is required. When teams do encounter an extremely sensitive piece of environmental intelligence, a phase of empowered execution may need to be interrupted. Properly managed, though, decision space is the capstone of a hybrid organization, providing a final control on risk and empowering teams to move quickly but within boundaries that you control.

If you've incorporated an aligning narrative, created an effective operating rhythm, built up interconnection among silos, and established lanes of autonomy, you are well on your way to handling a complex environment.

But how do you extend the model? How do you influence and build bridges to other parts of your global organization, across distributed geographies, or into business units that you don't control? Or, as in the Task Force, what if there are independent organizations that are critical partners in a complex fight? In these cases you may want to consider sending out ambassadors to spread the message of your mission.

QUESTIONS TO CONSIDER:

♦ When your organization misses an opportunity, how often is it the case that a team knew the answer but had to clarify whether they were permitted to act upon it?

♦ Do people in your organization have a true understanding of what decisions they are accountable for? How would you establish and communicate to your critical leaders the specifics of their authority and constraints—i.e., how would you create decision space?

♦ Do you believe hesitants and deviants exist in your organization? Which leaders, or groups of leaders, most embody these behavioral principles?

♦ Do you currently have the ability to identify and leverage positive deviants within your organization? How might the use of an O&I forum, and interconnecting technology, help ease this process?

CASE STUDY:
MEDSTAR

PREFACE

As you read the following in-depth look at MedStar's careful application of decision space, note how the organization began this initiative by drastically expanding the decision space of a carefully selected, small group of leaders at tactical levels, in order to better scale proactive action in the organization.

Moreover, note the ways in which these empowered leaders were prompted to network freely with other external stakeholders in patient care for better communication across conventional bureaucratic lines.

Finally, pay close attention to how MedStar identified undesirable personality traits hampering decentralized decision making in the organization. Note also how the implementation of decentralized decision making allowed positive deviant behavior to emerge, resulting in quantifiable results and operational improvements.

THE SETUP

On March 23, 2010, after what had felt like an endless period of divisive public and legislative debate, the Affordable Care Act (ACA) was signed into law by President Barack Obama, thus ushering in an exceptionally complex series of changes to the already-bewildering health-care industry of the United States. The new legislation had many detractors, sometimes hyperbolic, from both sides of the political aisle, and it still does to this day.

Many on the right have framed the law as an implicitly nefarious government intervention into health care on an unheard-of scale, with some describing it as "a pure income redistribution play . . . a hallmark of socialism." On the left, criticism has been defined by the ACA's failure to provide a public "single-payer plan" that would provide universal health care, the absence of which has left millions of Americans uncovered.

To the public, the law's most noteworthy and debated features included provisions on things like individual mandates, state-hosted health insurance exchanges, and the so-called guaranteed issue of insurance (which prevents insurers from denying coverage to applicants with "pre-existing conditions").

But for Matt Zavadsky, a senior director at an emergency medical services (EMS) organization in Texas, and many peer EMS providers around the country, a detail of the law more worthy of their attention seemed to escape broader public notice. In the case of Zavadsky's organization, this overlooked legislative detail—which we will delve into soon—would usher in a dramatic opportunity for operational reform and improvement, the delivery of which would involve reinventing the functions expected of its tactical-level paramedic teams.

In the fall of 2016, I was invited to give a presentation to a group of health-care professionals in Dallas and, in short order, found myself in a private club behind the owner's box of AT&T Stadium preparing to give a talk. Granted, it was a Tuesday morning and the stadium was empty, but it was still a fun moment for someone who grew up in a household where the Cowboys-Steelers rivalry was one of the most important discussions at the dinner table.

After my talk, I'd taken a seat in the audience, assuming I'd learn a bit about health care in Texas when, much to my surprise, Matt got onstage and said, "Okay, let me tell you how we implemented the *Team of Teams* model." He then went on to explain, with incredible data to support the business case, how he'd leveraged the principles we shared in that book.

The enterprise Zavadsky works for—MedStar—was founded as a regional governmental agency in 1986 as the Area Metropolitan Ambulance Authority of Fort Worth, Texas, and today it remains the region's exclusive EMS responder. Financially self-sufficient, MedStar draws no tax subsidy from the public, instead relying on what its employees call "hoped-for" payments from those it serves—following a "public utility model" of funding, whatever financial returns MedStar sees from care provision go entirely into covering costs and investing in new equipment for its teams to use in the field.

Walking around the organization's 85,000-square-foot headquarters in late 2016, I repeatedly heard one phrase thrown around by insiders. MedStar employees use the six-word quip to refer to the *traditional* jurisdictional limits of its employees: *You call, we haul, that's all.*

The narrow set of duties implied by this compact phrase summarizes all that was historically expected of the organization's core personnel:

frontline paramedics and EMTs. In the pre-2010 world of EMS provision, employees of MedStar all filled a relatively constrained series of functions: respond to emergency calls, take those patients they deemed in need of care to local ERs, then repeat.

You call, we haul, that's all.

While this role is still performed by MedStar's employees, a separate, unique, and far more experimental one has since been created by the organization.

THE PROBLEM

Why was payment for MedStar's (certainly limited) services traditionally "hoped for" rather than expected? The answer has much to do with the increased strain that the exceedingly fragmented and complex American health-care system has faced over time, which Zavadsky and his peers at MedStar—as well as local profit-focused hospitals—have held front-row seats to.

Between 1996 and 2006, ERs in the United States saw a 32 percent increase in use, reflecting a mainstream trend of low-income, often uninsured Americans relying on them as a health-care safety net. This pattern has apparently been fueled by a combination of many contributing factors—including chronic physician shortages in certain parts of the country, the "treatment now, pay later" nature of ERs, and a general rise in health insurance premiums.

Moreover, the prevalence of chronic illnesses like congestive heart failure (CHF), diabetes, emphysema, obesity, and chronic obstructive pulmonary disorder (COPD) means that ERs are often being used not really as a locale for urgent, lifesaving treatment but rather for treatment that would typically be administered in a primary-care context. A 2010 RAND study estimated that between 14 percent and 27 percent of all ER visits were for non-urgent care, whereas others have put this figure as high as nearly 40 percent.

This trend, combined with the inability by many of these patients to pay for the full cost of these visits, makes the fundamental financial viability of EMS provision seem questionable—not only for the health-care systems that provide the necessary treatment once patients get to the ER but also to EMS providers (like MedStar) that are trying to get paid for delivering them safely to hospitals and clinics.

In Zavadsky's words, MedStar "doesn't do wallet biopsies"—if one of Fort Worth's roughly one million residents makes a 9-1-1 call, they will get a response and, if necessary, a ride to the ER, regardless of their ability to pay. That is, until the signing of the ACA into law.

Recall that there was one provision in the ACA that escaped public notice but was of considerable note to health-care systems and EMS providers like MedStar. This part of the law is called "Section 3025," and it changed the financial incentives of MedStar and its peers dramatically. Through amending the Social Security Act of 1935, the ACA's Section 3025 empowered federal Medicare and Medicaid regulators to realign their payment models to American health systems around patient health benefits, rather than the number of procedures patients had undergone.

As a result, these entities began instituting incentive-laden programs to govern how Medicare and Medicaid would make payments to hospitals: if a system's patients were seeing high readmission rates for certain chronic illnesses, federal authorities would now respond by proportionally withholding Medicare and Medicaid payments to that system. The patients' treatments would be paid for, but now the hospital system would effectively see a net financial loss for their readmission—even if the patient was able to fully compensate the hospital.

With the 2010 passage of the ACA, suddenly the incentives of patients and EMS providers and private health-care systems were aligned: a decline or stalling of the long-term health of patients would now negatively impact the financial well-being of everyone involved. They now had fiscal incentives to ensure truly patient-centric, value-based care, rather than pursue an incident-centric approach of maximizing procedures offered to patients.

This was a welcome change for Zavadsky's teams—as Douglas Hooten, MedStar's CEO, puts it: "Philosophically, we certainly like now having a model that aligns the interest of patients with those of our systems."

Similarly, MedStar's local health-care systems also had reason to feel more open to partnership with MedStar. Dr. David Lloyd, a medical director at one of these now-partner systems (North Texas Specialty Physicians), welcomes the new rationale for-profit institutions like his were motivated to operate under: "The most expensive way to give someone health care is to put them in the ER, and it is often not the best thing for them."

With Section 3025 in place, these once-unaligned stakeholders now had reason to share information and unselfishly work together to mutually solve for health issues in the lower rungs of the local population—the question now was how MedStar might be able to help make the most of this opportunity.

THE SOLUTION

The answer was to expand decision space at MedStar's tactical levels. The organization's approach to decision space is not precisely the one we have outlined, but the principles MedStar used to vest and encourage decentralized decision making among its teams offer terrific examples of how to manage decision space.

Shane Ansel has been on the front lines of these initiatives since their inception.

Sitting in his medically equipped, MedStar-branded SUV in the parking lot of a central–Fort Worth hospital, I asked him about the chronically ill patients he typically sees in his line of work. There were a few terms I had heard being used by others that day in reference to patients like his— "frequent flyers," "rewards program members," and "superusers"—and I was interested in hearing Ansel's thoughts on his function.

A wiry transplant from Metairie, Louisiana, Ansel represents what MedStar's leadership believe is the future of their industry. One of the organization's elite Mobile Healthcare Paramedics (MHPs), Ansel represents a drastic reinvention of the traditional responsibilities of paramedics in EMS. In contrast to the aged "you call, we haul, that's all" approach to paramedicine, the responsibilities of MedStar's MHPs are summarized in a new phrase used by those inside the company: *clinicians, not technicians.*

MHPs are a crucial centerpiece of what MedStar refers to as its "Mobile Healthcare Initiatives"—a series of programs designed to proactively identify and solve high-risk patients' health-care problems *before* they end up in an emergency situation. Initiated in 2009 by Zavadsky as the ACA was percolating its way through Congress, these programs revolved around ensuring that nonacute cases of chronic illness among the sickest members of the Fort Worth area were solved where they should be— preferably in home or primary-care settings, rather than in expensive, often unnecessary emergency-care ones.

At the forefront of these programs, which range in name from "9-1-1 Nurse Triage" to "EMS Loyalty," are MHPs like Ansel, who act as integrated, autonomous primary-care providers to chronically ill, elderly, or otherwise ER-prone individuals in the Fort Worth area.

It begins when a patient starts being hospitalized frequently in one of the dozen or so health-care systems in Fort Worth and their provider starts to take notice. The way Zavadsky explains it, these programs rely on "referrals" they get on individuals who seem to be ending up in partner systems often and who commonly lack the means to pay for it. When these referrals come through, an MHP from MedStar will go meet with the patient and their caregivers in the hospital and enroll them in a program.

The decision-space lanes invested in MHPs by MedStar, as compared with those of traditional paramedics, are remarkably wide. Like doctors, MHPs can administer primary-care treatments and prescription medicine to patients in a home setting, work autonomously with primary care providers (PCPs) in various outside organizations, and generally interact over extended periods of time face to face with patients.

With an initial contact established not only between the MHP and the patient but also between the MHP and the patient's PCPs in partner health-care systems, MHPs like Ansel will then go visit these patients periodically in their homes. There they will provide primary care when needed and look for and address root causes of the problem sets the PCPs said they were seeing in this individual's health—causes that were not necessarily perceivable in an ER setting.

Says Ansel: "We go through the home itself and try to find contributing factors to their problems—are there any trip hazards—loose rugs, junk in the hallway? Are there smoke and carbon monoxide detectors, and is pet dander lying around? Do their lights work? What kind of food are they eating, or do they have enough of it? What medications are they taking, have they been prescribed it by different doctors, and are they labeled clearly?"

MHPs then meet with the patient's PCPs in a communal setting and relay what they found and tried to solve on the patient level.

So far so good—but how did MedStar create this role and learn to select individuals like Ansel to fill it initially? It was apparently very hard, as Zavadsky summarized:

> [When we initially piloted the program] it was hard to get our paramedics to join. . . . It had never been done before, and they weren't necessarily convinced that it was going to work. As a result, we had to incentivize applicants. We offered them a pretty

significant salary increase; we offered to pay for their training, and even to keep paying them as they attended the training. But from all of these incentives, we were only able to convince *eight* of our paramedics to take on this role.

MedStar currently has nearly five hundred employees, so it's difficult to picture this dramatically low turnout for such a heavily sponsored program back in 2009—but, upon deeper thought, it's no surprise. As we discussed earlier, the *potential* for decentralized authority can initially intimidate those seeking it. Yet Ansel was a member of these first few generations of MHPs, as was Desiree Partain, who has since become a director at MedStar.

Which parts of the vast realms of responsibility new MHPs struggled with varied from one MedStar employee to another: for both Ansel and Partain, the "social" aspect of the new role often had a particularly steep learning curve.

Both Partain and Ansel were part of the second MHP class trained by MedStar in 2009, and they separately noted that despite a universally high level of clinical expertise among their peers, those who were "just not able to articulate things in a manner that was conducive to a friendly environment" struggled the most in adapting to this new, often nonclinical role.

I ask for a less diplomatic answer, and Partain clarifies: "I've learned now, as a manager, that it is impossible to teach some of the nonclinical *personality* requirements of this role—and trust me, we've tried." Of the initial group of MHPs assembled by MedStar, some fell out due to the "culture change" required to balance the nuances of interacting autonomously and socially with patients, communicating effectively with the networks of PCPs for each case, and remaining patient in the face of often-frustrating behavior.

Partain describes some MHPs as having a tendency toward "compassion fatigue," which in turn leads to substandard performance. This can manifest in many ways and became extremely apparent to other MHPs when it did occur. Partain recognized the symptoms of this fatigue as apathy about reaching out to PCPs or a failure to follow up with patients. This hesitance to fully act on the expected extent of authority was difficult to ignore when it did manifest.

For Ansel the behavioral lack of fitness of some of his peers emerged in different ways. He remembers a case of one MHP "disconnecting his vehicle's GPS" for unknown reasons and disappearing for extended stretches of time while on duty. In this case the technological resources offered for this individual's use helped allow others to identify this behavior. In another case, Ansel recalls, an MHP was seen to be providing unequal, sometimes excessive attention to certain patients, doting on them in ways that didn't sync with her defined duties.

In contrast to these early examples of negative deviant or hesitant behavior, other MHPs showed themselves to be the positive deviants of the system. Members like Ansel learned to test their decision-space bounds in a proactive, reasonable way. Ansel says his autonomy as an MHP is, at this point, "pretty limitless . . . and if I do need something else, just one call to the doc and they can yea or nay it."

What Ansel means is that while MHPs can administer medicines and treatments beyond the scope of a traditional paramedic, there are still known limits to their empowerment. Whenever experienced MHPs hit the reaches of their authority, they are required to quickly refer either to the patient's PCP or up MedStar's solid-line bureaucracy to its medical directors. Provided that the clearance comes through, which it most often does, MHPs can then address the issue on the spot, lowering time and cost for both parties, as Ansel says, "without even having to leave the house."

Similarly, when an MHP like Ansel sees a patient's chronic illness take a turn for the worse or notices a new condition, the MHP can connect directly with the patient's PCPs—either to loop them into the MHP's thinking or to find a resource to solve the patient's problem.

But occasionally clearance for treatments from doctors don't come through, and MHPs can be frustrated by these bounds, particularly when they've previously gotten permission to exceed their decision space from either the doctor they're currently talking to or a different one.

Says Ansel: "Calling different doctors will give us different answers to the same requests we put in . . . so that becomes very aggravating, because here I am, trying to do what's best for the patient, and for our system. But today one person above me will tell me yes, and tomorrow I'd get in trouble for doing the exact same thing as yesterday?"

But in the face of these challenges, Ansel and others like him have learned which methods they can use to get the clearance needed to proceed with a certain treatment pathway.

"If I'm calling regarding something ventilator related," Ansel says, "and something odd plays up, I've learned to always go to 'Dr. X' for clarification on it." During some of these interactions, when "protocols are not helping," MHPs are empowered to "talk with doctors and see if we can't come up with something that we can do in that home"—and thus the lanes of decision space for MHPs are moderated and controlled by MedStar's bureaucracy. MedStar is able to increase the speed and accuracy of care while reducing its cost, but it leverages decision space to control risk in the system.

By proactively interacting with a variety of high-risk patients and being empowered with new levels of trust to act in fresh realms of authority, MHPs in MedStar's system can (in theory) learn to solve problems across Fort Worth–area medical systems.

How did these initiatives tangibly play out, though?

THE OUTCOMES

Speaking with Zavadsky over the phone about the consequences of Med-Star's Mobile Healthcare Initiatives, seven years after their initiation, he makes one point clear: "Across all of EMS, there are three key outcome domains health-care payers look for, and which MedStar has always measured itself by: health-care system utilization, patient health status, and overall patient satisfaction."

Across these key metric groups, MedStar's programs—spearheaded by the empowerment of MHPs—have delivered.

Since 2013, 475 "superuser" patients have had MHPs integrated into their primary-care network, helping improve average patient perceptions of their health status (including self-perceived levels of pain, anxiety, and mobility) by 32.2 percent and avoiding more than 1,917 ER visits by them over that time frame. The second-order effect of this empowered, preventative care has been the avoidance of 462 hospital admissions of superuser patients.

Naturally, what follows is the questions of cost—given the impact of the ACA and the preemptive nature of the MHP job function, how did MedStar's external health-care providers benefit from allowing their doctors, patients, and data to be used by MHPs? As the Mobile Healthcare Initiatives were launched with an eye to reducing the costs of these private organizations by reducing superuser reliance on their systems, this is an important consideration to take on board.

In total, for this small but ER-active group of 475 patients, close to

8.8 million dollars of savings have been accumulated by MedStar's local partners, thanks to MedStar's MHPs. In allocating a proportion of their saving to the nonprofit MedStar for its services, they can ensure that this cycle is maintained, and MHPs can continue proactively solving problems before they manifest.

As we've discussed, when MedStar began this program in 2009, it could convince only eight of its already highly trained employees to pursue an MHP role. Even at that point, these MHP candidates could be convinced to participate only through promises of salary increases, free training, and education.

Fast-forward to 2011; two new MHP slots opened in the middle of the year. Despite no longer being able to offer free education and paid time off for study to those who took up the role, MedStar now saw nearly two dozen candidates apply.

That change of heart may have a lot to do with the continued efforts of veteran MHPs like Ansel to demonstrate to other MedStar leaders what they're doing: "Anybody's allowed to come ride with us [on our duties]—there are no limits or anything. As a matter of fact, I just had a couple of part-time paramedics that have been interested in this [role] for a while. They've made it very [clear] that they have been interested for a couple of years, and we just started hiring part-time MHPs [which they will apply to become]."

The implication is that the enthusiasm for these roles—among both patients and wannabe MHPs—has now outpaced the supply, and further growth in the numbers of MHPs and patients MedStar can integrate to the program will depend heavily on scaling considerations. Nevertheless, the successful public practice of these roles by MHPs like Ansel and the reinforcement by MedStar's strategic leadership of the importance of this decentralized decision making mean that enthusiasm for this type of autonomy may increase further.

But more growth in demand may yet emerge outside Fort Worth. Since the inception of MedStar's Mobile Healthcare Initiatives, the organization has hosted more than 190 health-care delegations from forty-two states and six foreign countries, who have each sought to take the "lessons learned" from the Fort Worth area and apply them to their own health communities.

Ansel, like many other MHPs, has also helped play host and teacher to these types of external witnesses. Sitting in his SUV, driving through downtown Fort Worth, he reminisced with me about how he had been able to take two South African paramedics on duty with him recently, and how he enjoyed showing them what being an MHP offered him the ability to do, outside of paramedicine norms.

Just before I got out of his vehicle, I asked Ansel what he thought still remained to be understood about being an MHP by those outside of the role. He thought for a second, his sunglasses perched lightly on his forehead, then responded. "Most of them know what we do, as far as the critical-care side—they understand the medicine part; they know that sick patients exist. But on the MHP side, the limit of their knowledge [often] ends when it comes to understanding all of the programs we have, and *why* they're there, then applying that to the way we do our job."

I thought I picked up what he was getting at, maybe—that at the end of the day, there is an instinctive behavioral element to this job, mixed with a necessary level of higher-level thinking, which makes its practical completion so difficult. A wise leader will recognize who has the personality and high-level thinking needed for each level of decision making and will set decision-space boundaries accordingly.

CHAPTER 7

LIAISONS

"I need to talk with McChrystal," the voice on the line said, without a hint of hesitation. "It's Mike D."

I had picked up a ringing, secure phone line that sat on my plywood desk around the corner from the Balad SAR, introduced myself, and gotten this curt response from a confident voice. It was late 2007, and I was still in my first few weeks as McChrystal's aide-de-camp. I found the exchange a little strange.

I considered the voice's request: to be put straight through to our commander. Maybe this was a prank? Or some kind of hazing thing for rookies? A test, perhaps?

"Wait one," I said. Feigning confidence, I muted the line and quickly found a more seasoned member of our staff to help me out. "I've got a Mike D? Asking for McChrystal?"

Please don't be in on the joke, if this is one, I thought.

My fellow staff officer responded quickly, poker-faced. "Oh sure, he's one of our liaisons. When they call, they go to the top of the list. I'll explain later; just go grab the boss."

Still uncertain of the action I was taking, but heeding the guidance I'd been given, I entered our SAR and interrupted an ongoing discussion between McChrystal and several other senior Task Force members.

Approaching them, I cleared my throat. "Excuse me, sir." McChrystal stopped suddenly and looked over at me with a raised eyebrow, saying nothing.

"Mike D is on the red line," I continued, with a clear lack of confidence. It was probably obvious that I had no idea who Mike was or whether patching him directly through was the right decision.

But McChrystal nodded at me upon hearing this and picked up the phone in front of him, accessing the secure line I had been on just a few seconds earlier.

"Mike, what's up?" He paused to listen to whatever response he was hearing from the caller. "Hold on—putting you on speaker for the rest of the SAR. . . . Thanks for pulling us in on this early." He put the call on speakerphone, then addressed the larger group in the open room.

"Hey, team, Mike D is on the line and needs to update us on something happening at the embassy in his neck of the woods." The other senior leaders around the SAR's front table looked up from their laptops and lent an ear to the pending discussion.

Whoever this "Mike D" was, I thought, he was clearly significant enough to quickly gain the attention of our most senior personnel.

I took a seat in the SAR's back row and also tuned in. I didn't want to miss this.

LEVERAGING LIAISONS

The operating rhythm of an organization dictates the operational cadence of teams *within* an enterprise, and decision space gives them their lanes of autonomy.

But what about an organization's external stakeholders and critical partners? The difficulties in alignment experienced by teams within an organization can still apply on a broader scale. So how might external stakeholders be exposed to an organization's aligning narrative and be brought into collaborative problem solving? Similarly, what about globally distributed regional teams or their business units in a larger enterprise? If you're applying a team of teams model to a vertical business unit, how might you better connect with your peers throughout the enterprise?

Ahead we will explore how bureaucratic barriers to cooperation exist among different functional silos and external organizations, as well as how those barriers can be mitigated through the careful selection of *liaisons*. These individuals, as you'll see, are trusted members of their own organizations who can promote trust, cooperation, and understanding among different groups. They are culture carriers, well versed in the aligning narrative and strategically positioned and empowered to facilitate the interconnection of entire divisions or organizations.

As we've established, in a complex environment there is no possible way to accurately predict every contingency or problem set an organization might face—by definition, when cause and effect can be predicted, then you're not operating in a complex realm. This was true on a micro level among our tactical teams and on a macro scale between the entire Task Force and its peer organizations.

For the Task Force, these external stakeholders included key intelligence and law enforcement agencies, political authorities, and other military commands that had their own unique jurisdictions, resources, and capabilities. Each organization, of course, was free to run itself as it saw fit. Some remained steadfastly bureaucratic, whereas others were more naturally flat or networked.

Regardless, we were all autonomous players, and the key partners we needed to connect with were immune to the organizational shifts that the Task Force had implemented, as we would have been to any changes they were making to their leadership and decision-making structure. We all worked to be respectful of one another, but no organization's members were truly answerable to the rank-based authority of the other's strategic leadership.

Nevertheless, our respective problem sets were often causally linked. Whereas free information flow and cooperation could be achieved through social networks fostered among our internal tactical teams, creating organizational interconnectivity between these staunchly independent organizations was both challenging and critical to our collective success.

In the private sector, the challenge is similar—what if a division within a larger enterprise, having itself adopted an aligning narrative, colocation efforts, an O&I forum, and a set operating rhythm—nevertheless comes across a problem set that requires coordination with the organization's manufacturing division, logistics team, or adjacent region?

In the case of Under Armour's supply chain division, it was operationally dependent not only on the company's strategic leadership but also on multiple peer divisions—such as marketing, product design, and sales. Its Win at the Shelf forums would be severely constrained if these peers weren't active participants in supply chain's initiatives, but Hardy had no authority to enforce such a structure. He certainly couldn't *order* the stakeholders in these adjacent bureaucratic lattices to contribute to the operational changes that his division was creating. There is stress associated even with polite invitations in such a case—a normal by-product of internally focused teams not wanting others to tell them their business. An invitation to change can be easily interpreted as a critical judgment on current performance.

This is not to say that cognitive biases of these kinds are irrational. As we've established, Weberian bureaucracies make it easy for narratively divided teams to hold us-versus-them mentalities regarding one another—which are informed by genuine past negative experiences, including attempts at working across bureaucratic divides.

All it takes to create such a permanent relationship divide is a spoiled collaboration effort, or poorly considered comments by one leader in a meeting, or internal competition over resources, or the office rumor mill. In military and business cultures alike, culturally disparate tribes can easily be drawn into generations-long conflicts with one another based on long-past slights.

Just one negative interaction can condition an ingrained but operationally challenging hesitancy in leaders to trust or cooperate in future attempts at cross-functional solutions. Psychologists Amos Tversky and Daniel Kahneman summarize this problem well, referring to this tendency toward instinctive rushes to judgment as *judgmental heuristics*—internal shortcuts or rules we adopt that make the world around us easier to interpret.

Both Tversky and Kahneman received their undergraduate degrees in psychology in Jerusalem and their doctorates in the United States. After their mutual return to Hebrew University, this time as faculty, they embarked on a professional collaboration that would greatly impact the study of human judgment and cognitive bias. They elaborate on the concept of cognitive heuristics in a 1974 article they co-wrote entitled "Judgment Under Uncertainty: Heuristics and Biases":

> People rely on a limited number of heuristic principles which reduce the complex tasks of assessing probabilities and predicting values to simpler judgmental operations. In general, these heuristics are quite useful, but sometimes they lead to severe and systematic errors.

We all interpret the vastness of the world around us through these heuristics. We are hardwired to use what we already have heard about or experienced (either positively or negatively) with a population or an institution (say, the DMV) to assume the outcome of a pending interaction. We enter the DMV in a bad mood, perhaps, not because of any one memory but because of society's constant reminder that your experience there will be horrible.

Hardy encountered this when he initially tried to get Under Armour's design, sales, and marketing teams to show up to Win at the Shelf forums. The Task Force, similarly, found it challenging to gain genuine cooperation from peer military commands or civilian intelligence agencies. It is less a judgment of the change itself and more an aversion to being told how things should be done by a peer organization, division, or function that one has had past disputes with.

So how can this instinctive hesitance to cooperate be overcome among various parts of the enterprise or, in the case of the Task Force, with critical external partners?

There are two solution pathways available to leaders in this situation—a solid-line, bureaucratic method and a dotted-line one.

First the solid-line approach. Senior leaders can leverage their position in the bureaucratic hierarchy to press for freer communication and cooperation among resistant subordinate silos, adding pressure to move ahead with the initiative. In Under Armour's case, Hardy's initial mandate came through the solid lines of the enterprise, in the form of Fulks, who had both the positional and influence-based authority to establish cooperation and participation as key priorities.

This jump-started Hardy's ability to convince influencers in these silos of the merits of supply chain's new efforts. Eventually he could win over their full-hearted trust, but only after positive interdivisional experiences began to outweigh the negative scars. Tversky and Kahneman might frame this as the creation of a positive judgment heuristic—an instinctive future appreciation for the benefits of cooperation among these silos and leaders. In the Task Force, our leadership constantly reminded us that *we would need to make the first move, every time, to establish trust,* as there were years of negative memories to overcome.

But whereas this default method to press for cooperation is fairly intuitive, you'll find it a necessary but insufficient solution. Bureaucratic pressure alone is an inherently flawed method for ensuring genuine, long-term cooperation—as no one appreciates being *told* to play nice with others. When the pressure is removed for whatever reason, cooperation is likely to diminish.

It is the bureaucratic equivalent of parents forcing siblings to share, which can work fine in the moment but also risks reinforcing negative judgmental heuristics between those involved in the sharing. The likelihood of future cooperation without parental intervention can go down, unless those participating see positive results for themselves and begin to take ownership of the process.

And if pressure is the only driving force, then any early missteps will be leveraged as evidence against the change. With one negative outcome, naysayers are armed to return to their mutual solid-line leadership and say, *Look at what just happened. This isn't a good idea.* The preexisting negative heuristic has been reinforced. And, of course, early mistakes are inevitable.

Creating multiple dotted-line ties to supplement bureaucratic guidance is the second critical component for organizations to incorporate into this type of change. The creation of a liaison network was the Task Force's answer to establish powerful and genuine relationships across boundaries. Bureaucratic pressure to collaborate on complex problems was part of the effort, but liaisons offered a completely different channel for connectivity, a human-to-human personal network that was accountable for the creation of cross-boundary, dotted-line relationships among independent entities.

This creates the opportunity for a dual approach for connectivity. Whereas an enterprise's leadership persistently, directly, and honestly communicates with key partners, *liaisons* are positioned to create and maintain trust-based relationships, protect communication channels, and ensure transparency of information sharing.

The best messenger and advocate for a team's new operational needs from others is likely to be the *individual who needs them,* rather than the distant solid-line leadership, who would be simply passing along a message. In this way the intent communicated to an external stakeholder is accurate but, more powerfully, free from the dehumanizing, decontextualizing, and forceful effect of bureaucratically delivered mandates.

A liaison network allowed the Task Force's strategic leadership to earn trust and cooperation from otherwise-hesitant external partners. Having witnessed many of these external discussions during my year as McChrystal's aide-de-camp, I saw firsthand how this initial dialogue was always framed within the aligning narrative of the Task Force, while also anchored to tangible mutual priorities shared among our enterprises.

When ambassadors between nations begin a new assignment, they deliver their official credentials, signed by the head of state of their home government, to the head of state of their host country. This serves as an official endorsement of the ambassador as a representative of their country.

Similarly, McChrystal's endorsement of the Task Force's liaisons served to reinforce the liaisons' support from and clout with our senior leadership. In time I witnessed several such discussions between McChrystal and various senior leaders from partner agencies. These paraphrases of our organization's core narrative would often go as follows:

> We clearly share a determined adversary—one that, unlike our organizations, is networked and thus moves with incredible speed.
>
> In the Task Force, we are now trying to forge a new type of model based on relationships among individuals and organizations like yours—and we'd like to be more closely connected with your organization. Winning will come from leveraging our mutual strengths, sharing insights and nuanced understanding of the problems, and respecting one another's positions.
>
> To help our partnership, we would like to give you one of our best people as a liaison. I expect our liaison to be an asset to you, sharing anything we're doing, providing our most timely intelligence, and seeking out ways that we can help your organization accomplish its goals.

This honest, humble relationship reset was generally paired with the introduction of an empowered liaison officer or was timed to reinforce the significance of a liaison already working with the partner organization.

In the Task Force model, liaisons were highly experienced members of our organization, deployed to our partners' physical locations and integrated into their enterprise. The logic was similar to that which informed the boundary spanners among the Task Force's internal tactical teams. Liaisons helped reduce the degrees of separation between critical organizations working parallel to one another and enabled better information sharing among them.

A primary difference between liaisons and boundary spanners is that liaisons played a formalized role. They filled an official position, were often geographically removed from their original team, and operated with a broader and far more defined scope of responsibility. Liaisons represented an entire organization, not a single unit. These representatives answered directly to our organization's senior leadership and were expected to constantly interact with the leadership team of their host enterprise as well.

Simply put, when they called, our senior leadership answered—which is exactly why "Mike D" knew he could interrupt our leadership's scheduled activities. He was tasked with being a direct information conduit between the Task Force's strategic leadership and his host, and if they were having a crisis and needed Mike's help, he needed to demonstrate that he had direct and immediate access to our senior leadership, lest the aligning narrative seem more hyperbole than reality.

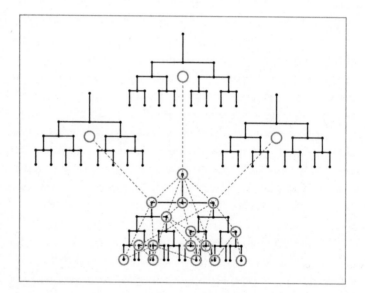

In theory, liaisons become prime dotted-line facilitators of our external partner. They interconnected our hybrid organizational structure with the key leadership of external partners, without the need to change anything about how those partners were running their organizations.

Liaisons already had become trusted figures in our own organization before they were assigned a duty like this, and they were therefore well positioned to gain trust, understanding, and participation from outside partners. This, in turn, increased the likelihood of contributions by these partners to Task Force practices needing their input—like O&I forums and cooperation with our teams during phases of empowered execution—

while mutual assistance was offered by our teams in response to their needs.

By helping establish these relationships, liaisons could enable the interconnection of our teams with the resources they needed to succeed in the field—a lesson that can be applied to the challenges civilian organizations face.

THE ISLAND OF MISFIT TOYS

The concept of liaison officers in the military far predates the Task Force's reformation. Many lessons about how to leverage them in any organization can be inferred from their often-suboptimal utilization in these historic contexts. But as you consider creating a similar model, keep in mind a simple rule: *unless liaisons are selected from among candidates equipped to seamlessly represent your senior leadership, their utility is limited, and they may be counterproductive.*

In early 2003, just ahead of the outset of the Iraq war, I'd been deployed as a SEAL liaison—before I was part of the Task Force—to the headquarters of an Army Special Forces group as they prepared to launch operations in the country's western desert.

This was the location where I first heard that call of "Shots fired," witnessing the start of a conflict that festers to this day. My experiences on that deployment showed me how a haphazard approach to the selection and deployment of liaisons can limit the benefits that can come from such a posting.

My onboarding as a liaison officer to that Army Special Forces group in 2003 was typical of what most liaisons in the military experience and was reflective of the low expectations that are traditionally associated with such a role. It's not a result of bad people, just of dated systems that have historically had low requirements for exchange officers. When industrial-age problems could be compartmentalized among divisions of an organization or units on the battlefield, liaisons were there simply to deconflict actions. But the interconnected nature of a complex world alters this significantly, a lesson we had not yet learned in 2003.

Arriving late at night onto a darkened and remote airfield, I scanned around to see whether there was anyone there to meet me. Realizing there wasn't, I hitched a ride with a vehicle heading toward the brightest lights on the base, which I assumed was a good place for me to start.

After an hour, I finally arrived at the correct compound but, lacking a proper identification badge for their headquarters, I made my way to the badging desk. There I met a young civilian contractor who told me without a hint of irony, "You're not arriving this week. You arrive next week."

In the moment I couldn't help but imagine that I was swirling in the mindless bureaucracy of Joseph Heller's *Catch-22*. One of my favorite characters in the novel, Doc Daneeka, has his combat flight records altered before the plane that he is "officially" on crashes in combat. His squadron receives news of his death as he sits among them, alive and well, now described as "the new dead man in the squadron who most certainly was there and gave every indication of proving a still thornier administrative problem." Heller's experience as a bombardier in World War II helped inform his writing of the literary classic, and the scene of my confused arrival at this base would have surely evoked a knowing grin from the author.

Eventually I proved to the badging officer that I had in fact arrived, was given my new identification, and made my way to my host's JOC—a gigantic arena with stadium-stacked seating. Filling these rows of chairs were at least two hundred people hard at work. I felt like the new kid in the cafeteria on the first day of school. Looking above their busy heads, I spotted elevated placards hanging above each ring of chairs—with huge block writing on each denoting which sections of the room were the sovereign territory of which functional group.

COMMAND sat at the front and center of the room, while OPERATIONS, AIR SUPPORT, and FIRE SUPPORT were all located in the next-highest ring of seats—being functions that, per the fastest-moving parts of the battlefield, had to be in closest communication with the organization's senior leadership. Next, at a higher altitude and greater distance from the front of the room, came functions that were slightly less time critical to mission execution—COMMUNICATIONS, LOGISTICS, and PERSONNEL.

Taking these in, I finally spotted my new home—in the far back right corner of the room. Tucked away, adjacent to whirring printers and heavily trafficked coffee stations, was the sign I'd been looking for: LIAISONS. Separate from the operations-related action at the center of the room, behind logistics planners and human resources desks, I found my tiny workstation, a speck among a vast array of other functional teams in the giant space. I took a seat next to the handful of other analysts and soldiers who looked as out of place as I did.

My tour had begun. I began to settle into my place on this island of misfit toys. Theoretically I was there as a facilitator of trust and communication, yet I was far removed, both physically and figuratively, from a position where I could hope to add any real value.

My daily reality of passively exchanging mundane, limited-utility information started, and would go on for six months. In time I would integrate with other parts of the staff and become an active member of their planning teams. Those experiences, from the perspective of understanding how a full-scale invasion is executed to seeing a very mature military staff do its work, was invaluable. But that was a circumstantial benefit for me as a leader. When it came to my *assigned* position, I added little value in helping create any actionable synergies between my parent and host organizations.

ISSUES IN SELECTION AND PREPARATION

What lessons can be learned about the best use of liaisons from my initial experience on the job?

First is the importance of selecting the right person for it—a candidate reasonably well connected and influential within the senior leadership of *their own* organization, who can thus earn the respect of, and offer genuine insight to, the external stakeholders hosting them as liaisons. The *gaining* partners need to see a liaison who they believe is personally close to their own leadership, understands how they think, and is empowered to speak on their behalf.

At the time of my deployment in 2003, I had none of these qualifications. Instead, I happened to be between tours with different SEAL Teams, having just finished a two-year rotation as a tactical-level platoon commander. I was a free agent, waiting to be placed in an operations-level position and adrift on the solid-line org chart, not quite belonging to one team or the other. This lack of an active position, however, made me a candidate to deploy overseas to fill a liaison job for a SEAL element that would be part of the initial invasion force into Iraq.

I was bolted onto the SEAL unit, and while I was from their tribe, I had no formal ties with the leadership and had never worked closely with any of the personnel.

But I was excited—a staff position, I knew, was likely my best shot at deploying to Iraq ahead of the invasion, and my lack of responsibility at the time made me easy to give up to another organization.

208 • ONE MISSION

A second lesson can be drawn from the lack of definition or importance placed on the job by each organization's leadership: liaisons need to
be given an appropriate amount of genuine responsibility. Liaisons were
traditionally under-empowered in the military, with very little accountability or responsibility placed upon their shoulders, in large part because
the role was always seen as very transactional.

The lack of sway held by the uninfluential individuals who would
inevitably occupy these liaison roles would (effectively and occasionally
intentionally) communicate a subtle message between the organizations:
*We'll keep each other informed, but we're not really interested in deep
cooperation or synchronization of efforts.* This would lead host organizations to hold lower expectations of liaisons, which in turn would limit
their ability to do their jobs effectively.

Thus a negative judgmental heuristic was formed, ensuring the functional constraint of the position moving forward. The only thing that
could have broken this cycle would have been a strong, clearly communicated demonstration from my own solid-line leadership to indicate that
they were taking this role more seriously, with an eye to doing more than
exchanging wave-top information: adding genuine benefit to the partner
organization.

But if that *had* been the view of these positions, I still wouldn't have
been the right fit for the job. I was not well connected in my parent command; I lacked a direct connection to our senior solid-line leadership, had
inconsiderable dotted-line influence among our teams, and had yet to
have any significant experience in the field.

In other words, I was learning all of this for the first time and had very
little to offer my host organization as an emissary, aside from focus and
work ethic. I was benefiting from the experience far more than they were
benefiting from having me in their headquarters. I was not a "Mike D."

Worse yet, the preparation I'd received to inherit this role as a liaison
was heavily overlaid by what I've now taken to calling *whisper guidance*—
the advice of influential peers from my SEAL command, given with an eye
to our unit's interests, as I left to be emplaced within an external command. This was a subtle agenda, provided to me on the way out the door,
but similar conversations were undoubtedly had with liaisons across the
battlefield.

Of course, my official role was to generally ensure that parallel efforts between my host and parent units didn't conflict with each other
and relatedly brief my original leadership on any upcoming critical mis-

sions by the Special Forces group. But considering the several hundreds of open-desert miles that separated the units, such overlap was unlikely.

My more subtle functions were summarized to me by the operations officer I would be communicating with every day from the Special Forces compound. Before my departure, this officer brought me to his desk and gave me my first exposure to what the *other* expectations of this role would be from my immediate leadership, all with a cocked half smile: "Look, you're sort of a mole for us. It's standard practice. Nothing bad, just keep us looped in on what they're thinking."

Of course, I was informed, I should act in accordance with my official duties . . . but this was just a friendly reminder about what also mattered: providing insights for my home unit, rather than acting as a conduit only for information sharing.

He continued, "Try to give us a sense of things. What's their mood? What are they planning that they're not talking about with anyone else yet? What intel are we missing about their activities? That sort of thing. It's normal practice and very helpful for us."

I wish I could say I had the foresight at the time to contextualize what this interaction represented, but the conversation was actually *comforting* in the moment. It reiterated that I was part of the tribe, even if embedded with another unit, and I was being sent there to serve the narrative of my own team and to act on behalf of *my* unit. There was almost an apologetic tone—*Sorry you have to leave and go work with that other tribe*—which in the moment, as a naive young leader, I was appreciative of. In contrast to the more generous, closely watched and nontribal role that would eventually define being a liaison in the Task Force, my early experiences had no mention of fostering new relationships, of helping others, or of making the first move toward establishing trust. The limited official guidance ensured that each unit's *whisper guidance* could usurp the intended function of these jobs.

Therefore, for this early deployment, I was a bit of a "Manchurian candidate": not necessarily there to build bridges, to translate chatter between bureaucracies, to develop trust-based relationships—all of the things that I would see firsthand several years later in Baghdad throughout the Task Force. Rather, I was there to benefit my parent unit—the SEALs—and act in accordance with the shared narrative that drove our teams. Instead of considering how *we* could help *others,* my mind was constantly referring back to the same question above my home station's doorframe:

There are certainly countless historical cases of excellent liaison relationships adding critical value to the fight, but I would argue that most of those were the result of a lucky coin toss, rather than a well-executed supporting framework.

My experience was in line with the historical norms of liaison roles in the military—an imperfect method of interconnecting peer bureaucracies, as ensured by the setting of low standards for candidates and the removal of any real official authority or accountability from the position.

The tour ultimately went very well. The outcomes weren't *negative* in any way, and it was one of the best learning experiences of my career. I made great new friends and gained a much deeper understanding and appreciation of the army, their Special Forces units more specifically. But despite that personal growth, as a traditional liaison, I certainly wasn't positioned to have the exponential impact that the role was capable of bringing to a complex fight and that the Task Force would expect of its liaison officers in the years to come.

CHANGE

Long before I was aware of the shift, the Task Force's strategic leadership began proactively changing the job expectations of its liaisons and actively communicating these fresh requirements to the subordinate solid-line silos in their hierarchy—in contrast to the open-ended definitions that had existed in earlier contexts in various military commands, as my own experiences had shown.

The change was grounded in commitment that the *parent organization* would make the first moves toward reforming relationships and deepening trust—with the role suddenly tied directly to the universal aligning narrative of the Task Force:

Credibility = Integrity + Proven Competence + Relationships

Credibility was what we needed in the eyes of our peer organizations, and in order to achieve it, we needed our liaisons to demonstrate integrity, competence, and a focus on cultivating positive, non-transactional relationships with these stakeholders. This would have a second-order effect on the types of individuals who would be selected for these roles, as our strategic leadership began communicating the heightened expectations of the role and distributing this awareness to all subordinate silos in charge of selecting liaisons for external partner organizations.

Two traits became key in selection of liaison candidates: their level of influence within their home unit and their individual personality type. Organizations considering a similar model should start with these variables as well.

Liaison positions were soon being staffed by middle- to senior-ranking officers—those who were somewhere between operational and strategic levels of leadership on the bureaucratic org chart—who were highly experienced on the battlefield, well versed in the functionality of both the solid-line bureaucracy and the dotted-line networks of the Task Force, and respected by their peers for their proven competence in the fight. Liaisons needed qualities similar to those that Barabási assigns to hubs, as "hubs create short paths between any two nodes in the system."

At what would seem like the peak of their careers, these individuals would be removed from the front lines of the Task Force's fight and embedded in a seemingly distant tribe. Once there, it would be their job to build and maintain difficult, trust-based relationships—the tracks on which information sharing among peer organizations would be enabled.

In various functional silos and units, factions were now asked to offer up their best members to be embedded with other units, with an unknown return on investment. This was, naturally, a difficult initial step for our strategic leadership to sell to subordinates.

The running joke in these circles soon became "Do a great job on the battlefield, and you'll end up wearing a blazer in an office someplace." The joke—although made with an undercurrent of exasperation—was a confirmation of the intent of our senior leadership. Leaders who displayed a strong battlefield acumen, plus an understanding of how our hybrid model worked, *plus* a natural ability to build relationships, would find themselves dressed in a suit and tie and working from an intelligence agency's headquarters, a remote embassy, or some other nonstandard environment around the globe.

This, naturally, wasn't an easy transition for many to accept—either the deployed liaison or their parent unit. Despite the communicated intent of our senior leadership, no one wanted to give up their best talent to fill what appeared to be a remote position, especially as the intensity of the war increased. Moreover, few high performers would want to leave their familiar, intimate home unit in favor of this isolating job.

On top of these concerns, the logic behind this shift didn't seem to make a lot of sense to most either: *how will pulling our most seasoned talent from different corners of our organization help us win the war?* If anything, the idea seemed to some to be likely to cut in the opposite direction.

What helped tamp down this risk—that of insubordination and continued whisper guidance informed by the unit-level narrative—was the fact that McChrystal himself would become personally responsible for approving and considering new nominations for liaison roles. This was not only helpful in ensuring that the individuals selected held the right personal qualities but also (naturally) forced unit leaders in charge of nominating new candidates to pay close attention to whom they put forward for the job.

During my deployment as McChrystal's aide-de-camp, I would occasionally get a call from a subordinate unit tasked with filling a liaison nomination. In the aide position, I was a safe sounding board to them, as I had no formal authority within our bureaucratic org chart but could still offer some insight as to what qualities were being selected for among candidates.

The core of these conversations always circled around the same themes: *Does this actually need to be one of our top people, or can we send a free body? We're busy here, we don't know the people this person would be working with, and we're trying to minimize the impact this would have on our own operations.*

These were all talented folks with an appreciation for the Task Force's aligning narrative, but there was still a natural and understandable desire to hold on to the very best.

My response to them was always roughly the same: "Here's what I've seen," I'd say. "These people become some of the most influential players in our entire organization. They're positioned such that they can walk into the offices of directors of the major agencies, ambassadors, and generals and act as a direct communication line to the Task Force. Those leaders have learned to trust that we're sending our most informed and capable players, so one bad liaison rotation will hurt that credibility, damage relationships, and slow down our operations."

Informing these criteria was the desire to reduce the degrees of separation among our leaderships and to lay the path for positive heuristics among once-rivalrous, untrusting commands. Though this logic wasn't necessarily exactly what was in the minds of our leaders at the time, subordinate silos had to be reminded of what caliber and significance of individual they were expected to put forth.

I'd often hear a sigh of acknowledgment in response to this—a grudging recognition that this requirement was indeed being taken seriously by our solid-line leadership. Still, that didn't mean they'd not need any further guidance on whom to pick.

Later in my tour, with just a few months left on the job, I received a similar call from a former commander of mine in the SEALs. He was looking to clarify the type of person to put forward for a liaison spot he'd been asked to provide for.

"Bottom line," he said to me over the secure line. "How should I be looking at this?"

"It's pretty straightforward, sir," I replied from my small seat outside the crowded Balad SAR. "You will know it's the right person if it hurts you to see them leave, and if you'd recognize their voice when they called you at two in the morning."

He paused. "Yep, got it," he said. There wasn't much else to ask.

"Sir," I offered, "these folks are more impactful than I would have ever suspected a year ago. Whoever you send will get a quick PhD in how this organization runs—this will benefit you guys in the long run."

These had to be people who were known and trusted on a personal level. They had to have battlefield bona fides. They were going to be moving fast, speaking on the behalf of our seniormost leadership from hour one, and unless they had relevance to their parent organization, they wouldn't have any significance or utility to their hosts.

These individuals would be in a place of great authority, where they'd not only get a sense for the nature of how our partner enterprises cooperated and shared information with us but also be able to practice it for themselves.

This leads into the second new quality of liaisons selected—the personality types that were deliberately selected for candidates in these roles. This is critically important for an organization that is considering adopting a similar model.

In his 2013 book *Give and Take,* organizational psychologist Adam

Grant advanced the idea that personality types in society and the work-force could be divided into three categories: *giver, taker,* and *matcher.* The nuances of these different types of individuals are implicit in their naming, for where takers "tilt reciprocity in their own favor, putting their own interests ahead of others' needs," givers "tilt reciprocity in the other direction, preferring to give more than they get," while matchers simply practice transactional interactions with others.

Givers, per Grant and others' research, can fall on both the bottom *and* the top of professional success ladders and can be easily taken advantage of by takers in their workplace—nevertheless, in these scenarios true givers generally find inventive ways to continue demonstrating aggressive generosity to others in the face of initially disadvantageous relationships.

Our argument in favor of liaisons relies on similar logic. Ideally, the messenger between an organization and an external stakeholder falls somewhere between Grant's matcher and giver categories.

It would be naive to suggest that these relationships in the Task Force were intended to be non-transactional, for obviously our organization was looking to access the human or physical resources held within other bureaucracies, and our leadership expected some degree of mutuality from the relationships they were trying to forge.

Nevertheless, by selecting individuals with reputations for selfless-ness and excellence in their fields and encouraging these liaisons to cease-lessly continue such behavior on a formal inter-organizational scale, once-adversarial and stilted relationships could be gradually molded into mutually beneficial ones.

As a matter of fact, these personal qualities are also what make liai-sons influencer-type individuals in their home units—their generosity and willingness to go the extra mile underlie their connections to their imme-diate peers. By relying on different tiers of a solid-line lattice to identify these dotted line–rich individuals within a bureaucracy and using their testimony to distinguish these candidates from selfish bottleneck-type in-fluencers, ideal liaison candidates can be selected. It's why they were hard to give up, and also why they were so effective.

But once they are emplaced, how can an organization's strategic lead-ership best support and leverage these individuals?

ACCESS TO (AND ENDORSEMENT BY)
STRATEGIC LEADERSHIP

Midway through my year with McChrystal, I found myself in the back-seat of a well-worn and dented SUV. We were driving from a landing zone outside Baghdad through the Coalition-secured "Green Zone" of Iraq's capital, and I was thinking about the next steps McChrystal and the rest of the leaders needed to take on this trip.

The Task Force's commander, in the passenger seat, and a teammate of ours behind the wheel talked about what was on the agenda for the day. This latter figure, who drove through the blackened streets with the familiarity of a local, had been waiting by this vehicle as the Task Force's helicopters had landed on an airstrip outside of the city.

He was a highly respected member of our organization, well known to many of the Task Force's personnel from his previous battlefield tours—but pertinent to tonight's events, he was the Task Force's liaison to Multi-National Coalition–Iraq (MNC-I), an external military command whose headquarters were in the capital. An experienced U.S. Army lieutenant colonel, he was representative of the type and quality of individuals who had been placed in these positions—he was a giver, an influencer figure in his home unit. He and one other liaison would spend the next year rotating in and out of this critical position, with one forward-deployed and another back in the United States at all times.

As we drove, the Task Force's tactical units were in a window of empowered execution—our O&I had ended a few hours prior, so now the teams were moving, networking, and driving operations freely with one another, aligned on strategy and narrative.

Hence our strategic leadership was free to focus on external relationships with our peer organizations. This trip would focus on the one we held with the key conventional military leadership of the Iraq war, MNC-I, while simultaneously supporting the reputation and activity of our liaison who was integrated with them.

Like all of the other liaisons the Task Force had emplaced within different organizations around the world, the officer behind the wheel filled two critical functions for our organization.

First, he was a critical lifeline into MNC-I and a facilitator of trust with them: if any activity involving the Task Force was impacting the operations of regular Coalition troops in the country, or vice versa, this officer would keep the senior leadership teams of both the Task Force and

MNC-I informed. He ensured that no actions of either organization caught the other unawares, proactively identified opportunities for mutual collaboration or information sharing between them, and, most important, was familiar enough with the tribal norms of his host organization to interpret our actions from their perspective—and vice versa.

During a pre-meeting drive like this, a great liaison (which this officer certainly was) would often be saying to McChrystal, *Okay, boss, when we did X, they were really pissed. That made no sense to them, because here's how they see that problem . . . and it contradicted their view in this way.* In doing so, the liaison was demonstrating his ability to speak the languages of both organizations and quickly translate back and forth between them in a way that a telephone-tree bureaucracy would not be able to accurately or efficiently match.

Then, freshly armed with our *host's* perspective on a recent action or incident, McChrystal could enter a conversation with our partners, with the liaison in tow, saying, *Okay, let's talk about X. I've had a long talk with our liaison about how you interpreted that action, which I completely understand. He gave me a great sense of your perspective, so I can see why that action would create tension. What we were trying to accomplish was Y and Z . . . and this is why. We understand your thoughts on this type of action better now, and in the future I guarantee you that it will inform our decision making, and you'll know before we take any action.* A brushfire extinguished before the forest is ablaze.

Again, only seasoned members of the organization could become truly effective liaisons with our most critical partners. Moreover, only a liaison with a well-grounded understanding of our complex battlefield could provide this type of information contextualization between our most senior leaders around the world. This was the reason that our organization had begun to place such an emphasis on their careful selection and why—as exemplified by this visit—our strategic leadership spent so much time engaging directly with them.

Combat operations were already ongoing for the night, yet the Task Force's highest-ranked leader had made the conscious choice to focus on a point-by-point discussion with this liaison officer, confident that it was the best use of his energy. This understanding of priorities also sent a deliberate message to our tactical teams during periods of shared consciousness: *you fight the war on the ground, and we'll manage the relationships needed to support your efforts.*

In some cases a liaison would circle back a few weeks into the job with complaints about how different our organizations were and how hard it was to establish relationships, looking for someone from the old tribe to say, *Oh yeah, they're a pain!* Instead, the response from our leadership was direct and consistent: *You're not there to let us know they're hard to work with. You're there for them to like you and to become a trusted part of their team. Get over yourself and make that happen.*

The message was clear and direct but critical to the broader success of the liaison network. Only after a trust-based relationship was established with the host organization was there any value in a liaison executing the second critical function of the position: interacting with the rest of the Task Force's liaisons constellated across other organizations.

Our enterprise had dozens of liaisons deployed around the world, each emplaced in their own partner entity. Whereas each of these individuals had to connect their home organization and someone's chain of command, they were also expected to act as a network in and among themselves, across a mosaic of different bureaucracies. These individuals, as a result, could quite literally synchronize the leadership of many external organizations on an emerging development with unparalleled speed when required.

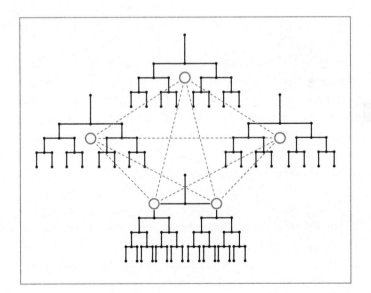

Forewarning of an upcoming operation that might impact conventional Coalition forces would need to quickly reach the MNC-I senior leadership. A time-sensitive intelligence grab from a conventional army unit in Afghanistan might tie to a threat stream in Africa that the embassy there should be made aware of immediately. An upcoming policy decision in the Pentagon might impact operations of intelligence agencies around the world. All of these were critical developments that the broader liaison network could quickly disseminate and contextualize across vast bureaucratic distances.

By having a well-acquainted, expansive dotted-line network of liaisons—external to the networks that interconnected the Task Force's silos—this could be accomplished. The best liaison officers would sit through a host organization's discussion, then subtly approach their leadership and say, *Can I connect your planners with so-and-so at the Department of X? They have great insights into what you're talking about . . .* It was no wonder that, as time went on, many additional partner organizations were more than happy to open their doors to one of McChrystal's liaisons—knowing that they added value.

Back in Baghdad's Green Zone, the benefits of these individuals were exceedingly clear—as was the trust that the Task Force's commander placed in them, which reinforced their use.

"Anything else we should be thinking about, going into this thing?" I heard McChrystal asking from my spot in the vehicle's backseat. "Are they comfortable with the Task Force's tempo of operations these days? We're really cranking."

He wanted to know whether the MNC-I leaders were getting anxious about the pace of our missions in the field. As a result of the team of teams operational approach, the Task Force was launching hundreds of decentralized missions every month, an unprecedented pace—and consequently, our leaders had learned to look for early indicators that our relationships with outside organizations were getting overstressed by lack of effective communication between their leaderships and ours.

Damage inflicted on our dotted-line relationships wasn't uncommon nor entirely avoidable, but the Task Force's leadership was always interested in quickly repairing damage, being careful not to let these relationships fray to the point of permanent animosity. Having a liaison on the ground, embedded in these bureaucracies, helped anticipate when things might be approaching a dangerous edge.

"They're good, sir," our liaison replied. "The pressure we're applying is forcing AQI to keep its head down here, and there's more room for engagement with local civilian leadership than there was a few weeks ago.

This could change, but right now our tempo is great from their view. Once things are more settled with some of the local militias, I'm guessing they'll want things to back off a little bit on our end."

We pulled up to the former Hussein palace that now housed MNC-I's headquarters, and McChrystal and our liaison officer exited the vehicle. Getting out as well, I handed them each a condensed briefing packet for their meeting with MNC-I's senior leadership and support staff.

Once we passed through the building's grand, marbled entrance, I took my cue to leave their side, splitting off to check in on personal contacts of mine in the building. The two of them walked in the direction of a conference room across the open foyer, where I knew they would be occupied for the next thirty minutes.

With my half hour of independence, I said hello to a few contacts in the building before navigating the sea of plywood cubicles the building housed. Finding a spare space, I plugged a secure Ethernet cable into my Toughbook laptop.

I sat and watched e-mails flow into my inbox and logged on to our organization's intranet portal, which brought our chat rooms online on my screen. Through this interconnecting technology, I could monitor the real-time actions of the rest of our organization's tactical teams during this phase of empowered execution—while our senior leaders were shoring up relationships with MNC-I here.

Our liaison structure was working behind the scenes, moving information, aligning leaders, and driving decisions in a personal—and thus very effective—way. Organizations are not a collection of buildings, technology, or assets; they're a collection of individual humans who take advantage of these tools to a common end. Finding, empowering, and connecting the *right* individuals in an enterprise with key outside partners is a secret weapon, a simple and effective way to break down barriers and leverage the power of networks without disrupting your existing structures.

Properly utilized, liaisons help a successful hybrid organizational structure spread its reach. They are culture carriers who deliver your narrative across regions or business units; they are ambassadors to your key partners. Liaisons can pull these partners into your aligning narrative, interconnect with their teams, and become *givers* in the information economy. Ultimately this will help both you and them "win the war" and thrive in a complex environment.

And the world isn't getting any simpler. During our excursion to Baghdad, it turned out that something new had started to develop in our external environment. Our teams were adapting in the moment, and our organization would need to realign sooner than our operating rhythm dictated.

QUESTIONS TO CONSIDER:

♦ How could various parts of your organization benefit from having liaison relationships that interconnect their traditional verticals or geographic boundaries?

♦ What partner relationships does your organization depend on that might benefit from a similar model?

♦ What process would you implement to select these individuals, and how would your organization encourage or facilitate their better function?

CASE STUDY:
EASTDIL SECURED

PREFACE

In the Task Force's case, liaisons like "Mike D" and the individuals our organization had placed in MNC-I's headquarters were used to connect different external bureaucracies to our own. But the principle can also be applied to connecting various parts of a global enterprise. As you'll see, Eastdil Secure—as informed by the experiences of employee Walker Gorham, a former Ranger in the Task Force—created similar relationship networks among its geographic and product specialty teams. By instituting and leveraging an O&I-like forum, Eastdil Secured created a space where the organic exchange of information across boundaries was possible, and its liaison network became the nervous system of the organization.

As you read how Eastdil Secured leveraged liaisons to drive interconnectivity, consider the way in which these individuals were selected and used to magnify aspects of this organization's original culture and strategy—as its strategic leadership had long desired—and were also trained as future firm leaders.

Moreover, take note of how liaisons were used in conjunction with other practices discussed so far in this book, such as an inclusive communication forum, for the better contextualization of data and information across an organization's structure.

Finally, you'll note how Eastdil Secured's liaisons were able to disseminate "best practices" among themselves through their own social network and thus continuously improve their original function.

THE SETUP

"Now I know why you love these guys," Holly, my wife, said, as we mingled with the group of Eastdil Secured senior leaders. "They're like SEALs, but in really nice suits." She laughed, took a sip of her wine and stared across the skyline of downtown Washington, D.C. We were guests at a cocktail reception hosted by the leadership of their firm; she'd heard me talk about the members of the Eastdil Secured team on count-less occasions, so I was thankful that she was finally able to meet some of them. And she was right; this was a highly focused and disciplined team, hardwired to win, but with a familial tightness when they were together in a social setting. It's a special organization; her description was accurate.

According to those on its inside, Eastdil Secured had always pos-sessed a uniquely flat, elite, and collaborative culture—qualities that re-main rare in its industry of real estate investment banking. These guiding principles had been held communal across its myriad product and region-specific teams ever since the company was founded by Ben Lambert in 1967. When Lambert first started Eastdil Secured, he intended for it to be distinctly and dramatically unique from competitors in the field.

Miles Theodore, a younger retail specialist with Eastdil Secured in Atlanta, had felt this distinction ever since he joined from another finan-cial services firm. "We'd never used the term 'networked organization' in the past . . . but we have always prided ourselves on being more flat, more prone to collaboration and more unified, so to speak, than other people in the real estate capital market space." In contrast, he says, "others come at the field with a brokerage mentality, and kind of sharp elbows."

If Theodore had to clarify what he meant by "sharp elbows," how would he phrase it? Jealous cultures of "These are my cookies" mind-sets between functional teams or leaders, he answers succinctly. "Limited in-formation sharing and collaboration by peers."

Theodore's views are reflective of a wider consensus in the firm, that a top-down strategic emphasis on tight ties among teams had always been the norm in Eastdil Secured. Sue-Lin Heng, a London-based officer for the company's hotel group, recalls that "relationships between offices have always been quite close," as they've always been emphasized by the firm's senior leadership.

Stephen Van Dusen, a managing director (MD), points to the "shared compensation structure and combined bonus pool" that the firm has al-ways maintained as a tangible example of this. Van Dusen refers to this effect as financially incentivized "collaborative motivation," consistent with the values Eastdil Secured's leadership have long looked to priori-tize. "Whereas," Van Dusen goes on to explain, "the industry standard is an 'eat what you kill mentality'—reinforced by a commission-based system." Not exactly good ground for trusting, collaborative relation-ships between high performers.

In short, Eastdil Secured's long-standing equivalent of an aligning narrative emanated from the founding principles established by Lambert and resulted in a shared dedication to client success, a flat structure, and the generous sharing of data across it.

Yet in the years immediately before and then after the global financial crisis of 2008, the traditionally North America–focused firm saw its external environment change dramatically. Once the smoke had cleared from the chaos, opportunities for international expansion were plentiful for players that were still standing—especially nontraditional markets like Asia, Europe, and the Middle East.

Concerted efforts by many helped the company avoid being drawn into an uncontrolled "boom" cycle by this newly target-rich environment, thus avoiding the deterioration of Eastdil Secured's long-standing collaborative emphasis on the prioritization of client experience. In Van Dusen's words, the periods that bookended the crisis were a "magical time to be in the industry," with new, tempting opportunities seemingly growing from all corners. Yet Eastdil Secured stayed a careful course, not wanting to be carried away from the collaborative culture that had served it well.

But over the next few years, Eastdil Secured's offices around the world swelled with new teams staffed by new hires, as emerging opportunities in fresh fields like debt markets had proven too tempting to not explore. Sourced from outside the firm, this talent represented a potential departure from the long-standing interteam-oriented culture of the company, on an office by office level.

Collins Ege, an MD for the company in Washington, D.C., remembers this period as a bit of a blur, where "it was all new people we were dealing with, and all new personalities" within a "twenty-four- to thirty-six-month period." The result was the danger of an emerging culture clash, but at these tactical levels, decision makers like Ege "spent a lot of time trying to figure out how this would all work together."

The complexity of Eastdil Secured's dramatically changed environment—both internally and externally—couldn't be avoided, no matter how careful and strategically aligned the company's leadership may have been.

It was only a matter of time before this changed the long-standing culture of the firm.

THE PROBLEM

In 2013 a large in-depth poll was conducted of Eastdil Secured's major clients, asking for their critical feedback regarding their experiences working with the firm. It was titled the "Kingsley Survey," and its results held some inconvenient truths for the organization's leadership.

To put it simply, the company's clientele all responded with surprisingly, alarmingly consistent feedback. They had each independently identified a problem that Eastdil Secured's strategic leadership couldn't perceive, given that it existed at the lower tiers of the firm.

What the Kingsley Survey revealed was that, by 2013, clients had felt that the company had reached an operational "ceiling"—small errors and pitfalls in service were occurring at a greater frequency in their experiences with Eastdil Secured, despite continued high overall performance. Worst of all, there was a growing sense among clients that Eastdil Secured's culture seemed to be getting "indistinguishable" from that of its competitors.

That last part stung—apparently, the cultural uniqueness of the company wasn't at its historical strength, and it was now at risk of impacting the operational side of the firm.

But how exactly was this happening? One officer in Eastdil Secured found a good explanation for the impact this cultural hang-up was having in an unexpected place—a military memoir he'd picked up recently.

This was *My Share of the Task*—McChrystal's memoir. In it he elaborates on the multistep process by which operator and intelligence analyst teams in the Task Force would traditionally target and eliminate insurgent cells.

Labeled "Find, Fix, Finish, Exploit and Analyze"—for the steps in the procedural chain, abbreviated to "F3EA"—this cycle summarizes how a counterterror mission would be carried out by operators ("Find, Fix, Finish") and how intelligence subsequently reaped from that operation would inform the next one ("Exploit and Analyze"). It was visually represented as follows in the book:

Randy Evans was a longtime senior officer of Eastdil Secured, and as a result he reported directly to the company's governing Executive Committee. By mid-2014—his mind fresh from the sobering results of the Kingsley Survey—he read *My Share of the Task* and was struck by how the process outlined above could be applied to the difficulties his organization was experiencing.

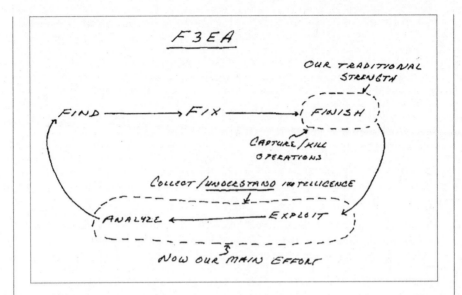

Applying the F3EA formula to the cultural and operational state of Eastdil Secured, he observed that his company was great when it came to its version of "Find, Fix, Finish"—quickly executing on varied market opportunities whenever they managed to be flagged to the right team at the right time.

But, like the Task Force in its bureaucratic heyday, Evans felt that Eastdil Secured fell short in the "Exploit and Analyze" parts of its internal process at the *junior* levels of the organization—in other words, dredging up, distilling, and distributing critical information to the *right* team remained constrained by a lack of networking among parallel teams that might have relevant market intelligence to share with one another.

Internal data, collected retroactively, confirmed Evans's suspicion that not only was information being "bottlenecked at the operational-level spots on the organization's solid-line" hierarchy, but very few people in the organization felt incentivized to "proactively" share relevant intelligence from their market with other teams.

Evans, with the results of this data and the outcomes of the Kingsley Survey in the back of his mind, was inspired by reading about the re-invention of the F3EA process. As it happened, he knew somebody who might be able to help him further understand how to apply the Task Force's experience to Eastdil Secured's problem set—someone with an inside line on what had happened inside the Task Force's reformation.

A slightly younger team member in the company, Walker Gorham had been a captain in the U.S. Army Rangers before joining Eastdil Secured. During his service, he'd deployed to Iraq, had led ground forces in some of the harshest conditions of the war, and thus had borne first-hand witness to the Task Force's reformation from a bureaucratic organization.

After finishing *My Share of the Task*, Evans sought out Gorham and was direct with him: "Was this all for real?" he asked.

Gorham didn't have to think hard about his answer. "Yes." Then he paused, maybe reading Evans's mind, hesitating. "But this would be tough for us to do." Gorham had been present in Iraq and Afghanistan and recognized the tremendous senior-level commitment to change that would be required for Eastdil Secured to really embrace this initiative—and he wasn't entirely sure it was possible in the private sector.

But Evans was confident the company needed this. He'd heard what he needed to from Gorham: this was for real, and it *might* work.

THE SOLUTION

Like our other featured case studies in this book, Eastdil Secured pursued a mix of different practices when trying to reform itself into a team of teams. These included improvements on the strategic alignment of its different silos and the reinvention of their Market Intelligence Call (MIC, pronounced "Mike"). But a critical centerpiece that brought these other two practices together was the company's use of a liaison network, which featured heavily in both complementing the content of MICs and better unifying Eastdil Secured's teams. We will focus in this writing on how its liaison network was established and how it was used in conjunction with these other practices.

The first step Evans took—as he should have—was to make the case for and gain permission from his solid-line superiors in the firm on his ideas on how Eastdil Secured's culture might be reestablished: Eastdil Secured's Executive Committee composed of Roy March, Lambert, and Michael Van Koynenburg ("VK")—the company's strategic triumvirate.

Roy March had been the CEO of Eastdil Secured since the merger between the company's previous component halves—Eastdil Realty, a New York–based real estate capital markets firm, and Secured Capital, a similarly focused West Coast–centric firm—had joined in 2005 to become greater than the sum of their parts. As a member of the firm's Executive Committee, March was directly reported to by Evans.

At Evans's scheduled performance review in 2014, March remembers hearing Evans's pitch for a way to become a more effective information franchise, a need highlighted by the Kingsley Survey.

Laughing, March recollects this initial exchange as being "a little unusual."

Why? "Well, I think he actually brought in an excerpt from *My Share of the Task* . . . during his review. Most people in those situations come in and try to talk about their accomplishments for the year. When they don't . . . well, it was actually productive, and heartening."

Mike Van Koynenburg was also active in the day-to-day strategic leadership of the company on the Executive Committee, as the former chief of secured capital. Evans's pitch stuck out to him as well, distinguishing itself from "the usual chest pounding" that VK had gotten used to hearing at meetings like these from subordinates over the years: "He decided instead to talk about having read *My Share of the Task*."

Evans's approach was unusual, but it worked, and the Executive Committee was tentatively on board—they saw the logic in his thinking. But they all wanted to hear Gorham's concerns out first, before going any further. They needed to know: *What would this take to work?*

As March recalls, "His comments were essentially *I think it could— but everybody in this firm is an operator, so you are going to have to be committed to the behavioral change needed to make this work*." Gorham wanted to make sure that the firm's leaders were taking what was being suggested seriously and were considering the implications of it heavily.

March got the message. "He candidly didn't think we should start it unless we were fully committed to finishing it, because it would be disruptive but also disrespectful for what could actually be accomplished, if we weren't really committed to it at the most senior levels of the firm." But he and VK were now believers, and they were willing to provide the commitment that Gorham deemed necessary. Soon enough, Gorham and Evans had their formal mandate for change.

The next step was to create buy-in among the solid-line leadership of different product teams that could be counted on—for this the Executive Committee turned to Van Dusen and Ege, among others, who were established managing directors from parallel functional silos in Eastdil Secured.

Unlike the hesitation that was seen in the case of Jim Hardy's peer divisions at Under Armour, or Matt Singleton's attempts to prompt

OMES's directors to participate in their O&I, Eastdil's solid-line leadership bought in enthusiastically to Gorham's and Evans's overtures. Fortunately, they too had noticed the impact of the informational bottlenecks among their silos.

With this buy-in, Eastdil Secured went about taking tangible steps to interconnect its teams.

This began with heavily investing in the creation of multiple video teleconferencing (VTC) forums, all set on a specific cadence—these ranged from the biweekly, company-spanning, mass-attended Market Intelligence Call to smaller-scale forums that certain product groups would undertake on a more frequent operating rhythm (exemplified by the office asset class group's dramatically dubbed "SWAT" call). The MIC in particular ensured that scattered teams now could be familiarized with one another, establish better lines of communication, and be better exposed firsthand to the strategy of Eastdil Secured's strategic leadership.

As discussed earlier, technology is certainly of *some* utility in creating dotted-line relationships among teams—it certainly was in Eastdil Secured's case, and proved to be necessary for their change. Van Dusen, as the designated controller for some MIC forums, saw firsthand how these technological "mechanisms" eventually "allowed [for] . . . *familiarity* between . . . the people on our team in Atlanta, in New York, in Boston, and so on."

VK somewhat agrees, characterizing these forums as critical for expanding the range of Eastdil Secured's strategic thinking: "Installing the [MIC] system was a game changer for getting buy-in from our lower levels. The senior guys had always got lots of exposure from the top leadership of this firm, but the VTC in the MIC allowed some of our younger people to be engaged more directly, [get] more involved, and allowed them to be showcased earlier."

But with familiarity and connection initially made possible through this interconnecting technology, how might this opportunity for collaboration be best exploited by participants? If the desired outcome was for strategically minded, organic information sharing to happen freely among teams, without the intervention of senior leadership, then that desire had to be demonstrated.

VK continues, "What I think impacted us the most was discovering that the technology in and of itself was not what was necessary to create the change." Instead, the solution would lie in changing "the behavioral aspects" of the broader organization.

March agrees, touching on an expectation that seemed to exist among Eastdil Secured's ranks: "Most of our people were waiting for some big technological breakthrough at the firm level, that would ultimately infuse a sharing of information" across the teams. But gradually, they realized a technological silver bullet to solve the firm's challenges just didn't exist—it had to be complemented by an elite human element.

So Gorham and Evans decided to use specially selected *liaisons* from across the company's functional teams to populate the content of MICs and be physically emplaced within different product groups in the company. The first "tranche" of liaisons was handpicked by March and VK, with the input of the various product group leaders, such as Ege and Van Dusen, who had to decide what qualities to select for in these individuals.

Ege had a clear picture in his head of what type of thinkers, and individuals, Eastdil Secured needed as liaisons: "Sometimes we get a little bit too nerdy in this office—we're a very quant-centric business, by definition." What Ege thought was missing among this habit of "nerdy" thinking was a widespread consideration of the "so what?" to contextualize and make relevant and actionable the traditional number crunching that had driven the firm's earlier attempts at promoting tactical information exchange.

This type of thinking would then be broadcast through the various forums and technological investments that Eastdil Secured had made in this effort. Ege: "We needed someone to answer these kinds of questions for us: *What do these rental rates* mean? *How does this exit-pricing trend influence the projected total return for a separate project? How can one team's experiences in a market inform another one down the road, in another region?* We had to get into these granular ideas of how you use the data, and then apply it to market opportunities."

Ege's framing was the idea that a qualitative connecting of the dots among different teams was needed and would be prompted, through social learning, by the initial demonstration of this behavior by liaisons. Liaisons would be selected based on their perceived capacity to think strategically and qualitatively about market data, with the intention that they'd promote similar behavior across all of Eastdil Secured's teams, as boundary spanners.

Eastdil Secured's creation of a defined liaison role—an individual *formally* designated to build *informal* relationships—and their tapping of trusted individuals to fill this first tranche ensured a sound approach to creating these relationships.

Theodore and Heng would both end up being among this first tranche of liaisons, and experience would prove a powerful teacher regarding their ability to analyze data that they perceived in one market and publicly apply it to another during discussions on the MIC forums.

Naturally, there was a learning curve associated with this. Theodore's initial experiences as a liaison leading presentations on the MIC and interoffice forums were trying: he found "being the arbiter of all retail data," to put it mildly, very "enlightening." For the first time, he and other participants could clearly "see the way other teams were operating their day-to-day business and the way they were using data, and interpreting it, and recording it."

Mistakes were also common. Theodore says: "There were one or two MICs where I just wasn't ready to present . . . but it only took one time being on camera and flustered in front of two hundred of my colleagues to appreciate the value of preparation." Liaisons soon learned to exchange best practices among themselves, as they became progressively better at filling the role Gorham and Evans had first envisioned them occupying.

Per Theodore: "It's funny, because if you looked at the sixth or eighth MIC presentation by some of us, you'd see a lot of similarities in the way content was presented, and the formatting of different slides from each team." Noting what format of presentations and discussions worked best within the context of MIC forums allowed this new network across Eastdil Secured's functional groups to develop methods by which to best disseminate market intelligence across teams.

What helped Theodore and other liaisons during this learning period was the use of "dress rehearsal calls" for forums and honest off-line dialogue with other liaisons in their own clustered network. As he puts it, "amongst the liaisons, we were our own little sort of team of teams."

This also applied when it was time for a new tranche to take over—Theodore remembers engaging heavily with "Shannon and Kerry—the newly appointed liaisons on the retail team" ahead of the handoff to them and advising them on everything from how to collect data to how to interpret it, while providing them with some of the resources he had used to come up with ideas to present.

The normal length of a tranche deployment for Eastdil Secured liaisons was set at nine months, although there have subsequently been exceptions to that rule—as of late 2016, a third tranche has taken up the mantle, yet Heng still remains—a veteran but infrequent hand in the liaison program, happy to pitch in on the occasional presentation on a MIC forum, but a less frequent contributor than the newer arrivals.

THE OUTCOMES

On a recent visit I paid to Eastdil Secured's central D.C. office, I asked Ege what he thought were the critical takeaways from his company's experiences in reforming its bureaucracy: "What were really the key few difference-making aspects of what the company had done, when distilled to bare elements? What had made it all come together so far?"

Looking around, the office he shared with a good few dozen other employees didn't seem out of the ordinary to the untrained eye. We were surrounded by glass cubicles ringed by a perimeter of corner offices, while live market graphs and TV screens showing Bloomberg tiled the office's pillars and walls—a typical setup for a financial services firm.

Ege took his time thinking through what I had asked, and his response to my question was twofold: "The number one thing that was taught was that we (our teams) didn't need to see the senior people speaking on our forums. We wanted these liaisons to take on this level of accountability and leadership. They were playing a meaningful role in the firm that ultimately would be some sort of legacy planning."

By empowering the firm's various tranches of liaisons to consider their teams' market data on a strategic, qualitative plane of thought, and applying that perspective across different teams, the company was sowing future leadership of the company as shared consciousness was being developed. It was these types of individuals, employees that could think on strategic qualitative planes, who were best positioned to benefit from more exposure on MIC forums.

"Second," Ege went on, "we're retraining our habits—once we've ingrained this type of communication, this information sharing, these networks as not just tasks but habits, then it becomes unstoppable."

He pulled up a slide on a laptop perched on his standing desk—part of a PowerPoint presentation that had been featured in a recent SWAT forum with Eastdil's Office group. On one side it showed the front page of Charles Duhigg's 2012 best seller *The Power of Habit*. On the other it showed a formal definition of "habit," likely taken from the book: "an acquired behavior pattern, regularly followed until it becomes involuntary."

Ege looked over at me. "That's what we've learned to hit with our liaisons—the whole concept of doing, demonstrating, and reinforcing something done right, so often that it becomes subliminal and timeless." This development of a "habit" has facilitated the scaling of Eastdil Secured's original culture.

Heng sees the efforts of Eastdil Secured to become a "team of teams" as a building-upon of the culture that existed in the company beforehand. "Eastdil's always been a type of team of teams—historically flat, with easy access to leadership, but what things like the MIC call and liaisons did was provide a *structure* to extend and expand that around the company."

She is right—using these practices in conjunction with one another, their mutual effect can be complemented and augmented. Noting that the original strategic culture of the firm—one focused on easy information sharing and closeness among leaders—has been expanded through the use of liaisons and forums reinforces a central point of these practices.

Still, enough time and practice have passed that constructive critiques of Eastdil's approach to connecting its teams through this "structure" have emerged from a variety of sources—while a greater number of the company's teams now are working together and sharing intelligence, certain liaisons and officers have started to recognize just how much work it is to maintain the momentum that has been built.

The general theme of this constructive feedback is that the current cadences of market calls and the work required of liaisons to identify these qualitative trends across quantitative data are highly demanding. Unlike pure number crunching for a single team, strategic-level qualitative analysis of market trends is uniquely time-consuming and stressful for the liaisons.

Says Theodore: "The challenge of one person trying to come up with fresh content and independent research every other week—that was hard." During the first tranche of liaisons, every product group had one liaison in charge of presenting for that team every other week—this has since changed, with up to four liaisons now being nominated by each product group. But Heng and Van Dusen also acknowledge that the cadence and manual preparation of the data may need some adjusting.

Leaving Ege's office, I asked him for an example of what the "acquired habit" he thought had been created in Eastdil might look like.

In response, he pointed over to a glass-windowed conference room right next to his office—I peered in and saw a smattering of men and women gathered around a central oval table, talking with one another while one drew up notes on a whiteboard. "Those are representatives from our local multifamily team, our office team, the hotel team, and the retail one, plus all of their liaisons, all volunteering to brainstorm the redevelopment of a hotel site here in the city.

"I was just in there before you came in—they're talking through best practices used by other teams in the past, how the lead team should approach this, using all of the intellect and power of everyone in that room . . . but if you had been here a year ago, the only people in there would be the lead team."

What Ege was describing was what I had seen so long ago, back in the Task Force—networks interacting organically among functional silos, free from excess reliance on senior bureaucratic leadership to facilitate information flow.

Speaking with other figures in the firm, a more dramatic example emerged of how Eastdil's liaison networks, combined with MIC forums, had helped the firm adapt to external conditions or new danger in its external environment: the firm's response to Britain's referendum to exit the European Union, an event that created what March referred to as "perfect storm conditions" in international financial markets and confusion among clients.

As previously noted, in the lead-up to June 2016, scientific polling indicated that Britons would decisively vote to remain a part of the European Union. But to the shock of pollsters, politicians, and economists, voters elected to leave. Markets crashed, currencies showed dramatic fluctuation, and clients were left confused and uncertain of the safety or future of their investments.

March categorizes this event as just one of a broader tapestry of market-shifting developments that year, saying that "you could probably title 2016 as a year of surprises—the oil price collapse, simultaneous with the sell-off of the Chinese stock market had equally dramatic effect. . . . Brexit and our own [U.S.] election all had incalculable outcomes that forced us to move quickly." These global disruptions made investors nervous, and they wanted answers quickly about how Eastdil Secured was approaching the turbulence.

The temptation for many organizations in this type of environment would be to speculate, but that was not the case for Eastdil Secured—per March: "The liaison network and MIC allowed us to move immediately and be the 'steady hand on the tiller' for our industry."

The outcome of having a liaison network in the midst of multiple crises was "shared intelligence, not speculation." Much like the Task Force's approach at the peak of its operation, a disciplined approach to information sharing, decision making, and cross-boundary connectivity during normal times allowed them to weather these storms with calm and discipline. As disruption emerged around the globe, a traditional organization would have scrambled to connect teams and patch together solutions in the moment. But Eastdil had built this muscle preemptively, so global synchronization was not a new behavior for it. Hearing directly from senior leadership did not mean it was time to panic, just business as usual. Sharing insights and trusting the views of your teammates around the world was an established behavior, not unfamiliar territory. Where many organizations might have been caught in a frantic mode of putting out seemingly endless fires, Eastdil maintained a long-term and steady view on the market, a perspective not lost on its clients.

Sounds like a pretty good habit to maintain.

CONCLUSION

During my visit to MNC-I's large Baghdad headquarters, I waited in a cubicle as McChrystal, with our Task Force liaison leading the way, briefed several of his peers behind closed doors.

Per standard practice, I remotely accessed our classified portal to check on the current state of our organization's operations and to quickly gain awareness of any issues that might have arisen since our departure. As soon as I went online, I received a quick chat-room note that requested we return to Balad.

Though the organization was in a phase of empowered execution, there was a highly nonstandard contingency arising.

A specific high-value target ("Objective Raven") had been spotted—an X_1 moment. He was a key node in Al Qaeda's global network, and this rare opportunity to remove him from its ranks would be fleeting. There was no time to waste, and our commanding general would need to oversee the operation that would follow, as addressing this development would cross geographic boundaries, require coordination with multiple agencies, and necessitate the leveraging of well-cultivated partnerships with external organizations.

I unplugged my Toughbook and jogged down the palace's marble hallways toward the meeting location. By the time I got there, the meeting had finished, and various generals and senior civilian leaders from multiple agencies were already flowing out of the room. McChrystal caught my eye and knew that I had something time sensitive to report.

After a quick update, we turned for the exit. During our brisk walk, I explained to him that the rest of the meetings we'd had planned for that

day had been notified of our change and that our helicopters were spin-
ning up for a rapid return to Balad.

The flight back was uneventful—a temporary respite as we flew low
over the blackened desert until the faintly shimmering lights of our compound became visible on the horizon. Our helicopters landed just fifty
meters from the unassuming back fence of our compound. Jogging ahead,
I opened the cipher-lock gate and held it for McChrystal and the rest of
our team as they entered the interior of our headquarters.

When we finally walked into the Balad SAR, the room was more
abuzz than normal. On the twelve screens at the front of the room, the
normal feeds of current operations in Iraq and Afghanistan had been replaced by ones showing individuals from various Task Force and external
partner bases around the world—displays similar to what we'd see during
our O&I forums.

"What's the current situation on the ground?" came a voice from a
civilian headquarters in the United States.

Looking up at one of the screens arrayed in front of the Task Force's
leadership in the Balad SAR, I could see a female analyst in plain clothes
staring back.

As was the case with presenters in our O&I forum, we in Balad weren't
her only audience—when she spoke, the analyst was interacting virtually
with an audience of hundreds of critical personnel, located in dozens of
rooms around the world and scattered across once-impermeable tribal
boundaries. That she was in a civilian headquarters somewhere along the
eastern seaboard was no longer a limiting factor to her being a present,
integrated, and trusted member of our global team.

She spoke up again: "I'm asking because we've just received some
new intelligence that seems to contradict the update given at the top of
the hour." This got everyone's attention.

"What are you seeing, Karen?" an intelligence officer in our SAR
replied. "Bob, are you and your team getting this?"

As senior intelligence analysts gathered around the Balad SAR's table, we waited for Bob and his staff to do the same in their small headquarters on the other side of the world—from where they were expecting
to oversee the operation.

Bob, not unlike a liaison officer who might be assigned to a critical
spot in Baghdad or Kabul, had an exceptional reputation as a tactical
leader. For his reward, he had not been asked to assume a conventional

role but was tasked to change out of his body armor and deploy to the far edges of the Task Force. His new unit was a collection of similarly qualified individuals, an ensemble of talent from varied units—civilian and military—now deployed as a unified team.

They would be controlling the tactical side of this operation, and this update from Karen might impact their next moves.

"Hey, Bob here . . ." In front of us, another screen went live. Through the crackling, tenuous display, we could all see a picture of Bob's sparse headquarters, his picture less clear due to the weaker bandwidth at his location.

From back in the United States, Karen further explained her update: "I just got some intel that at 1700 Zulu, the target was identified leaving an apartment complex downtown. Our previous understanding was that we had him pinpointed at his safe house outside the city at that same time. Only one of these can be correct. We're trying to deconflict the reporting now."

This was a problem—apparently the target was in two places at once, if both of these reports were to be believed. Contradictory intelligence like this would, per standard practice in this field, be reason to abort the operation.

This cancellation would be hugely inconvenient and come at great opportunity cost: wheels were already in motion at multiple levels; credibility with a suite of partners was in the crosshairs. Support systems and additional resources were now being maneuvered across the Task Force's multiple theaters of operation. Strategic leadership from an array of outside national security organizations had already assembled to oversee the execution of this mission.

These types of dilemmas are common in most industries—the aching choice of whether to pull the plug on an existing initiative, once new information comes to light that challenges its likelihood of success.

If the mission was executed and the house was empty, Objective Raven would go back underground, finding a new hiding place within our opaque environment and evading apprehension. Our organization's credibility would take a blow, affecting not just Bob's team, but the success of future efforts around the world.

McChrystal spoke up. "Bob, can you hold everything in position?"

"Yes, sir. We can hold in place for forty-five minutes, but no longer." Bob had a complex situation on his end to monitor—too long a list of nuances to verbally inform everyone in Balad and around the world. Everyone on the line trusted his judgment. If he said forty-five minutes, then that was the time line our teams had to work within. Every second spent checking Bob's math would be a second not spent solving the problem facing our entire network.

VOICING CONCERNS

Had our organization been a traditional hierarchy, the analyst who raised this new, conflicting intelligence would not have had direct access to our organization's senior leadership and decision-making apparatus in order to voice her concern.

Moreover, even if she had, the behavioral norms in a bureaucratic system would have incentivized her to keep her head down—a feeling we can all instinctively identify with. Karen would have been incentivized to seek out her direct supervisor, then rely on his capacity as an information pump to "own" the update for her, rather than risk appearing to go over anyone's head.

From there, maybe her boss would have decided to bring it up one more level, or to instead sit on the information. This boss might have reflected: *Isn't this contradictory to our thinking? Won't our leadership get frustrated with a last-minute injection like this? Is it worth the disruption?*

Human nature takes hold in these situations, and bureaucratic self-preservation instincts too easily win out. This is for good, psychologically grounded reasons—taking an action route that enables an individual to avoid *owning* an outcome is quite a relieving feeling, and thus is an easy temptation to give in to.

Though moral hazard is commonly associated with decision making in the financial or insurance worlds, having been breathlessly described by economist Lawrence Summers as "central to every policy discussion in response to the financial crisis," it is actually endemic to the general handling of information in any large organization, no matter the industry.

A savvy bureaucrat will know how to play this game: how to e-mail new, possibly disruptive information to a wide array of folks they're connected to via the solid-line hierarchy, knowing that the ten people on the ever-handy "cc" line are likely overwhelmed by information requests at the moment but, having received this e-mail, will have to share "ownership" if something does go wrong.

Well, this manager would think, *I've received contradictory intelligence from Karen and forwarded it along to everyone who needs to see it. If it's correct and they don't stop the operation, then I'm covered because I sent them the data. If they cancel the operation but the new intelligence is still proven wrong, well . . . I didn't recommend they stop the mission; I just sent along the new intelligence.* This would be a safe and understandable play.

Not only do bureaucratic models enable this type of default behavior, but their impermeability can passively encourage it among even those who would otherwise *try* to share information. The real-world penalties in this type of culture can be tragic, as management professor Amy Edmondson recalled in her 2012 book *Teaming* when detailing the aftermath of the 2003 *Columbia* space shuttle disaster:

> The next day, shuttle engineer Rodney Rocha reviewed a video of the launch and became deeply concerned about the size and position of a chunk of insulating foam that appeared to have . . . struck its left wing. . . . To determine whether damage had occurred, Rocha hoped to obtain photographic images of the shuttle's wing from spy satellites.

Rocha's initial attempts failed to gain traction past his immediate superior, and he was "discouraged by his earlier efforts to call attention to the . . . issue, and convinced that voicing concerns was career limiting." Rocha decided to keep quiet in the larger team meetings, a fault of the organizational structure of which he was a part.

This failure to share information, due to a lack of what Edmondson calls "psychological safety," contributed to the deaths of all seven *Columbia* crew members as their aircraft burned up upon reentering Earth's atmosphere. The nonlinear outcomes of poor behavioral norms, which an organization's leadership methodology can influence, are striking in a life-and-death environment.

Though the potential consequences to other organizations of accepting this moral hazard may be less dramatic, creating an environment where relatively low-ranking individuals like Karen feel safe speaking to multiple levels of leadership in open settings is critical in a complex world. Psychological safety, described by Edmondson, is a "climate in which people are free to express relevant thoughts and feelings . . . that produces a sense of confidence that the group won't embarrass, reject, or punish someone for speaking up." It does not mean that everyone will agree or be friends or that such an environment organically exists without the active efforts of strategic leaders in the system. Rather, it acknowledges the need for individuals to feel safe contributing in a constantly changing situation where there is an inherent risk of imperfection.

Achieving this state requires a deliberate and consistent communication of an aligning narrative that emphasizes trust and transparency, as well as public displays of these actions by others—the more senior the better. You've likely seen this type of social learning in small, high-performing teams, but it's a rare behavioral attribute to replicate on an organization-wide scale.

Creating the environment for this type of behavior requires consistent access to an inclusive communication process, a regular resynchronization on the overarching mission of the organization, and confidence among the members that senior leaders are willing to accept transparency and debate.

When our analyst, Karen, turned on her microphone to address our various teams, several things were taking place. She was leveraging a global communication infrastructure that had taken years to build, she was accessing the collective expertise of a globally distributed team, and she was demonstrating trust in a culture of transparency that was protected and reinforced every day by our senior leaders.

There's a constant reminder in the special operations community that you need to "build relationships before the firefight." Similarly, an organization cannot *suddenly* connect hundreds of teams around the globe without creating some level of chaos and countering traditional norms. Contributors will not *suddenly* feel safe speaking in a transparent fashion without prior conditioning. In Karen's case, years of disciplined management of our team of teams model ensured that she had the space to be transparent with the organization.

The end result was that our analyst had the psychological safety to know that the response from a three-star general wouldn't be *Who the hell are you, and what makes you think you can talk to me?*

She could interject, prevent a major error, and be rewarded for the behavior. She would encounter a leadership team that trusted her competence and assumed her positive intent. And most important, the response wouldn't be a condescending *pat on the head*. The organization would react to this new intelligence, sending a message to others watching that Karen's behavior was exactly what made us a unique organization.

RESPONSE

"Okay, everyone on the net—we need your full attention here." The Task Force had to pivot to react to Karen's new information, so our senior intelligence officer in Balad—a member of our strategic leadership team—took center stage.

"Let me summarize what I'm hearing, and correct me if this is off. Based on what we just heard from Karen, we can't be one hundred percent sure of our target's current location. We're ready to launch on Bob's end, but he will not initiate the operation until we can confirm or deny what we've just heard. Based on the time line we've heard from Bob's team on the ground, we have forty-five minutes to sort this out, or we will need to abort. Karen, we're now waiting to hear from you and your folks."

He finished with a question: "Does anyone think I've missed anything?"

It was this last comment that was probably the most important of everything that had just been said: something had changed, the situation was fluid, and our strategic leadership had just given everyone a new baseline of where things stood.

But in the end, this was just one senior leader's interpretation of events. This situation was like a constantly shifting Rubik's Cube, and our leadership needed viewpoints from every angle to get an accurate picture. Asking the group for counter-interpretations was a critical step in preventing groupthink, and it taught every member of the team to be willing to engage the rest of the organization with new information if they had it.

This time everybody was in agreement as to how this new intel changed what we had to do as an organization. Bob gave a thumbs-up into the camera, acknowledging his understanding, and we could see his team continuing to move quickly in the background of his video feed.

McChrystal spoke for the first time since our return, directly to the young analyst who had first identified the contradictory intelligence,

"Karen, great work. Please get the report up on the portal so everyone can take a look. All outstations, please have someone give it a quick read so we're all seeing the same information."

From there, discussions went on around the room and around the world: senior interagency liaison officers informed key players who would need to be aware of the potential of aborting the mission. From Iraq to Washington, D.C., Europe to North Africa, rooms went into an immediate buzz of motion, phone calls, and e-mails as members of our networks reached out to their dotted-line contacts and partners.

Seated in the back row of the SAR, I was playing whatever small part I could to help facilitate these efforts, keeping tabs on who had yet to be informed of this update and whether new intelligence was coming in, and chatting directly with folks I knew on Bob's team to see whether they needed any support.

To an outsider it might have looked like chaos, or perhaps just another busy day of war. To an insider it was instead the image of a well-functioning ecosystem, purpose-built to enable the productive collaboration of once-stand-alone specialists and units—with the end result of rapid adaptability.

Sitting in the Balad SAR during those late hours, I watched as a senior analyst with the FBI reached out to personal contacts in his organization, trying to summon new intelligence that might clarify the situation; as our State Department liaison connected with the local U.S. embassy team and ensured that the ambassador was aware of the current state of the operation; as myriad groups that often lived in natural competition with one another instead cooperated as fluidly as any sixteen-member platoon I'd ever been a part of.

But this team of teams, as opposed to the small tactical units where I'd seen this behavior in the past, was positioned to reach, inform, and influence national leadership—not simply by breaking down bureaucratic silos but rather by demonstrating that there was an entirely new, interpersonal method to approach this type of conflict.

"Thirty minutes down. Our assets are only good for another fifteen," Bob piped up on the net, as a reminder to everyone listening that we were running out of time.

A phone in the SAR slammed down. A senior interagency partner turned on his microphone and spoke to our global network.

"Team, just spoke with an agent familiar with the mission. Our target has a cousin who is often mistaken for his twin. He's sending me a picture right now of the cousin—he was in police custody last summer. Karen, I'm having it forwarded to you. Can you show the picture to your source? The cousin is heavier-set than our objective and has a distinct burn on his left side and face. Maybe it was the cousin that was spotted downtown."

Seconds mattered: our assets would be shutting down in just over ten minutes, and our window would be lost. The picture of the cousin, potentially the cause of the confusion, bounced around the world. From the United States to Iraq to Karen's inbox to intelligence officers on the ground nearest to the objective, this new information was shared rapidly.

Everyone waited. Assets were held in position. We counted down.

Four minutes were left before our window would close and the mission would have to be canceled. I watched as the room, typically abuzz with background motion and noise, went into an eerie calm.

"Okay, just back in from our source." Karen had come back online. "That's who he saw downtown. Source positively identified the cousin as the individual he spotted downtown. No contradictory intelligence."

"Great work, everybody," came McChrystal's voice in Iraq. "Bob, you're cleared hot."

The mission was a go. Hundreds of people around the world had synchronized around new information, in real time, and solved a complex issue. A potential reason to abort had been identified, analyzed, and disproven. Karen, a young analyst, had done the right thing, networks around the world had reacted, and Bob's operation was a go.

The mission would succeed. A few hours later, the enemy network would be weaker than it had been the day before—a critical node would have been removed—and it was made possible only through our hybrid model functioning at peak.

Earlier we considered Donald Sull and Kathleen Eisenhardt's *Simple Rules*, which recommends battling complexity with simplicity. Human nature tends to pull us in the opposite direction, adding complexity to complexity, and soon the way that an organization functions is just as difficult to understand as the world it is interacting with. You've likely felt this throughout your career.

Reflecting on the major components of the team of teams model that we've discussed to this point, one final look at how we can combine them into a single *simple* model will serve us well. This is intended to combine the key levers that are at your disposal to find the right balance between

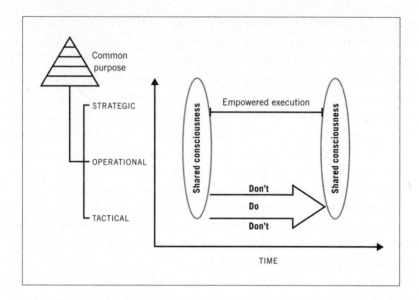

speed, decentralization, and risk—knowing, of course, that the levers to control or loosen can be adjusted as makes sense for you, your leadership team, and your organization.

First, creation of the aligning narrative establishes the organization's focus. A sufficiently powerful narrative will break down the tribal barriers that exist in a large enterprise.

Armed with a *one mission* focus, you are ready to thoughtfully consider the tempo of your environment and structure your operating rhythm accordingly. In the Task Force, our leadership discovered that this needed to be a daily cadence, as that was the speed with which Al Qaeda was changing. The rhythm that is right for your organization should be based on the environment around you; but know that a truly adaptable organization must consistently realign (reestablish *shared consciousness*) as fast as or faster than the problems it is facing.

This cadence, your operating rhythm, becomes the first of your two major levers for controlling risk. Extending or reducing the time between periods of shared consciousness allows you to control the windows of *empowered execution*. During those windows of empowered execution, *decision space* is a simple-rule approach to establishing boundaries for what your teams *can* and *cannot* do.

A simple model, these practices allow you to tell your organization, *Things are changing [this fast]. Therefore, we'll realign ourselves [this often]. Between realignments, do [this] with speed and autonomy, and don't do [this] without asking permission. When we resynchronize, be honest and transparent about what you've learned.*

In a highly complex environment, the Task Force maintained a disciplined, consistent, and easily understandable model to address the constant change that surrounded us. There is beauty and power in simplicity.

HEROES AND LEADERS IN NARRATIVES

Complex missions like the ones we've featured in this book—in both military and civilian contexts—succeed when great teams interconnect with a powerful, one mission focus. The practices and behaviors that this book has detailed make this possible.

But there is one final and important point to consider, and that is how an organization's senior leadership should perceive their role in this type of model. As silo-spanning, dotted-line networks begin to complement and relieve pressure on an organization's solid-line bureaucracy, what temptations and norms will leaders need to fight off for the good of their newly empowered teams?

Throughout the first several decades of the twentieth century, Swiss psychiatrist Carl Jung put forward the strange idea of the *archetype*. An extension of Jung's broader framing of a "collective unconscious" that exists among humans, archetypes are "universal images that have existed since the remotest of times." These are concepts "inborn" to all people, which hold inalienable definitions that we all seem to grasp intuitively from our birth, and which remain ingrained in each of our minds.

Though Jung's larger concepts are (to say the least) eccentric, a generalized take on his theory of archetypes may explain why "Great Man"–esque understandings of successful leadership are so resilient in pop culture. When we think of "leaders," per Jung, our instinct to credit them as commanding, self-reliant, omnipotent figures (like Genghis Khan, Margaret Thatcher, or Rupert Murdoch) is an extension of a universal archetype we hold for what leadership *should* look like.

The power of this instinct is reflected in both legend and reality. From Homer's characterization of Odysseus and Tolkien's of Aragorn to continued idolization of real-life figures like America's George Washington, General Electric's Jack Welch, Apple's Steve Jobs, and Alibaba's Jack Ma, there is a stubborn tendency from the outside to wholly credit the genius or special gifts of an individual figurehead-type leader with an entire institution's success.

There are cases in history that might warrant this type of surface-level description; but this line of thinking risks overlooking the significance of the grander processes these leaders created and benefited from. Great teams, great culture, and great discipline will all be the dominant forces moving forward. Any leader trying to fight these twenty-first-century organizations from a lone hilltop will quickly perish in an effort to hold on to norms of the past.

When I left my position as McChrystal's aide-de-camp, I enrolled directly in the Naval Postgraduate School in Monterey, California, to pursue my master's degree in irregular warfare. Once there, surrounded on the Pacific coast by peers from different pockets of the special operations community, I found myself regularly answering questions that mistakenly framed our organization's successes around McChrystal and a few of his better-known senior team members. Their comments from a perspective outside the system suggested a belief in myth, in leaders who had somehow surpassed human limitations, who could do things that others couldn't. My answers, knowing the organization from the inside, were based in reality.

How does he get by on four hours of sleep? (Answer: stress and adrenaline are terrific stimulants.)

How can he eat only one meal a day? (Answer: he has a weird metabolism.)

How does he remember everything and know everyone's name? (Answer: he reads his briefing books and listens when people introduce themselves.)

The list of what I was asked could go on, but the underlying assumption of these questions was always the same: that our organization's success was due to an invulnerable leader who single-handedly directed the organization from atop our bureaucratic org chart.

It's important to not misconstrue my thinking here. The Task Force's operational improvement was certainly due to McChrystal's initial vision, his willingness to take the personal risk of driving change, and his initiation of a top-down move to redefine our processes and behaviors. But attributing the success of these practices to the singular presence of a commanding strategic leader overlooks what our other leaders had done, and is a lazy approach. The heroic-leader myth ignores the truly hard work that makes systems like this function. It ignores how our leadership had empowered and interconnected younger teams and leaders; how they'd pulled diverse voices and perspectives into the conversation; and how they'd modeled a humility-based leadership archetype for the rest of us to embrace. These were not leaders on a hilltop, but servants to the mission.

In honestly answering these questions from my peers, instead of catering to their preconceived notion of a heroic, all-knowing leader, I would tell them about a very mortal *human* who was willing to demonstrate behavioral standards and facilitate the interaction of teams rather than pretending to know all answers to their many problem sets.

In short, our leaders did things that many of us could, provided we are willing to humble ourselves to the insights of others, have deep respect for the complexity of the fight, and work harder than most. These are actions that any leader can decide to take, but he or she must consciously do so. As I learned early in my career, you're not *made* a leader; you decide to *become* one.

There is nothing simple about that combination; it's certainly attainable, but many still prefer to believe in the myth. In my experience, it's not the leader who places him- or herself in the hero's role who creates a truly adaptable organization. Today's world is far too complex for such an approach. Our best leaders, regardless of rank or position in an organization, must assume the role of the mentor and guide, rather than seek the hero's spotlight.

As you move up and achieve ever-greater success, the world will constantly push you to assume the archetype of a lauded, lone hero. The world will inflate your ego and give you individual credit for battles won by shared effort. Giving in to this temptation will be a detriment to your enterprise.

Today's leaders must clearly and consistently explain to their organization that no single person is truly the stand-alone hero; rather, team members must collectively strive to listen, learn, and share with one another if they hope to navigate the turbulent waters of the twenty-first century. *They* are the ones who must connect to solve problems. *They* are the ones who must assume new and uncomfortable levels of empowerment and accountability. As an interconnected team of teams, *they* are the organization's secret to overcoming its greatest challenges.

An executive leader can build and sustain the means for teams to act upon their own problem sets, shepherd the organization in the right direction, and protect its members from outside forces. But ultimately, success and failure will depend on the tactical and operational members of the enterprise—a truly humble leader will watch their capabilities emerge, resist calls to take credit for them, and publicly acknowledge that the newfound capacity of the organization's systems is far greater than anything one person or team could ever hope to produce.

Today's best leaders are those willing to say to their organization:

> *I understand the complexity of the environment. I understand that you must move faster than our structures allow for and that you understand your problems better than I ever could. I will create spaces for you to organically communicate and share information. I will empower you to make decisions and execute. I can help guide us on the path, but only you can win the war. I trust you to do that.*

In response, members of organizations must fulfill their equally important part of the agreement:

> *We understand that you're building us the space to thrive but that it is ultimately our journey to take. We see you humbling yourself to the reality of the complex fight. We trust you to protect our ability to move with speed and adaptability. We will rise to the challenge and hold ourselves accountable to the outcome.*

A team of teams model is exactly that—a model. When executed well, with the correct application and demonstration of behaviors and practice, it is a true differentiator in organizational performance. I've experienced the culture it creates firsthand and have watched others do the same. But, as in any decentralized network, it is ultimately the organic interactions of similarly motivated *people*—individual humans who are willing to discard myopic, unit-centric views on organizational issues and commit to a broader aligning narrative—that make its practices produce value and unleash a massive competitive advantage.

Aligning teams, communicating with transparency, decentralizing decision making—these stand-alone concepts aren't new. But if organizations are willing to truly embody them together, linchpinned by leaders who can assume humble, nonheroic roles and individual team members who embrace new realms of responsibility, they will set the standard for effective enterprise in the years to come.

If you wish to prompt your organization to pursue this state, I wish you luck on this path and hope that this book will prove a resource to you as you move ahead. After more than a decade of observing the battlefield and a wide range of industries, I have no doubt that driving this change is a critical calling of today's leaders.

Those who survive this transition into the information age will set the standard for decades to come, and those who hold tightly to their twentieth-century playbook will be a footnote of history.

APPENDIX: CHIEF OF STAFF

In 2007, on a cold and windy March afternoon, I crossed an open field at the National Defense University (NDU) in Washington, D.C. I was there to interview for an aide-de-camp job under then–Lieutenant General McChrystal, who had given a brief lecture to the students while home from Iraq for thirty-six hours.

NDU was founded after World War II in order to create cross-functional relationships among our various services, an ability I'd have to demonstrate should I get this job. As a result, the location was more fitting than I appreciated at the time, given the year ahead of me and the lessons it would hold about overcoming tribal barriers. The university's brick buildings, set along the Potomac River, had a stately appearance, and I was anxious about the interview.

At the end of our relatively straightforward discussion, McChrystal had asked me simply, "Do you want this job?" Of course, any interviewee should see questions like this coming, but I hadn't expected it to be put to me so bluntly. Frankly, it had never crossed my mind that a three-star general would be interested in what I did or didn't *want* to do.

My response to this question was as honest as it could be, and I made sure to not be disrespectful to his current staff officers, one of whom sat in the room with us.

"Sir, I don't think anyone in our community dreams of being an aide, and it's certainly never a position that I've sought." I paused. "That said, I've felt something change in our organization over the past few years— we're running differently, and better. An opportunity to see behind the curtain and understand how this is working . . . Well, that's fascinating to me."

McChrystal's face was blank, unreadable, and I assumed that he might have found my answer weird. Maybe, I thought, I was totally wrong: maybe there weren't any new practices to be understood but rather just a fortunate distribution of leaders who were responsible for our improvement. If this was indeed the case, then my answer had probably seemed nonsensical.

McChrystal and I talked about that interview a few years later, and he remembered that answer, saying it "was the moment I decided to bring you onto our staff." I hadn't known at the time how passionate the Task Force's leadership team were about the unifying practices they'd put in place, and the fact that I'd expressed interest in seeing things up close, he told me, sealed my fate.

One week later, after an all-too-short discussion with my wife explaining the significance of this opportunity (which would in reality be a one-year deployment away from my family), I was notified that the job was mine. After this was announced to my solid-line leadership, I received a simple one-line e-mail from the commander of my SEAL team: "Welcome to the show . . ."

Since leaving the military in 2012, I have noted an ever-increasing interest in the chief of staff (CoS) function within various parts of private-sector industry. My formal title for McChrystal was "aide-de-camp," but the functions the job would entail were akin to those of the current chiefs of staff whom I've interacted with in the corporate world.

The aide-de-camp position has a long history within the military—an early example of this in the American armed forces was between Founding Fathers George Washington and Alexander Hamilton. Aides are historically used for a wide range of work, and the experiences of any one aide are unique to the command they are assigned to and, more important, the individual officer they are working for. On both of these fronts, I was incredibly fortunate.

In Iraq, I was observing an extremely prominent general lead a wartime counterterrorism organization during a period of peak need—which resulted in my taking on unusual functions for an aide. As I've discussed throughout this book, McChrystal allowed me and other staff to be exposed to strategic discussions, to sit through key interactions, and to be granted broad access to the clear majority of information crossing his desk. We were limited less by our rank, and more by our personal judgment—and with that level of empowerment came high expectations.

Members of McChrystal's immediate staff were expected to listen, think, connect dots, and drive actions in line with the same level of empowered execution that was taking place within the battlefield units. We were his filters against complexity, expected to act when appropriate, or deliver clear and well-framed information to our organization's senior leadership when the situation demanded.

The titles might be different, but the functions that I and other staff members filled were akin to some of the best practices I've seen in the CoS role in civilian contexts. In the best examples I've seen among aides within private industry, C-suite executives leverage their staff in a similar fashion to what was practiced in the Task Force. I've seen an exceptionally wide range in how these staff positions are leveraged by senior leaders in industry, sometimes within the same organization.

In an organization with a confused approach to developing their chiefs of staff, one CoS might be focused on transactional efforts, such as scheduling or briefing books; another might focus more heavily on daily administration, removing smaller tasks from the executive's daily responsibilities; whereas a third might be acting as a strategic adviser, helping a CEO think through the next quarterly report or a pending merger. Each of these can be critical jobs, but in my experience, most senior leaders with a CoS hope for a different vision of this role, but leave the desired outcome of getting there to chance.

If you're a newly appointed CoS or, perhaps even more critically, a senior executive who is trying to best utilize a CoS position on your team, the following model may be a helpful guide.

It is broken into four quadrants, each defining a different phase of a CoS's development into fulfilling the potential of their role. For example, a newly assigned CoS, regardless of experience level, should be expected to start their job in quadrant one, and then develop clockwise through the quadrants presented in the graphic on page 254.

The timeline for that progression will vary depending on the individual and the leadership culture, so some may never reach quadrant four, or may be there only for brief moments in their career.

I define the four quadrants along the lines of what the CoS is expected to accomplish in each phase. They steadily build the scale of their

	EXECUTIVE	ORGANIZATION
	1 *Bridging to the organization* ▶	**2**
EXECUTION	**Primary focus of CoS:** Using tactical decision making to support execution of CEO's initiatives. **Impact on the organization:** Ensuring the effective management of operating rhythm (scheduling, content, pre- and post-planning) to demonstrate value of CoS. **CoS's role in information flow:** The CoS remains in a learning phase, and so should build relationships with different leaders in the organization to study their respective challenges and opportunities. **Communication priority of CoS:** Learning the communication norms of the CEO and trying to anticipate what might be required of the CoS.	**Primary focus of CoS:** Coordinating short, medium, and long-term strategy execution on behalf of the CEO. **Impact on the organization:** Bridging communication gaps between senior leaders, business units, functions, or regions. Starting to demonstrate monetary value of having a dedicated CoS to the rest of the organization's senior leadership. **CoS's role in information flow:** Monitoring, supporting, and indexing information sharing in favor of the CEO's intent. **Communication priority of CoS:** Demonstrating an ability to offer insight into the CEO's perspective, but not speaking on his or her behalf.
PLANNING	**Primary focus of CoS:** Helping manage the CEO's time allocation towards internal and external issues according to an 80/20 rule-of-thumb. In contrast, the CoS should dedicate more time to resolving internal issues. **Impact on the organization:** Working closely with the CEO to ensure his or her strategic vision and intent are properly communicated and effectively measured. **CoS's role in information flow:** Establish and monitor the CEO's critical information requirements. Set the CEO's priorities and allocation of focus based on his or her stated objectives. **Communication priority of CoS:** A CoS should be able to quickly prepare correspondence in the CEO's voice/pen for all audiences, internal and external.	**Primary focus of CoS:** Coordinating short, medium, and long-term strategy planning for the organization. **Impact on the organization:** Managing the strategic planning process in the following ways: 1) Identifying decision opportunities; 2) Determining decision space responsibilities; and 3) Presenting key information to and forcing decisions by CEO. **CoS's role in information flow:** Cascading key decisions after they are made by the organization's senior leadership by: 4) Communicating the decision to the organization; and 5) Monitoring and reporting back on execution/implementation. **Communication priority of CoS:** Communicating to the organization on behalf of the broader executive team and being a definitive voice within it.
	4 ◀ *Becoming a thought partner*	**3**

Optimizing decision making

duties, but the actions detailed in each quadrant are critical to supporting the success of a task-saturated senior executive.

However, a CoS cannot abandon the responsibilities of one quadrant as they move to the next. As the CoS progresses, some of the actions in the previous quadrant(s) may be distributed to other chiefs, or be accomplished organically, but the CoS is still the "owner" of their execution.

Each quadrant has four pieces of subject matter that a CoS *must* focus on and master before effectively executing in the next quadrant. These pertain to how they spend their time, how they engage with the organization, how they impact information flow throughout the executive team and broader enterprise, and the role they play in communications coming out of the executive's office.

Primary focus of CoS relates to the CoS's own expenditure of time; what aspects of work should take up their day. *Intended impact on the organization* considers what the CoS's role should be in the eyes of others within the enterprise; this will prove critical as the CoS moves through the quadrants. *CoS's role in information flow* shows the CoS progressing to increasingly critical roles in the movement of data around the organization and the making of decisions based on those insights; the CoS is not a strategic decision maker but has the positional capability to ensure executives are making decisions with the speed and accuracy that the situation requires. And finally, *Communication priority of CoS* suggests the role that the CoS should play in helping to shape and broadcast the executive's intent to the executive team, broader organization, and outside audiences.

Quadrant 1: Ensure the CEO Is Executing with Efficiency

- *Primary focus of CoS:* Most of the CoS's time is spent getting to understand the executive and ensuring that the CEO's time is being used efficiently and effectively. The CoS is being effective when the executive is no longer a logjam, is on time and *present* for meetings, and has the necessary "white space" to look at the organization's strategic horizon.

- *Intended impact on the organization:* The CoS is seen to be filling a transactional role, ensuring that scheduling, task assignment and follow-through, and meeting content and agenda are all working well.

- *CoS's role in information flow:* The CoS is listening to other executives, understanding their problems, and becoming knowledgeable on their perspectives of the business. Relationship development is key in this phase.

- *Communication priority of CoS:* The CoS is developing an understanding of how the executive prefers to receive and digest information, as well as learning the executive's preferred approach for transmitting intent or simply communicating broadly with the executive team or the enterprise. Importantly, the CoS should be looking for gaps in this structure. Are there places where different business units are talking past one another, and how can the CoS help fill these seams?

Don't force your CoS to get ahead of their skis at this point. Forcing them to become a decision maker or forcing them to assert control over other executives will create short-term momentum but undermine the long-term potential utility of the position.

Quadrant 2: Ensure the Organization Is Executing with Efficiency

- *Primary focus of CoS:* The CoS should be spending more time on decisions and actions related to the execution of strategy. This builds, and requires, sustained stability in the executive's schedule.

- *Intended impact on the organization:* The CoS will be seen to begin to straddle the gaps between silos, connecting data and decision points between product teams, business units, regions, or any other bureaucratically compartmentalized areas. This is the starting point of other senior leaders seeing the deep value that could come from the position. The CoS is becoming a selfless, well-placed member of the team who is proactively connecting dots across the organization to the great benefit of other executives.

- *CoS's role in information flow:* At this point in his evolution, the CoS is monitoring the flow of information and assessing where and how it is being used to support strategic intent.

- *Communication priority of CoS:* The CoS should be comfortable representing the executive's views on key topics to a broad range of audiences but should stop shy of interpretation or forecasting. Authorizing a CoS to move to that level should be a conscious decision by the executive.

The goal in quadrant 2 is for other executives to self-discover how the CoS can help the organization function more effectively. The CoS should be positioned as a neutral broker solely focused on helping the organization execute.

As a senior executive, your goal in developing the CoS's position should be to get your peers comfortable with the coordination efforts that this individual is capable of driving. They must see consistent accuracy when the CoS describes your position on a topic. If you're changing a viewpoint without informing your CoS, you are undermining their credibility and slowing their evolution toward quadrant 4. Your organization must develop trust in the CoS before he can move to quadrant 3. In quadrant 3 the CoS will be positioned to truly shape the decision-making process.

Quadrant 3: Help the Organization Make Decisions and Execute with Greater Speed and Precision

- *Primary focus of CoS:* The CoS is shifting their focus from execution to strategic planning. With trust developed in quadrant 2, and other executives now understanding the impact that this position can have, the CoS can become a focal point for coordination of cross-functional and complex decision making within the organization.

- *Intended impact on the organization:* The CoS is identifying cross-enterprise decisions that need to be made, clarifying decision space, and presenting opportunities for decision to the appropriate mix of executives.

- *CoS's role in information flow:* The CoS is communicating strategic decisions and monitoring and reporting back on their execution.

- *Communication priority of CoS:* Similar to quadrant 2, but now the CoS's ability to represent positions has expanded to the entire executive team. This will give them the ability to communicate with the enterprise, as well as external stakeholders, and demonstrate the clarity of voice and thinking within the C-suite. It is no small step, of course, for the CoS to earn this level of trust from the executive team. In many organizations this will be the most challenging step in this model.

By this point, your CoS has become a thought partner and trusted resource for your executive team. They are not driving decisions, but are rather identifying decisions that need to be made in support of strategy, passing information among the appropriate executives, ensuring that decisions are made by the right cross-functional leaders, and monitoring progress so that executives can move to the next large issues. Your executives see the CoS as an invaluable member of their network. They trust the CoS to not only represent your voice, as the senior executive, but also their collective voice as a C-suite. The CoS has the ability, therefore, to put down rumors and clarify issues long before they ever reach your desk. They are a truly empowered actor in the organization at this point.

Quadrant 4: Help the CEO Make Decisions and Execute with Greater Speed and Precision

- *Primary focus of CoS:* The CoS has moved through the first three quadrants and now can add great value as a thought partner. They should be spending roughly 80 percent of their time addressing internal matters so that you, the senior executive, are free to spend 80 percent of your time focused "up and out". For this work, the CoS must be empowered with some level of influence on decisions "down and in" to the organization. Of course, if you've helped them navigate quadrants 1 through 3, this should not come across as a threat to the enterprise but rather as a valued asset.

- *Intended impact on the organization:* The CoS's organizational focus is at the highest levels. Is the executive team allowing daily decisions to pull them away from the organization's vision? Is strategic focus being lost based on down-and-in issues? The CoS has become the trusted "devil's advocate" in the room, a critical function that far too many executive teams lack.

- *CoS's role in information flow:* The CoS can establish boundaries around critical information requirements and ensure that they are supportive of long-term objectives. In other words, what are the pieces of incoming data that should pull the executive team down and into the enterprise, and which should be handled at a lower level so that the CEO can maintain an 80 percent external focus?

- *Communication priority of CoS:* The CoS is able to anticipate the executive's response on a broad range of topics and prepare correspondence, messaging, and talking points for quick review. In some areas the executive may authorize dissemination of messaging prior to full review. The CoS has truly become, in this case, an extension of the executive they represent.

Quadrant 4 is the goal that so many executives hope their CoS will reach, but they'll often hire a person who lacks sufficient experience or background to move past quadrant 1 or 2. Alternatively, when they do have a quadrant 4–capable person—and I saw this often in the military—they move that person *immediately* to the bottom left of the model and do not allow time and space for the CoS to develop the sufficient relationships and understanding of the executive culture needed to succeed. This type of CoS may have the ear of the CEO, but without the trust of the other executives and a track record of creating cross-functional value, their impact will be limited.

If you intend to leverage this model, and you are either an executive with a CoS, or a CoS reporting to an executive, I would recommend the following approach.

Both the executive and the CoS should review the model proposed here, then map each quadrant and subsequent line of effort to their own institutional leadership: what is currently going well, what isn't working, and where are the proverbial "blind spots"? Use this mapping as a starting point for a discussion between yourself and your CoS, and discuss a plan for moving forward.

I would then recommend using that mapping as a baseline for periodic check-ins (I'd recommend at least monthly, perhaps more often). At these points, ask yourselves where progress is being made and where you should focus next. If you're an executive, remember that this is a tool designed to help your CoS earn credibility and build relationships with the staff so that they can become your quadrant 4 partner. If you're a CoS, remember that you shouldn't try to tackle every gap at once; start in quadrant 1 and work your way around.

If you do have these types of positions in your organization, ask yourself how you might benefit from tying them together as a social network within the organization—similar to how liaisons could be familiarized with one another. Surely they're connected, but what is that network accountable to achieve? What collective authorities do they have? Most networks like this that I've observed are simply expected to coordinate and deconflict. Even if their members are in quadrants 3 or 4, their empowerment as a connected network can fall into quadrants 1 and 2.

Ultimately, your organization should also have a view on what it is trying to use this position for—as an example, the U.S. military has a long-held vision that has served its chiefs of staff well for generations.

I recall a moment, when I was still early in the job, when I tried to apologize to McChrystal for a mistake the day prior. It was nothing catastrophic, but he'd had a suboptimal meeting with one of the Task Force's outstations the previous night that I'd been responsible for arranging. I had failed to give the team on the ground good insight into how to best structure their briefing to our senior leadership, and the interaction had been less productive than usual—which was my fault, not the tactical team's. McChrystal brushed off my apology.

"Have you ever thought about why we have aides in the military?" he asked rhetorically. "You might think it's so senior officers can have our lives planned out perfectly, but that's not the idea. If I wanted true perfection in this job, I'd hire someone that could stay in my leadership team for my entire tour. Then I wouldn't have to put up with onboarding new people who screw stuff up when they start."

He smiled.

"The job you're doing," he continued, "exists just as much for our organization and you as it does for a senior officer like me. It exists, in large part, so the next generation of leaders—officers like you—can see how things function at the strategic level and learn how this machine works. Everything's hard the first time you do it, and you'll make mistakes. I just expect you not to repeat them. But most important, I expect you to learn." It was a one-time discussion but entirely reframed my view on the job ahead.

Similarly, if you're willing to take this type of approach in your chief of staff model, you'd be investing in the future success of your organization's leadership.

As this book has stated often, today's environment is simply moving too fast for any one individual to sift through the complexity alone. Building a truly empowered team around the executive suite will prove to be an increasingly important value differentiator, in which having a well-considered approach to developing a CoS is critical.

ACKNOWLEDGMENTS

A book, I've come to learn, is more than words on paper. It's a complex project between *people*. At the center of our narrative sits the battlefield, and the fights that continue to this day: I'd like to acknowledge the on-going sacrifices being made by the men and women in service to our nation and our partners, and their families who make that possible. The world is changing, and the members of our armed forces have been sitting in the crosshairs of that change for well over a decade. Their learning cannot be underestimated, nor can the intensity of the lives they each live. We are in their debt.

I owe thanks to each of the members of our team at McChrystal Group who helped us wrestle this idea set into an approachable narrative, and who brought us powerful examples from the field. I've spent my life on high performance teams, where every day means sprinting to keep up with the person on your left and right. This team has all of that and more.

The case studies in *One Mission* involved interviews, iterations, and in-depth collaboration with the organizations we describe. Each of them is a special enterprise, with leadership that understands the world for what it is—a place in transition. We're in their debt, and we look forward to the continued success that lies in front of each of them.

In the broader network of friends, there are countless individuals that have provided outstanding feedback throughout this process, but I would like particularly to thank Spencer Bradley, Simon Sinek, Louis Kim, Lea Carpenter, Chris Hylen, Tom Gentile, Steve Hoffman, Teddy Collins, Sam Ayers, Jason Graefe, Peter Bergen, Jim Levinsohn, Laura Bosco, Mary Ann Fussell, and Sarah Younger. The most important feedback, of course, came from Bria Sandford, our exceptionally talented editor who guided us through this project with an equal mix of patience and red ink.

Amongst the many talented people who contributed to our writing, Antje Williams stands out. Her work ethic, diligence, and good humor proved invaluable to the fine-tuning of our work through its longest nights and most challenging iterations.

I owe special thanks to two others. I could ask for no better friend, mentor, and partner than Stan McChrystal. His thoughts and recommendations throughout this process, and more broadly throughout the past decade, have been invaluable. And in Charlie Goodyear I was gifted with far more than I could have hoped. Charlie is a uniquely talented mind and was the coauthor, thought partner, and positive deviant that made this project come together. The world will know his name.

Charlie would like to thank his family for their selfless love and support. They are the giants upon whose shoulders he tries to stand.

And I, too, owe the largest thanks to my wife, Holly, and our children. Their support is, and always has been, unwavering.

NOTES

CHAPTER 1: ONE MISSION

13 **"seem to feel trapped"**: Kartik Hosanagar, "Blame the Echo Chamber on Facebook. But Blame Yourself, Too," *Wired,* November 25, 2016, www.wired.com/2016/11/facebook-echo-chamber (accessed February 22, 2017).

15 **"Those fighters in Iraq"**: Ayman Al-Zawahiri, CNN transcript, September 10, 2003, http://transcripts.cnn.com/TRANSCRIPTS/0309/10/bn.03.html (accessed February 22, 2017).

16 **In early January:** Michael R. Gordon and General Bernard E. Trainor, "Weekly Attacks in Iraq, January 2004–May 2010," *The Endgame: The Inside Story of the Struggle for Iraq, from George W. Bush to Barack Obama* (New York: Random House, 2013), xvii.

18 **"revolution in Sapiens' cognitive"**: Yuval Noah Harari, *Sapiens: A Brief History of Humankind* (New York: HarperCollins, 2015), 21.

19 **coined the term "black swan"**: Nassim Nicholas Taleb, *The Black Swan: The Impact of the Highly Improbable* (New York: Random House, 2007), xxii.

20 **forseeable "grey swans"**: Philip E. Tetlock and Dan Gardner, *Superforecasting: The Art and Science of Prediction* (New York: Broadway Books, 2015), 239.

20 **"there is some truth to this"**: "Management Theory Is Becoming a Compendium of Dead Ideas," *Economist,* December 17, 2016, www.economist.com/news/business/21711909-what-martin-luther-did-catholic-church-needs-be-done-business-gurus-management (accessed February 22, 2017).

20 **"A letter carried on horseback"**: Joshua Cooper Ramo, *The Age of the Unthinkable: Why the New World Disorder Constantly Surprises Us* (New York: Little, Brown, 2009), 15–16.

22 **"an Eastern monarch"**: Abraham Lincoln, "Lincoln's Milwaukee Speech" September 30, 1859, U.S. Department of Agriculture, National Agriculture Library, www.nal.usda.gov/lincolns-milwaukee-speech (accessed February 22, 2017).

22 **"a new type of thinking"**: Albert Einstein, "Atomic Education Urged by Einstein: Scientist in Plea of $200,000 to Promote New Type of Essential Thinking," *New York Times*, May 25, 1946.

CHAPTER 2: THE HYBRID MODEL

26 **Weber was born**: Max Weber, *The Theory of Social and Economic Organization*, ed. Talcott Parsons, trans. A. M. Henderson and Talcott Parsons (Mansfield Center, CT: Martino, 2012), 4.

27 **"impersonal order"**: Ibid., 330.

28 **"specialists without mind"**: Tony Waters and Dagmar Waters, *Weber's Rationalism and Modern Society: New Translations on Politics, Bureaucracy, and Social Stratification*, ed. and trans. Tony Waters and Dagmar Waters (New York: Palgrave Macmillan, 2015), 7.

28 **"The development of bureaucracy"**: Weber, *Theory of Social and Economic Organization*, 340.

28 **"an objective organization"**: John Micklethwait and Adrian Wooldridge, *The Company: A Short History of a Revolutionary Idea* (New York: Modern Library, 2003), 106.

28 **GM seized more than 15 percent**: Ibid., 107.

29 **"by its very nature"**: Simon Sinek, *Leaders Eat Last: Why Some Teams Pull Together and Others Don't* (New York: Penguin, 2014), 96.

30 **"'What,' I wondered"**: Duncan J. Watts, *Six Degrees: The Science of a Connected Age* (New York: W.W. Norton, 2004), 275.

30 **"The answer, from an information"**: Ibid., 275.

34 **displaying record profitability**: "The Problem with Profits," *Economist*, March 26, 2016, www.economist.com/news/leaders/21695392-big-firms -united-states-have-never-had-it-so-good-time-more-competition-problem (accessed February 23, 2017).

34 **through gigantic mergers**: "United and Continental Airlines to Merge," *BBC News*, May 3, 2010, www.bbc.com/news/10095080 (accessed February 23, 2017). Brian Bostick, "Timeline: Major U.S. Airline Merger Activity, 1950–2015," *Aviation Week Network*, February 17, 2015, http://aviation week.com/blog/timeline-major-us-airline-merger-activity-1950-2015 (accessed February 23, 2017).

34 **According to 2012 estimates**: Clark Gilbert, Matthew Eyring, and Richard N. Foster, "Two Routes of Resilience," *Harvard Business Review* 90, no. 12 (2012): 65–73.

34 **Today, publicly listed**: Martin Reeves, Simon Levin, and Daichi Ueda, "The Biology of Corporate Survival," *Harvard Business Review*, January–February 2016, https://hbr.org/2016/01/the-biology-of-corporate-survival (accessed February 23, 2017).

35 **June 2016 Brexit referendum**: Nate Cohn, "Why the Surprise over 'Brexit'? Don't Blame the Polls," *New York Times*, June 24, 2016, www.nytimes .com/2016/06/25/upshot/why-the-surprise-over-brexit-dont-blame-the -polls.html (accessed February 23, 2017).

35 **"an explosive shock"**: "French PM Says Time to Reinvent Europe After

'Explosive' Brexit," Reuters, June 24, 2016, www.reuters.com/article /britain-eu-france-valls-idUSL8N19G42N (accessed February 23, 2017).

35 **Polling had predicted:** Nick Miroff, "Colombians Vote on Historic Peace Agreement 35 FARC Rebels," *Washington Post,* October 2, 2016, www .washingtonpost.com/world/colombians-vote-on-historic-peace-agreement -with-farc-rebels/2016/10/02/8ef1a2a2-84b4-11e6-b57d-dd49277af02f _story.html?utm_term=.e8e93261e3c3 (accessed February 23, 2017).

35 **the *New York Times* predicted:** Josh Katz, "Who Will Be President?" *New York Times,* November 8, 2016, www.nytimes.com/interactive/2016 /upshot/presidential-polls-forecast.html (accessed February 23, 2017).

35 **for all fifty states:** Luke Harding, "Numbers Nerd Nate Silver's Forecasts Prove All Right on Election Night," *Guardian,* November 7, 2012, www .theguardian.com/world/2012/nov/07/nate-silver-election-forecasts-right (accessed February 23, 2017).

35 **confident in a Clinton victory:** "Who Will Win the Presidency?" *FiveThirty-Eight,* November 8, 2016, https://projects.fivethirtyeight.com/2016-election -forecast (accessed February 23, 2017).

35 **David Snowden and Mary Boone:** David J. Snowden and Mary E. Boone, "A Leader's Framework for Decision Making," *Harvard Business Review,* November 2007, https://hbr.org/2007/11/a-leaders-framework-for-decision -making (accessed February 23, 2017).

38 **"To act on the belief":** Friedrich von Hayek, "Prize Lecture: The Pretence of Knowledge," December 11, 1974, www.nobelprize.org/nobel_prizes /economic-sciences/laureates/1974/hayek-lecture.html (accessed February 23, 2017). Original emphasis.

38 **"If man is not to do":** Ibid.

38 **"objects of pure structure":** Watts, *Six Degrees,* 28.

39 **A network's shape:** Nicholas A. Christakis and James H. Fowler, *Connected: How Your Friends' Friends' Friends Affect Everything You Feel, Think, and Do* (New York: Little, Brown, 2011), 14.

39 **"in which everybody knows":** Albert-László Barabási, *Linked: How Everything Is Connected to Everything Else and What It Means for Business, Science, and Everyday Life* (New York: Basic Books, 2014), 42.

39 **"repeated human interaction":** Anne-Marie Slaughter, *The Chessboard and the Web* (New Haven: Yale University Press, 2017), 83.

41 *"homophily* . . . birds of a feather":** Christakis and Fowler, *Connected,* 17.

42 **"when there are feedback loops":** Alex Pentland, *Social Physics: How Good Ideas Spread—the Lessons Learned from a New Science* (New York: Penguin, 2014), 37.

42 **anthropologist Robin Dunbar:** R. I. M. Dunbar, "Neocortex Size as a Constraint on Group Size in Primates," *Journal of Human Evolution* 20 (1992): 469–93.

42 **close relationships with approximately 150:** Robin Dunbar, "How Many 'Friends' Can You Really Have?" *IEEE Spectrum,* May 31, 2011, http:// spectrum.ieee.org/telecom/internet/how-many-friends-can-you-really-have (accessed February 27, 2017).

43 **"It came to be known":** Manuel Castells, *Networks of Outrage and Hope: Social Movements in the Internet Age,* 2nd ed. (Cambridge: Polity, 2015), 56.

43 **"calling for the resignation of Mubarak":** Ibid.

44 **"a leaderless movement":** Heather Gautney, "What Is Occupy Wall Street? The History of Leaderless Movements," *Washington Post,* October 10, 2011, www .washingtonpost.com/national/on-leadership/what-is-occupy-wall-street-the -history-of-leaderless-movements/2011/10/10/gIQAwkFjaL_story.html ?utm_term=.691457cf5c33 (accessed February 23, 2017).

44 **By November 15:** "Occupy Wall Street: New York Police Clear Zuccotti Park," *BBC News,* November 15, 2011, www.bbc.com/news/world-us-can ada-15732661 (accessed February 23, 2017).

44 **U.S. Senators Bernie Sanders and Elizabeth Warren:** Michael Levitin, "The Triumph of Occupy Wall Street," *Atlantic,* June 10, 2015, www.theatlantic .com/politics/archive/2015/06/the-triumph-of-occupy-wall-street/395408 (accessed February 23, 2017).

CHAPTER 3: AN ALIGNING NARRATIVE

47 **neurons are in its tentacles:** Peter Godfrey-Smith, *Other Minds: The Octopus, the Sea, and the Origins of Deep Consciousness* (New York: Farrar, Straus and Giroux, 2016), 67.

47 **Researchers can surgically remove:** Sy Montgomery, "Deep Intellect," *Orion,* 2011, https://orionmagazine.org/article/deep-intellect (accessed February 24, 2017).

48 **Robert Kaplan and David Norton:** Robert S. Kaplan and David P. Norton, *Alignment: Using the Balanced Scorecard to Create Corporate Synergies* (Boston: Harvard Business Review Press, 2006), 1–2.

49 **"Business performance therefore":** Peter F. Drucker, *The Practice of Management* (1954; repr., New York: HarperBusiness, 2006), 121.

49 **"translating strategy into objectives":** Donald Sull, Rebecca Homkes, and Charles Sull, "Why Strategy Execution Unravels—and What to Do About It," *Harvard Business Review* 93, no. 3 (2015): 60.

50 **84 percent of managers:** Ibid., 60–61.

50 **"rely on colleagues in other functions":** Ibid.

50 **"handled badly two times":** Ibid., 61.

54 **"7/8ths of the iceberg underwater":** "First Public Hearing of the Financial Crisis Inquiry Commission," January 13, 2010, http://fcic-static.law.stanford .edu/cdn_media/fcic-testimony/2010-0113-Transcript.pdf (accessed February 24, 2017).

CASE STUDY: INTUIT

63 **five years old and was still:** Alasdair Nairn, *Engines That Move Markets: Technology Investing from Railroads to the Internet and Beyond* (New York: John Wiley & Sons, 2002), 367.

63 **Apple's most recent venture:** Gabriel Torres, "Inside the Apple III," *Hardware Secrets,* May 31, 2012, www.hardwaresecrets.com/inside-the-apple -iii (accessed September 8, 2016).

63 **Founded by Scott Cook:** Suzanne Taylor and Kathy Schroeder, *Inside Intuit: How the Makers of Quicken Beat Microsoft and Revolutionized an Entire Industry* (Boston: Harvard Business School Press, 2003), 1.

63 **without pay at times:** Ibid., 37.

63 **and was denied:** Ibid., 65.

63 **would regularly call up:** Ibid., 73.

63 **for free to attendees:** Ibid., 80.

63 **Intuit had begun dispatching:** Ibid., 72.

64 **Excel programs), was looking:** Ibid., 92.

64 **should have been no competition:** Ibid., 91.

64 **more user-friendly than Money:** Ibid., 105.

64 **profit margins for retailers:** Ibid., 103.

65 **entertaining a nearly $2 billion:** Elizabeth Corcoran, "Microsoft Halts Merger with Intuit," *Washington Post,* May 21, 1995, www.washingtonpost .com/wp-srv/business/longterm/microsoft/stories/1995/intuit052195.htm (accessed September 10, 2017).

65 **Intuit bought Chipsoft:** Taylor and Schroeder, *Inside Intuit,* 160.

65 **Intuit bought Rock Financial:** Ibid., 254.

66 **"We started as a software company":** Tayloe Stansbury, interview with the author, August 22, 2016.

66 **"social media, cloud, mobile, and data":** Brad Smith, interview with the author, August 22, 2016.

67 **"how do you take a company":** Brad Smith, Internal McChrystal Group testimonial, 2014.

67 **"Are we the best":** Matt Rhodes, interview with the author, August 22, 2016.

68 **distribution of alignment triangles:** Intuit Strategic alignment triangle sourced from Internal McChrystal Group resources (accessed August 20, 2016).

70 **"air, water, and food":** Rob Lanesey, interview with the author, February 17, 2016.

70 **"I think the death knell":** Smith, interview with the author.

72 **"One Intuit Forum":** Ibid.

72 **"One of the things we did":** Rhodes, interview with the author.

73 **"It is a lot of detail":** Ibid.

73 **"If I am an investor":** Ibid.

74 **"The write-ins started to say":** Smith, interview with the author.

74 **"Back when I was at another":** Rhodes, interview with the author.

74 **"[Through this style of alignment]":** Smith, interview with the author.

75 **it was announced:** John Ribeiro, "Intuit Selling Quicken to Private Equity Firm HIG Capital," *PCWorld,* March 4, 2016, www.pcworld.com/article /3040723/intuit-selling-quicken-to-private-equity-firm-hig-capital.html (accessed September 8, 2016).

75 **"[Our new alignment] led":** Smith, interview with the author.

CHAPTER 4: INTERCONNECTION

78 **modern day "opinion leaders":** Albert-László Barabási, *Linked: How Everything Is Connected to Everything Else and What It Means for Business, Science, and Everyday Life* (New York: Basic Books, 2014), 129.

78 **"the attention to hubs":** Ibid., 64.

78 **"Though not necessarily innovators":** Ibid., 130.

78 **"social media offer brands":** "Celebrities' Endorsement Earnings on Social Media," *Economist,* October 17, 2016, www.economist.com/blogs/graphic detail/2016/10/daily-chart-9 (accessed February 24, 2017).

78 **explored in Christakis and Fowler's:** Nicholas A. Christakis and James H. Fowler, *Connected: How Your Friends' Friends' Friends Affect Everything You Feel, Think, and Do* (New York: Little, Brown, 2011), 16.

78 **related case of *social learning*:** Further description of social learning can be found in Alex Pentland, *Social Physics: How Good Ideas Spread—the Lessons Learned from a New Science* (New York: Penguin, 2014).

81 **"We call it the no-fly zone":** Chris Hylen, interview with the author, January 6, 2017.

81 **call "boundary spanners":** Rob Cross and Andrew Parker, *The Hidden Power of Social Networks: Understanding How Work Really Gets Done in Organizations* (Boston: Harvard Business School Press, 2004), 74.

83 **"when traders had the right balance":** Alex Pentland, *Social Physics: How Good Ideas Spread—the Lessons Learned from a New Science* (New York: Penguin, 2014), 33.

83 **identified a human tendency:** Further description can be found in Roderick M. Kramer, "Trust and Distrust in Organizations: Emerging Perspectives, Enduring Questions," *Annual Review of Psychology* 50 (1999): 569–98.

84 **"a newsroom format, as you've seen":** Trevor Hough, interview with the author, January 6, 2017.

84 **70 percent of companies today rely:** Lindsey Kaufman, "Google Got It Wrong. The Open-Office Trend Is Destroying the Workplace," *Washington Post,* December 30, 2014, www.washingtonpost.com/posteverything/wp/2014/12/30/google-got-it-wrong-the-open-office-trend-is-destroying-the-workplace/?utm_term=.8a832199cbfa (accessed February 24, 2017).

84 **accommodate *thousands* of people:** Julia Boorstin, "Inside Facebook's Futuristic New Headquarters," *CNBC,* May 22, 2015, www.cnbc.com/2015/05/22/inside-facebooks-futuristic-new-headquarters.html (accessed February 27, 2017).

85 **a building on Facebook's campus:** Kevin Kruse, "Facebook Unveils New Campus: Will Workers Be Sick, Stressed and Dissatisfied?" August 25, 2012, www.forbes.com/sites/kevinkruse/2012/08/25/facebook-unveils-new-campus-will-workers-be-sick-stressed-and-dissatisfied/#6e3ad7111335 (accessed February 24, 2017).

86 **framing of a "telephone tree":** Christakis and Fowler, *Connected,* 12.

86 **"Senior executives instituted":** Cross and Parker, *Hidden Power of Social Networks,* 73.

94 **Julia Hoch and Steve Kozlowski:** Julia E. Hoch and Steve W. J. Kozlowski,

"Leading Virtual Teams: Hierarchical Leadership, Structural Supports, and Shared Team Leadership," *Journal of Applied Psychology* 99, no. 3 (2014): 390.

95 **"In a random sample of recent":** Mark S. Granovetter, "The Strength of Weak Ties," *American Journal of Sociology* 78, no. 6 (1973): 1371.

96 **"Spartan . . . come back":** *300*, directed by Zack Snyder (Warner Brothers Pictures, 2007).

97 **"Either this, or upon this":** Plutarch, "Sayings of Spartan Women," in *Moralia,* trans. Frank Cole Babbit (Cambridge, MA: Harvard University Press, 1931), 465.

97 **"deprive of their status":** Plutarch, *On Sparta,* ed. Richard J. A. Talbert and Christopher Pelling, trans. Richard J. A. Talbert (London: Penguin Classics, 2005), 158.

107 **"state of emergent, adaptive":** Gen. Stanley McChrystal et al., *Team of Teams: New Rules of Engagement for a Complex World* (New York: Portfolio/ Penguin, 2015), 153.

CASE STUDY: OKLAHOMA OFFICE OF MANAGEMENT AND ENTERPRISE SERVICES (OMES)

110 **"Those are the phone systems":** Recollection of conversation on July 7, 2016.

110 **"How can you tell":** Matt Singleton, interview with the author, July 7–8, 2016.

111 **within specific time constraints:** OMES internal resources, provided and accessed in July 2016.

111 **"felt like a dictatorship":** An OMES IT director, interview with the author, July 7, 2016.

111 **deemed "cowboy IT":** A Service Quality staff member, interview with the author, July 7, 2016.

112 **"But it was exactly":** Singleton, interview with the author.

113 **"That made me go straight":** Ibid.

113 **"Yeah, we wanted to get":** Ibid.

113 **"He'd come find us":** An OMES IT director, interview with the author.

113–4 **"The elephant in the room":** Ibid.

114 **"We thought it was going":** Ibid.

114 **"We already had change-management":** Ibid.

114 **repeated by the IT directors:** OMES internal resources.

115 **"We had great, cool candidates":** Singleton, interview with the author.

115 **"We knew she was who":** Ibid.

115 **"I was all gung-ho":** Carissa Terry, interview with the author, July 8, 2016.

116 **"No—too ivory tower-y":** Matt Singleton, interview with the author, July 8, 2016.

117 **required urgent resolution:** OMES internal resources.

117 **"Be there. Attendance of these":** Ibid.

118 **The project's time line:** Terry, interview with the author.

118 **Verbally highlighted the people:** OMES internal resources.

119 "include the good, the bad": Ibid.

120 "Hmm, yeah, forty-seven": OMES internal resources.

121 helped hers get the job done: Ibid.

121 off to the side: Ibid.

121 "It's been a godsend": An OMES IT strategist, interview with the author, July 8, 2016.

122 help corroborate this: OMES internal resources, provided and accessed in August 2016.

123 risk levels associated with each: Service Quality staff members, interview with the author, July 7, 2016.

124 "discernment seems to have started": Ibid.

124 "Now we can respond": An OMES IT director, interview with the author, July 7, 2016.

124 "We've been looking": Singleton, interview with the author.

124 "the biggest complaints": An OMES IT director, interview with the author, July 7, 2016.

125 "We're a tech organization": Recollection of conversation on July 8, 2016.

125 "Maybe eight years ago?": Singleton, interview with the author, July 7–8, 2016.

125 one forum a week: OMES internal resources, accessed February 2017.

125 "This is how we're transforming": Singleton, interview with the author, July 7–8, 2016.

CHAPTER 5: OPERATING RHYTHM

126 "Football isn't a contact sport": Vincent Lombardi, quoted in Geoffrey Norman, "Contact Sports," *Weekly Standard,* January 7, 2013, www.weekly standard.com/contact-sports/article/694078 (accessed February 12, 2017).

127 "The team of '99": Jeremy Henderson, "John Heisman: Auburn 'the First to Show What Could Be Done' with the Hurry-up Offense," August 16, 2013, *War Eagle Reader,* www.thewareaglereader.com/2013/08/john-heisman-on -auburns-hurry-up-offense (accessed February 20, 2017).

128 "K-Gun" offense: Dallas Miller, "Dec. 2 in Bills History: The Birth of the K-Gun Offense," BuffaloBills.com, December 2, 2014, www.buffalobills. com/news/article-1/Dec-2-in-Bills-history-The-birth-of-the-K-Gun -offense/13cecac3-8f75-489d-8e23-47f8cd0c32eb (accessed February 22, 2017).

128 set the NFL record: James Dator, "Are 7 Touchdowns Created Equal?" SB Nation.com, November 6, 2013, www.sbnation.com/nfl/2013/11/6/5069168 /nick-foles-peyton-manning-seven-touchdowns (accessed February 21, 2017).

130 "a conquering army on the border": Otto von Bismarck, quoted in William Cook, "Europeans No Longer Fear Germany. But Do the Germans Still Fear Themselves?" *Spectator,* December 29, 2014, www.spectator.co.uk /2014/12/europeans-no-longer-fear-germany-but-do-the-germans-still-fear -themselves (accessed February 22, 2017).

130 "getting involved in the minutiae": Persi Diaconis, "The Problem of Thinking Too Much" (presentation, December 11, 2002 in Cambridge, Mass.), http://

statweb.stanford.edu/~cgates/PERSI/papers/thinking.pdf (accessed February 15, 2017).

135 **"evolved into a [newly] continuous"**: "Strategic Planning," *Economist*, March 16, 2009, www.economist.com/node/13311148 (accessed February 17, 2017).

137 **"more companies than not still view"**: Hal Lancester, "Experts Differ on the Merits of Going Over the Boss's Head," *Wall Street Journal*, June 17, 1997, www.wsj.com/articles/SB866499936586359500 (accessed February 22, 2017).

CASE STUDY: UNDER ARMOUR

147 **"Wow . . . well—it's like"**: Senior supply chain officer, interview with the author, November 10, 2016.

148 **"it all began in 1996"**: Edwin Dungy, "Under Armour Founder Breaks into Billionaires Club," December 6, 2011, *Forbes*, www.forbes.com/sites/edwin durgy/2011/12/02/under-armour-founder-breaks-into-billionaires-club /#12c52f045843 (accessed September 8, 2016).

148 **increased net revenue 24 percent**: 2010 Under Armour Annual Report, 3.

148 **"We are 14 years"**: Ibid.

151 **"lack of visibility"**: Senior supply chain officer, interview with the author.

151 **"Our Supply Chain logic"**: Denny Ward, interview with the author, January 31, 2017.

151 **"timing and lack of visibility"**: Ibid.

151 **"Time is of the essence"**: Ibid.

151 **"kept on slipping past"**: Jim Hardy, interview with the author, October 13, 2016.

152 **"couldn't control for those variables"**: Ibid.

152 **"four years ago, we couldn't"**: Peter Gilmore, interview with the author, November 8, 2016.

152 **"we were a one-billion-dollar company"**: Hardy, interview with the author, October 13, 2016.

153 **"a thirty-page binder"**: Ibid.

153 **"outlining the game plan"**: Ward, interview with the author, January 31, 2017.

153 **"locations jumped around a bit"**: Ibid.

154 **"a red, yellow, green stoplight"**: Ibid.

154 **"three and a half years"**: Hardy, interview with the author, October 13, 2016.

154 **"right product, right place"**: Ibid.

155 **"Look for opportunities"**: Senior supply chain officer, interview with the author, November 10, 2016.

155 **"identifying all of the key leaders"**: Ibid.

156 **"I really kicked that guy's ass"**: Hardy, interview with the author.

156 **"not quite sympathy, but empathy"**: Ibid.

156 **"participants were expected"**: Senior supply chain officer, interview with the author.

157 **"for the VPs and SVPs"**: Ibid.

158 **"It's treated as a deadline"**: Hardy, interview with the author.

158 **"a level of accountability"**: Senior supply chain officer, interview with the author.

158 **"In the old days"**: Hardy, interview with the author.

158 **"Indexing what happened"**: Ibid.

159 **"I think this help[ed] scale"**: Gilmore, interview with the author.

159 **"We're very different"**: Ibid.

160 **"and with all of the key leaders"**: Senior supply chain officer, interview with the author.

160 **"Millions of dollars saved"**: Hardy, interview with the author.

160–1 **"misread market trends"**: Dennis Green, "Under Armour Made Some Huge Mistakes That Are Turning into a Nightmare," *Business Insider,* February 19, 2017, www.businessinsider.com/under-armour-business-mistakes-2017-2 (accessed February 10, 2017).

CHAPTER 6: DECISION SPACE

162 **"All inquiries carry with them"**: Carl Sagan, *Broca's Brain: Reflections on the Romance of Science* (New York: Ballantine's Books, 1980), 13.

163 **"When bad men combine"**: Edmund Burke, quoted in David Bromwich, *The Intellectual Life of Edmund Burke* (London: Belknap Press of Harvard University Press, 2014), 175.

164 **"the sentiment extractable"**: Ibid., 176.

164 **"As the number of available"**: Barry Schwartz, *The Paradox of Choice: Why More Is Less,* rev. ed. (New York: HarperCollins, 2009), Kindle location 83.

164 **"in order to solve the problem"**: Ibid., 55.

165 **"creating multiple business"**: Stephen Pritchard, "Leadership Challenges: Risk of Information Overload That Threatens Business Growth," *Financial Times,* November 6, 2012, www.ft.com/content/a0cde056-1e1c-11e2-8e1d-00144fea bdc0 (accessed January 3, 2017).

165 **"Pieces [of information] fall"**: Nada Bakos, "How True Is Zero Dark Thirty? A Former Operative Weighs In," *Pacific Standard,* January 16, 2013, https://psmag.com/how-true-is-zero-dark-thirty-a-former-operative -weighs-in-3214e516e072 (accessed January 5, 2017).

166 **"it has been suggested"**: Claus W. Langfred and Neta A. Moye, "Effects of Task Autonomy on Performance: An Extended Model Considering Motivational, Informational, and Structural Mechanisms," *Journal of Applied Psychology* 89, no. 6 (2004): 936, http://mason.gmu.edu/~clangfre/Effectsoftaskautonomy .pdf (accessed February 13, 2017).

166 **below the malfunctioning aircraft**: Simon Sinek, *Leaders Eat Last: Why Some Teams Pull Together and Others Don't* (New York: Penguin, 2014), 72–73.

167 **"The air traffic controller replied"**: Ibid., 73.

167 **"intentional behaviors that depart"**: Gretchen M. Spreitzer and Scott Sonenshein, "Toward the Construct Definition of Positive Deviance," *Ameri-*

can Behavioral Scientist 47, no. 6 (2004): 828, www.positivedeviance.org /pdf/publicationgeneralpd/Feb2004ABS_SpreitzerSonenshein.pdf (accessed January 8, 2017).

168 **"The concept is simple"**: Richard Pascale, Jerry Sternin, and Monique Sternin, *The Power of Positive Deviance: How Unlikely Innovators Solve the World's Toughest Problems* (Boston: Harvard Business Press, 2010), 3.

168 **"deviates in a positive way"**: Ibid.

168 **"twenty-two Vietnamese provinces"**: Ibid., 5.

168 **an antiasthma medication**: Ibid., 17.

168 **"The 'positive' aspect"**: Ibid., 56.

169 **result of his actions**: Kim Iskyan, "Here's the Story of How a Guy Making $66,000 a Year Lost $7.2 Billion for One of Europe's Biggest Banks," *Business Insider,* May 8, 2016, www.businessinsider.com/how-jerome-kerviel -lost-72-billion-2016-5 (accessed January 17, 2017).

176 **"because they focus"**: Donald Sull and Kathleen Eisenhardt, *Simple Rules: How to Thrive in a Complex World* (New York: Houghton Mifflin Harcourt, 2015), 32.

181 **team's "boundary rules"**: Ibid., 49.

CASE STUDY: MEDSTAR

186 **industry of the United States**: Sheryl Gay Stolberg and Robert Pear, "Obama Signs Health Care Overhaul Bill, with a Flourish," *New York Times,* March 23, 2010, www.nytimes.com/2010/03/24/health/policy/24health.html?mtrref =undefined&gwh=3220D51455112600FF2714B8CDF8234A&gwt=pay (accessed November 25, 2016).

186 **"a pure income redistribution play"**: Bill O'Reilly, "Bill O'Reilly: Obama Care and Socialism," Fox News, July 23, 2014, www.foxnews.com/transcript /2014/07/24/bill-oreilly-obamacare-and-socialism (accessed November 25, 2016).

186 **On the left**: John Geyman, "Can Overuse of Health Care Be Managed by Giving Consumers More Choice and Responsibility?" Huffington Post, July 18, 2016. www.huffingtonpost.com/john-geyman/can-overuse-of-health -car_b_11050884.html (accessed November 2016). Greg Sargent, "Hillary Clinton Should Be Pressed on Health Care, Too. Here's How," Washington Post, January 21, 2016, www.washingtonpost.com/blogs/plum-line/wp/2016 /01/21/hillary-clinton-should-be-pressed-on-health-care-too-heres-how /?utm_term=.1f5c221e8221 (accessed November 25, 2016).

188 **created by the organization**: Internal MedStar resources, provided and accessed November 20, 2016.

188 **32 percent increase in use**: Harold Cross, "A Data Flow Sheet for Managing Unstable Patients in the Emergency Department," *Joint Commission Journal on Quality and Patient Safety* 32, no. 4 (2006): 221–24, http://patientsafety authority.org/ADVISORIES/AdvisoryLibrary/2010/dec7(4)/documents /123.pdf (accessed November 25, 2016).

188 **congestive heart failure (CHF), diabetes**: Margaret Jean Hall, Shaleah Levant, and Carol J. DeFrances, "Hospitalization for Congestive Heart Fail-

ure (2000–2010)," NCHS Data Brief No. 108, U.S. Department of Health and Human Services, October 2012, www.cdc.gov/nchs/data/databriefs /db108.pdf (accessed November 25, 2016); American Diabetes Association, "Statistics About Diabetes," May 18, 2015, www.diabetes.org/diabetes-basics /statistics (accessed November 26, 2016).

188 **treatment that would typically:** Robin M. Weinick, Rachel M. Burns, and Ateev Mehrotra, "Some Hospital Emergency Department Visits Could Be Handled by Alternative Care Settings," *Health Affairs* 29, no. 9 (September 2010): 1630–36, www.rand.org/pubs/external_publications/EP20100123 .html (accessed November 2016). Lori Uscher-Pines, "Applying What Works to Reduce Non-Urgent Emergency Department Use," The RAND Blog, May 22, 2013, www.rand.org/blog/2013/05/applying-what-works-to-reduce -non-urgent-emergency.html (accessed November 26, 2016).

189 **"doesn't do wallet biopsies":** Matt Zavadsky, interview with the author, November 29, 2016.

189 **patients had undergone:** Office of the Legislative Counsel, *Compilation of Patient Protection and Affordable Care Act,* May 2010, http://housedocs .house.gov/energycommerce/ppacacon.pdf (accessed April 4, 2017).

189 **"Philosophically, we certainly like":** Douglas Hooten, interview with the author, November 29, 2016.

189 **"The most expensive way":** David Lloyd, interview with the author, November 29, 2016.

190 *clinicians, not technicians*: Shane Ansel, interview with the author, November 29, 2016.

190 **unnecessary emergency-care ones:** Zavadsky, interview with the author, November 29, 2016.

191 **in the Fort Worth area:** Internal MedStar Resources, provided and accessed November 20, 2016.

191 **face to face with patients:** Zavadsky, interview with the author, November 29, 2016.

191 **"We go through the home":** Ansel, interview with the author, November 29, 2016.

191 **"[When we initially piloted":** Zavadsky, interview with the author, November 29, 2016.

192 **a director at MedStar:** Internal MedStar Resources, provided and accessed November 20, 2016.

192 **"I've learned now":** Desiree Partain, interview with the author, November 29, 2016.

192 **"compassion fatigue":** Ibid.

193 **"pretty limitless . . . and if I do":** Ansel, interview with the author, November 29, 2016.

193 **"Calling different doctors":** Ibid.

193 **"If I'm calling regarding":** Ibid.

194 **"Across all of EMS":** Matt Zavadsky, interview with the author, October 31, 2016.

195 **problems before they manifest:** Internal MedStar Resources, provided and accessed November 20, 2016.

195 **middle of the year:** Zavadsky, interview with the author, November 29, 2016.

195 **"Anybody's allowed to come":** Ansel, interview with the author, November 29, 2016.

195 **their own health communities:** Zavadsky, interview with the author, October 31, 2016.

196 **"Most of them know":** Ansel, interview with the author, November 29, 2016.

CHAPTER 7: LIAISONS

200 **"People rely on a limited":** Amos Tversky and Daniel Kahneman, "Judgment Under Uncertainty: Heuristics and Biases," *Science* 185, no. 4157 (1974): 1124.

206 **"the new dead man":** Joseph Heller, *Catch-22*, 50th anniversary ed. (New York: Simon and Schuster, 2011), Kindle location 6204.

211 **"hubs create short paths":** Albert-László Barabási, *Linked: How Everything Is Connected to Everything Else and What It Means for Business, Science, and Everyday Life* (New York: Basic Books, 2014), 64.

214 **"tilt reciprocity in their own":** Adam Grant, *Give and Take: A Revolutionary Approach to Success* (New York: Penguin, 2013), 4.

CASE STUDY: EASTDIL SECURED

222 **"We'd never used the term":** Miles Theodore, interview with the author, October, 18, 2016.

222 **"Limited information sharing":** Ibid.

222 **"relationships between offices":** Sue-Lin Heng, interview with the author, October 20, 2016.

222 **"shared compensation structure":** Stephen Van Dusen, interview with the author, October 19, 2016.

222 **"Whereas," Van Dusen goes on:** Ibid.

223 **"magical time to be":** Ibid.

223 **"it was all new people":** Collins Ege, interview with the author, October 12, 2016.

224 **abbreviated to "F3EA":** Stanley McChrystal, *My Share of the Task* (New York: Portfolio/Penguin, 2013), 153.

224 **he read *My Share of the Task*:** Randy Evans, in conversation with the author, September 2016–January 2017.

225 **parts of its internal process:** Ibid.

226 **possible in the private sector:** Ibid.

227 **"a little unusual":** Roy March, interview with the author, November 7, 2016.

227 **"the usual chest pounding":** Mike Van Koynenburg, interview with the author, November 7, 2016.

227 **"His comments were essentially":** March, interview with the author, November 7, 2016.

227 "He candidly didn't think": Ibid.

228 "allowed [for] . . . *familiarity*": Van Dusen, interview with the author, October 19, 2016.

228 "Installing the [MIC] system": Koynenburg, interview with the author, November 7, 2016.

229 "What I think impacted": Ibid.

229 "Most of our people": March, interview with the author, November 7, 2016.

229 "Sometimes we get a little": Ege, interview with the author, October 12, 2016.

229 "We needed someone to answer": Ibid.

230 "being the arbiter of all retail": Theodore, interview with the author, October 18, 2016.

230 "It's funny, because if you looked": Ibid.

230 "Shannon and Kerry": Ibid.

231 "The number one thing": Ege, interview with the author, October 12, 2016.

231 "Second," Ege went on: Ibid.

232 "That's what we've learned": Ibid.

232 "Eastdil's always been": Heng, interview with the author, October 20, 2016.

232 "The challenge of one person": Theodore, interview with the author, October 18, 2016.

233 "Those are representatives": Ege, interview with the author, October 12, 2016.

233 "perfect storm conditions": Roy March, e-mail to the author, November 27, 2016.

233 "you could probably title 2016": Ibid.

234 "shared intelligence, not speculation": Ibid.

CONCLUSION

238 "central to every policy discussion": Lawrence Summers, "Beware Moral Hazard Fundamentalists," *Financial Times,* September 23, 2007, www.ft .com/content/5ffd2606-69e8-11dc-a571-0000779fd2ac (accessed February 15, 2017).

239 "The next day, shuttle engineer": Amy Edmondson, *Teaming: How Organizations Learn, Innovate and Compete in the Knowledge Economy* (San Francisco: Jossey-Bass, 2012), 115–16.

240 "climate in which people": Ibid., 118–19.

245 "universal images that have existed": Carl Jung, *Collected Works of C. G. Jung,* vol. 9, part 1: "Archetypes and the Collective Unconscious," ed. Sir Herbert Read et al., trans. R. F. C. Hull (Princeton, NJ: Princeton University Press, 1969), Kindle location 238.

INDEX